In the Presence of Proof

A MEDIUM'S VIEW OF THE AFTERLIFE
AND HOW TO CREATE HEAVEN ON EARTH

Deborah Hanlon

little pink press

Published in the United States by Little Pink Press, New York.

ISBN: 0692160930
ISBN-13: 978-0692160930

PRAISE FOR
"IN THE PRESENCE OF PROOF"

"This is a book for anyone interested in living fully, here on earth, as a human being, NOW. You don't have to believe in the ability to communicate with those who have died to enjoy In the Presence of Proof. You can be a hard-nosed, science-based skeptic. You can be someone (like me) who has been fascinated with, scared of, puzzled by the meaning of death and the existence of an afterlife. There is so much in this book to help you travel through the maze of your human mind to the shore of something bigger, vaster, more beautiful that we can ever dream of. Deborah Hanlon is a mystic and a guide, and I recommend this book."

-Elizabeth Lesser, Founder, Omega Institute

"Deborah Hanlon is a talented medium who often speaks to those on the other side, but make no mistake, this is a book about LIFE. While filled with personal stories and experiences, including the loss of her brother when she was only three, this book is about much more than a medium's journey. Ultimately, it is a manual for living life. Highly recommended!"

-Kevin J. Todeschi, Executive Director & CEO
Edgar Cayce's A.R.E. / Atlantic University

"I found myself insatiably consuming every word, every page. Deborah answers our deepest questions about life and death. She is brilliant, real, and cares deeply that we suffer less and live more. This may as well have been called "How to Live.""

-Keryl Pesce, Author, Hello Beautiful and
Happy Bitch

"A phenomenal book ... beautifully written and enlightening. In the Presence of Proof is a must read for anyone seeking answers about "the afterlife," and the meaning of life in general. Most of us have lost a loved one, and some struggle with grief and finding peace. The kind of spiritual enlightenment this book provides, goes a long way toward finding that peace. I WISH I COULD GIVE IT MORE THAN 5 STARS!"

-Lynda P., Amazon Reviewer

"Changed my whole outlook on death! This book has given me so much peace after the recent passing of my beautiful 22 year old daughter. Author / Medium Deborah Hanlon is the real deal. If you are grieving, I encourage you to read this book. If you know someone grieving, this is a beautiful gift. If you are not grieving now buy it as it will give you this beautiful outlook that you will want to soak in before a loved one leaves us here on earth."

-Dorothy Lellek, Amazon Reviewer

"If you're fortunate enough to ever attend any of Deborah's galleries or have a personal reading, you'll know just how gifted she is very quickly. I personally believe that one of her biggest gifts is also how genuine she is and her to desire to help others. This book really reflects everything she does and is. It's written in such an honest and relatable way that really makes you feel like you're talking to a good friend. You finish the book with such a sense of peace and understanding that I don't think I ever really had before.

-Holly, Amazon Reviewer

"This book is truly life changing. If you have suffered a loss of a loved one, if you want to live a purposeful life and if you want to get in touch with your spiritual self in order to better understand life and death, then this book is for you. Absolutely inspiring!"

-M. Peters, Amazon Reviewer

DEDICATION

To Christopher George Hanlon:

November 17, 1974 - May 31, 1979
Your death has proven to me there *is* an afterlife.
You have given me the most magical answers to one of the
greatest mysteries of all time.
Not bad for a four and a half year old.
And our beat goes on.

ACKNOWLEDGMENTS

How does one write an acknowledgement page for her first book? There are simply not enough pages in the world for any one person to acknowledge those who have helped me along the way. Collectively, everyone I've ever met should be acknowledged, from the doctor who delivered me to those who do my dry cleaning. OK that may be a bit drastic, but when I've written a book about how I have come to see and understand the world, that it's really a collection of experiences, both human and spiritual that have helped me get to this point, I really ought to think of everyone. So in my heart, I am including everyone. For the sake of this book, I am making a few notable mentions. But those of you who know what we have shared and encountered, know. And I trust all of you will feel my sentiments of gratitude whether I list your name here or not.

I must thank my family of origin, no matter what courses we have all taken. Today, I am grateful to each of you. There were lessons big and small and at the core of all of us, I believe we all are doing the very best we can in a world filled with confusion.

To my dad, for showing me another side of life, even when I didn't fully understand it. For showing me that pain from the death of a loved one never really stops, and people need multiple methods to help them heal. Whatever ways we choose to heal and cope are simply the best we could do in that moment. I understand the multiple responses to pain because of you.

To my step-mother Nancy, whose persistent and consistent nature taught me how to function in life. No matter what, bills need to be paid, and life always needs to move forward. We may not always know what to do, but we ought to reach out for help and guidance. For showing me the world of manicures, pedicures, 401K's and stock options. For being a strong woman who doesn't get involved unless asked. A true role model.

To my brother John, for always being authentically himself. You are an intelligent dude who lives life precisely on his terms. For him waking me up in the middle of the night to watch Saturday Night Live, (when I fell in love with Mr. Bill and was devastated every time he was crushed by those around him!) to being a stable force to vent to about family and life. A true "zen guy," even though you smashed your iPad in frustration and easily go off in politically driven rants about governments and economies. You are one of the most level headed people I've met. My first true love in this world!

To my brother Chris, for being with us for such a short time and sending us all out into an orbit of life that none of us could prepare for. My first little buddy, my wrestling and mess-making partner. Thank you for teaching me about life, death and human potential. Thank you for never leaving my side. This is literally, *all* because of you.

To my sister Lauren, who has taught me what it's like to be a big sister. Thank you for your fun, loving heart, sense of humor, desire to learn and constant support! Thank you for growing our family to include Todd and Baby T - the newest Caveboy to our tribe!

To my three gorgeous inside and out, "Caveteens," Jack , Ben and Chris. This journey began because of all of you. You are all truly what have kept me going no matter what! Your presence in the world has been a tremendous catalyst for all I have become. You are proof that The Universe is smarter than I am, for It knew exactly what needed to happen at precisely the right times! I love you all and I'm ridiculously proud of you, more than you will ever know. I am confident you will all manifest the lives of your dreams!

Jack for your persistent sense of self that keeps us all on our toes! For always being proud of your mom and having no fear in showing it to anyone he knows. You are The Energy in this world that made it all come together for me.

Ben for "perfectly being you." Your authentic, hard working, strong, loving self are qualities that will always take you far. You taught me how to just "be." My young entrepreneur, the world has a lot more to see from you!

Chris for being the "baby" forever! Your deep sensitive soul is a gift for this planet! Your innate connection to and knowledge of music, lyrics and emotion stuns me every day. Your passion for basketball excites me into learning more about players, contracts, and the NBA franchise! I can't wait to see what you do with all that you are!

To my niece Chelsea, your presence in my life opened me up to oh so many emotions! To the one who got yourself back on top with softness and your authentic will to survive. "I'll love you always and forever" and ever and ever!

To my niece, Caitlyn, and nephews Connor and Ryan! No greater little beings on the planet to be the extended siblings to my boys! The six of you have been the most insane "rat pack" of children! You have all brought me to my knees with laugher at your raucous and fun loving ways! I'll forever see all of you in the double strollers as we spent hours trying to occupy your wild hearts!

To GK. I finally know what it means when someone says "so and so is my rock," because that is exactly what you have been to me—my truest 'rock'. Strong, stable, supportive and loving, all in your own brand. Your ability to always be open to new experiences and gaining insights, having a superior moral compass and the strongest judgment of character I have ever known is more valuable to me in a human than anything else! I could not ask for more! I only hope you now can see nice guys do not finish last! I look forward to more "what if's" with you.

To Samantha and Gregory, my "stepchildren" who have added so much to not only my life, but to my boys' as well. Life takes its twists and turns, and the two of you mean more to me than I think you can and ever will realize.

To Catherine Bilquin, my professor in college who literally is the one who put me on a path that made me love every moment of my career. Your class got me thinking about how to put all of what I love to learn into a neat package and how to teach it. Although I've lost touch with you, I'd love for you to know forever what a major and deep impact you made on my life!

To Antonetta A, another true and hilarious friend who helped me enjoy all aspects of life! Again, our meeting was cosmically arranged! Thanks to you I really learned how to play tennis!

To Lynda Parisi who spent countless hours filming my early days. Without you, not only would I not have footage of my early career, but I wouldn't have footage of my children at young ages! Thank you for believing in telling my story! Often times it is what kept me going strong!

To the Stiletto Girls. Wow! The support from all of you has been amazing!! Thank you all for adding another facet to my journey and for laughing, supporting and drinking our way to the top!

To Keryl Pesce. Do you see this book in your hand? It is only because of Keryl that it is done and in print in front of you! Keryl, a woman who is a true supporter for people to be, know and do their Highest Best. A true Angel on earth!

To Bonnie Hearn Hill for her dedication and expertise on editing this book! No small feat for sure!

To all clients, past, present and future, your support has truly been the vehicle that keeps me going. Without all of you, I would have ended up on a completely different path. There are literally *thousands* of you whose stories will stay in my heart forever and quite a few of you who have really taught me the value in my work.

To Eileen Scanlan. I've never met anyone stronger and more capable than you. What you endured in life astounds me. I am thrilled to know we can call each other friends, and even more so, "family." Gee, your mom, Patty, Kev and Chris are having a field day, now aren't they?

To Joan Simpson, for all the soup, nourishment and genuine love and care!

To Michele Bastian Taylor, Suzanne Lunham, Barbara Naparano. The "team" that keeps all things Deborah going! Grateful isn't even the word for all of you!

To Chuck Benfer who connected me with so many amazing radio personalities who have become true and forever friends.

To Laura Daniels, Chrissy, Brian, Joe Daily, Michelle Taylor - you are all such professionals in your field.

To Anne Quinn. The mentor I needed at just the right place and right time of my life. Thank you for helping me "sort myself out," over and over and over! There is so much gratitude for our friendship!

To all my teachers over the years, Doc Rick Huntoon, Lina Perez, Linda Richichi, Debra Sheafe, Paul Coleman, Intuitive Tara, Charleen Predmore, Dahlia Bartz-Cabe.

Dare I also write an acknowledgement to all the "greats" whom I have not yet had the pleasure to meet (yet!!) here as well. My gratitude is overwhelming for all of you! Thank you to Deepak Chopra, Panache Desai, Elizabeth Lesser, Joan Anderson, Pam Grout, John Edward, George Andersen, Tony Robbins, Oprah Winfrey, the late Wayne Dyer, Brian Weiss, Eckhart Tolle, and of course… The NY Knicks, (there is just something oh so magical about watching the Knicks with the boys at MSG! A true "peak moment" for me every time we go—even in the nose bleed seats!)

CONTENTS

Deborah Hanlon

Introduction

Nothing creates change and transformation more powerfully and forcefully than grieving the death of a loved one. Nothing. Losing someone you love deeply is the most painful and well, quite frankly the most horrific human experience we all must endure. No one ever says "Yay! So and so just passed on!" My maternal grandmother passed at 100 years old. We *knew* she was going to die. It was well beyond her time, she was ready to go and yet, there was a sadness when she finally did. Although we were relieved for her that her journey on this earth was complete, it's inevitable to feel the loss of a person's physical presence when they have died. Our frequent trips to the nursing home ceased. We still pass by it and can't help but think of all the time spent there. Now that's all a memory. I've met literally thousands of people over the years and have had a unique opportunity to be there at the beginning of many people's grieving journey. I am humbled on a daily basis by the courage and strength every person I've met has shown. I care enormously about how people are doing, and I work very hard at keeping in touch with everyone who needs my help and guidance along their way.

As a medium giving readings and talking with people for over 15 years, I started to realize that while people enjoyed receiving messages from their loved ones who have passed away, once they left our appointment they immediately returned to their regular lives. If they were unhappy, they continued to lead unhappy lives. If they were stressed at work, they continued to be stressed at work. If they were unsure about a decision, filled with self doubt, or wanted to make changes, but didn't know how, there were few places for them to turn to for guidance. Here they were, having to deal with their grief and move on with the daily stresses of life. I often wondered what more I could do to help people live a better life. This is when insight from beyond stepped in and helped me help so many others to create a life after a loved one's death.

As an intuitive, I'm often able to predict what is going to happen in the future for people. These "psychic" readings are a little more helpful in that people can get answers to specific questions or things they've been wondering about, but I knew that after receiving intuitive readings, people would return to their lives without any idea *how* to improve things or overcome the challenges they asked about. They continued to live as confused and unfulfilled—sometimes even worse than they were before the passing of a loved one. I often felt it was a poor use of our time spent together if nothing ever changed after they left! My purpose here on earth (as proclaimed by me) is to help people heal, help them see beyond themselves. I want to help them open up and transform themselves after losing someone or simply after experiencing any sort of loss, whether that loss was a job, a relationship, or a sense of themselves. I've learned personally that Loss is Loss. (I'm a believer that a teacher always teaches what he or she needs to learn!) And the old concepts of death have us stuck in the past.

When we survive a death, two things can occur: we can get sucked into the past or we can learn how to create a new future. All of that happens in the moment of the present. The potential for either outcome exists in the "afterlife." We can either understand death as a part of the process and see things as a constant flow of changes or, we can think of death as a punishment or the result of making a bad decision. An ending. Signed. Sealed. Delivered. We can let it consume us and keep a belief that is outdated that (death is the end), or we can upgrade our awareness and see things more closely as they are (life is in a constant state of change and flow!) How do we do this? Where do we begin? How can we be open to dying so we can see life in a new light?

I started learning about myself first. I had my own past to reconcile, and my own losses to understand. Some of my most painful losses weren't even a physical death, but the end of relationships that were once so important to me. I also endured my own spiritual death when I made decisions about my life that were not in the former comfort zone of myself; and even harder to overcome—the trying to convince those closest to me that I was making the right decisions. I lost those relationships. They died. New ones emerged, but the grieving process for the old ones was intense and filled with insights and opportunities for my personal growth. Sure, I would have preferred not to have had these experiences. But I did and I understand death on a much deeper level because of them. It all aligns as it needs to be. What did I do? I listened. I studied. I cried. I screamed. I yelled. I bargained. I rationalized. I tried to make some sort of sense out of it. I blamed myself. I blamed *everyone* else. I dug up my past. I threw an emotional fit, like, daily. I unleashed anger like an erupting volcano! I expressed. I dumped my heart , and mind all over anyone who would listen. I was vulnerable. Stuck. Sad. Sick. Hopeless. Wishing to be dead, not realizing at the time that I was among the "living dead." I was dead inside while my outer self appeared wonderful. The process was the greatest mindf*ck I've ever experienced. I resisted it. Tried denying my grief. Tried excelling at other things. Tried hiding from the world. I tried it all. I hated every minute of it. Then this book happened.

So, I am not going to start it off by telling you how great you will feel during the transformation process, because most times, it doesn't feel great. Well, unless you think being stranded on a tumultuous ocean during a storm in a rickety boat is fun, you probably will not like the process of becoming and transforming. It's scary. I never saw the light at the end of my own dark tunnel. Thankfully, others around me did. Thankfully, life after death does exist. I knew this in terms of having life after a physical death, but I didn't know there was an afterlife to every moment of our physical life here. We are constantly "dying" and re-creating a new Self. There is an afterlife to this very moment as you read these words. There is an afterlife to your unhappiness in this moment. There is a life after every moment and situation if we allow it to die in our daily life. Have you realized how many times you have already died in your current life? Can you begin to think of that right now? You are a being of evolution, a glimpse of energy housed in your current body with a story—an identity that you have the power and control to evolve or not.

Now, looking back at the process, I can see that in my fits of resistance to these losses and circumstances, I was also growing and learning. As my day job, I am a medium. I talk about the afterlife every day. I receive proof of it, literally every day. The reality of an afterlife and being able to be In the Presence of Proof every single day humbles me. It drives me to teach people about it! So literally every day, I was in the presence of new insights into the world of grief, life and death. I sat with people who were in the same emotional place I was in. But I didn't understand it this way, yet. I didn't see it. All I kept telling myself was how lucky I was. I was not affected by hard core death. No one had recently passed around me who was significant enough to me to miss on a daily basis. I didn't think I had a right to say my deaths' were the same. I didn't even think of my life as one that had loss in it. (Boy, was I wrong.) I had gratitude every day for what I didn't have—namely, the tragedies I listened to in other's lives. And yet I was failing to see that I was carrying the same personal devastation around on my own shoulders as most of those who sat with me. The universe is brilliant! I was being supported in ways I couldn't yet see. I had everything I needed all around me to get through it, and I had no clue! I "heard" and felt insights day in and day out about how to know that life survives after death. I listened to the wisdom provided to each client over the years and applied much of it in my own life. I also sought out the help of a few skilled mentors for additional insight. We all have blind spots and we all need others' wisdom to help us *see*. It's crucial for growth.

I did the work it takes to see the other side of death. And let me tell you, Heaven on earth exists! And it's been there the entire time, but has been clouded by past thoughts, beliefs, expectations and limitations. It's been covered by your grief. It is stuff you do not even realize is here, because, frankly, you thought that's all there is. Your thoughts, beliefs and past conditioning create the current you. Some of those beliefs are outdated. They are weeds that prevent a fresh new growth. We can let them die, so new and better growth can emerge, but first you must acknowledge what is currently present in your mind and whether it helps you or hurts you.

After many years of self discovery and trudging through my own personal hell which included dealing with a divorce with young children, working non stop to get my work "out there" to create a future for myself and my three Caveboys (later to become Caveteens,) and enduring a very painful family fall out, as well as start a new relationship and subsequently blending families, I started to rebuild myself. Little by little, I worked hard through the struggles. I learned how to have boundaries. I learned how to express myself and ultimately how to love myself, flaws and all! I learned I can live without having to know the outcome of every step I take. I learned how to be vulnerable and to allow people to show up for me when I need them. I learned how to really understand what my needs are, and I learned how much I didn't like doing any of that! However, I saw with proof how capable I am and also how quickly I can fall apart at a moment's notice. I learned to depend on people, even when that thought scared me. I learned how to fall in love and what love is. I learned that unexpected twists and turns in life are scary and fun, and that we can't get away from them and we can not control anything! I was being taught all along by those on the other side, how to be and how to live, and I had no idea. *This* is what I want to pass on to you!

I was able to actually witness my own death. No, I didn't have a Near Death Experience—at least not the kind you may be aware of. But I witnessed the death of my former self, former relationships, former beliefs, realities, and thoughts. The old me was so trapped in a mindset that was allowing constant dysfunction and anxiety to run my life. I felt inadequate and incapable in my own skin. I thought I was a horrific mother. I thought I couldn't handle anything. I thought some levels of dysfunction were normal and everyone had them. What a surprise it was to evolve from a mindset that anxiety and inconsistency were normal and incurable facets of life, to learn that is not true and life can be lived anxiety free and sans drama! It's OK to be boring! It's okay to not have a lot of crap going on. Who knew?! I always had to fight the proverbial wolves at my feet. I was constantly worried about money as a kid, or how I needed to help my mother, or worried when things were going well when the other shoe was going to drop. I did not know that life can truly be lived with a level of consistency and basic normalcy. Bills can get paid, weight can be monitored and lost, and not everything resulted in a tragedy! I never knew there didn't have to be only two realities or ways of living and existing—one that is depressingly low, or manically high. Life can be lived in a much more balanced way. I understand Moses' feeling of witnessing the burning bush! Holy Crap! My burning bush revelation saved my life. I'd write that on stone tablets too!

I want to make my abilities as a medium a little more useful to people, and offer more than an entertaining evening of readings from the other side, or an hour of career path guidance. I want to give people proof the afterlife exists. Proof that consciousness never dies and life exists after death. I want to actually help people deal with their grief after a loved one has passed; help people learn how to overcome their limiting thoughts and belief systems so that they can live a happier and more satisfying life. Meanwhile, all along, I thought I was helping people understand that we are still able to communicate with our deceased loved ones and I spent a ton of time and energy into finding 'proof' for that phenomena. Really, the proof of life after death existed not on the "other side," but right here, on this side! It exists in our living and not our dying! What a revelation for me! And this will all make sense when you get to the other side of this book— the end of it.

As my insights gained momentum for me, I started teaching Energy and Reiki classes that I "Deborahized!" Before you roll your eyes about Reiki, read on. I added to the traditional Reiki teachings the basic principles of energy, and created exercises where people could finally understand the connection between their thoughts, beliefs and their current realities. These are certainly not your ordinary Reiki classes. In fact, I swore for many years that I would never teach Reiki. Frankly, I thought it was for second rate people who needed to do some sort of fake energy work. How could someone take an energy class, for three hours, and then proclaim to be a practitioner? Ok, Ok. I can be a snob! I can be a downright asshole sometimes, but that's what I thought about Reiki until I put it all together!

Our thoughts and feelings affect our energy field. Our energy field dictates the life we will have, or at the very least, how we will respond to life. If this is true, we need to be more aware of how our thoughts are affecting our energy. I began holding a variety of workshops at my center, The Center for Being, Knowing, Doing and started connecting people with amazing teachers. I continued offering meditation classes that have dramatically helped people make sense of steps they need to take in their own lives. It was like taking a regular exercise class. With consistency, changes were happening for participants, big changes. I'm continuously seeking new opportunities that allow me to use my gifts and abilities to teach others how to enjoy their lives more and I believe everyone has the ability to experience a sort of "heaven on earth" and that there is proof it all exists. These Energy Awareness workshops and meditation classes have helped people finally make a connection between their thoughts and why certain aspects of their lives keep popping up. Most importantly, it gives some tools on how to change things to improve their lives.

I want people to understand the nature of who we are before we die! Why do we live such rough lives and never fully get it?! Why are we not understanding our nature to a point where we are empowered enough to create a life we love to live? We don't even know who we are! How can we really make good use of ourselves if we do not understand our true nature? How can we appreciate the now when we have no comprehension of how life moves and works together? Why wait until we have died to finally get it? What a waste if we finally understand how to live only after we have died! Right?! It's a bit maddening!

We're not just our current identity of somebody's mom or sister or a doctor or waiter. What we actually are is infinite energy. We've always been energy and we will always *be* energy. We are energy that is housed within our current bodies and sadly, we have taken on the belief that we are that identity we have created for ourselves. That's a teeny tiny identity. It's basically a small percentage of who we really are. Most people don't even realize that we ourselves create our identities. We believe a few limited thoughts about ourselves, and our world and then we live out our life with that knowledge. But is that enough? Have you expanded those beliefs? Have you challenged yourself? Have you allowed a former self to die off so a new one can emerge? Have you witnessed your own death? Have you grieved and honored the former you and embraced and celebrated the new you? Well it's time baby! It's time!

When a baby is born, we usually have a celebration to acknowledge this teeny new human's birth. Have you celebrated *your* new birth? We also come together after a person has died to celebrate and acknowledge the life they lived. Have you created a ceremony for your death? Have you set off a lantern saying goodbye to the old you? Do it!

How do we sort this all out and get to the heart of it all? What mindset do we need to adopt to live more authentically and closer to our "True Self?" What is it about the deceased awareness levels that we need to know? How it is they are in a place of pure peace, while we struggle here? How can we live as if we are already dead? How can we create Heaven on Earth? That is what this book is about. It's bigger than knowing "Is Uncle Stan Ok?" (He is, trust me. He's got the good spot). But your world and his world—it's all the same world! It's bigger and more connected than you have ever imagined! That's the good news!

The deceased have a consciousness, a knowing, a way of BEING that puts them directly in heaven! It's not a location or a destination! It exists in a mindset of Being, Knowing, and Doing, and we can get closer to that space and to them while we are still living here on earth! And we can do that through simple steps and awareness. How odd is it to think of the deceased as being? That's because it's completely contrary to how we view and perceive death. We always think of death as an end. A cessation of being. When rather, it's the ultimate source of Being! It's time to upgrade your understanding on what life, death, and the afterlife are. It's time to change your entire paradigm.

My goal is that this book will help you feel completely connected to yourself, to your loved ones and to the Collective Whole, where your loved ones reside. To understand you are more than your current human self and help you jump out of your comfort zone, work through your grief, battles with yourself, and really, *really*, learn to live. To no longer fear death and to alleviate all the "woulda, coulda', shoulda's" regarding the death of your loved ones. To experience no more guilt. No more regrets! Just consciously learning to BE!!

I'll share with you what I've learned from people who have passed on. I can provide you with the proof they are still around us, living right next to us. Not missing a single beat in our lives and they are truly more connected than ever before! But more importantly than that, **the dead truly can teach us how to live.** It's my hope that this book will teach you how to trust your own inner intelligence, or your intuition; and then you'll begin to see how everything is interconnected—both living and deceased. Once you understand that your true nature is *energy*, then you can learn how to interpret and harness that energy to start living a "larger life", or to create your own heaven *on* earth. It's real! I promise!

I am not an expert on any one religion or theology. I am neither interested nor prepared to argue religious points of view, dogma and the multitude of interpretations that come along with them. I respect absolutely all religions and what they seek out to do. I have included stories that I found intriguing from various religions, but chose them only because I love them and not because I am subscribing to any one dogma over another. This is an account of the afterlife in my own words. After reading and studying world religions in college, I see that what I have experienced and how I understand the "other side" most closely relates to a Hindu perspective, but really, all religions and traditions have similar—if not identical— threads within them. I honor all religions and have a deep profound respect for the true practice of any religion for the sake and comfort of the practitioner themselves. I do not view any religion as right or wrong. I personally see the practicing of any particular religion as a human expression of creating and finding meaning and a connection to a Higher greater Power. Some call that power God, Universe, Source, Higher Power, Divine All, Brahman, Energy, and many, many more. There are concepts that I discuss that can also be found in most religions that describe a smaller self (soul) and it's connection from a Larger Whole (God). Some see it as a disconnection, others see it as a continuation and one in the same. There are so many varying turns we could take in this book when comparing my words to any tradition, that I simply didn't want to get into it. I never claim my way is *the way*, and I only ask that mutual respect is given back to me. The two hardest things to discuss with close family and strangers alike are politics and religion. It figures my life's work would be one side of that "taboo topics" scale. Yay for me! Good thing I can handle it. I'm assuming if you have gotten this far into this book, that you are open to hearing my perspective. And you understand this is just that—my perspective!

The hardest thing about writing this book has been how to organize it. Every topic overlaps and flows into every other topic. I have spent months trying to find the right flow, cutting and pasting, moving paragraphs and entire chapters all around to somehow create some semblance of order. This was the worst part of the process. Then one day, I meditated on it. I begged to figure out how to set this up. The words, "Past, Present, Future" came to me. And voila! Duh! It all finally made sense to me.

My entire life, I've been obsessed with time and how physics clearly explains how there is truly no such thing as time. The illusion of time has been created or warped because of our position in the Universe. Humans perceive time and that's it: time becomes "real". However, in physics, the past, present and future are all happening simultaneously. They are occurring within us and manifesting outside of us. The "place where we go" when we die, is the place of "no-time," which really means, "all time". We re-enter into the "Collective Whole," which I will describe in later chapters. The reality of life as we know it is complicated. Time, growth and order. It's difficult, and making sense of it all, is, well, *impossible*. Much like writing this book and having it flow. It makes perfect sense that a book about everything that goes against our logic creates a hard task of wrapping a logical flow to it.

As a child, have you ever read "The Monster at the End of This Book"[1] by Jon Stone? It stars Grover—our lovable furry monster from Sesame Street. Well that book was one of my very favorites of all time. In it, Grover is talking to the reader. He reads the title and begs you, the reader to not turn the pages, because he is afraid of the monster at the end of the book. Each page presents a panicked blue Muppet frantically begging you to not turn another page. I still laugh at it. I remember as a kid feeling that very real connection with Grover. I felt he really was talking to me, the reader. After all, he knew every time I turned that page. He tries to prevent you from reading on, and yet, as the curious one, you the reader, just keep turning pages to see this monster. A natural curiosity of what and who this monster is, and how they will interact with Grover pulls you through. Grover is now screaming at you to stop. He's worried, nervous and doing everything in his power to stop you from getting to the end. But, that's impossible. And what happens at the end? The monster at the end of the book was Grover himself. It's a silly book, but one that popped into my head as I am writing this one. There is a "monster" at the end of this book too! And yes, it can be scary to think about who is there however he/she is there no matter how much you try to prevent yourself from getting to it. But I promise you—the anticipation of the journey is way harder than the reality of it. Embrace your inner monster. You just might really love him/her.

When people ask me what I do for a living, I'd like to say "I'm a transformation and communications expert. I help people transform their lives, change their limited belief systems and begin living authentically. I can literally bring the deceased back to life and I can help you change the way you view your space on this plane." But still I somehow cannot get my three Caveboys to stop peeing on the toilet seat. Some things will forever remain a mystery!

Thanks for your interest, and I hope you find it insightful.

Love,
Deborah Hanlon

1

Who I Am and What I Do

I guess what I do is recognized as being an Intuitive Medium, although many people call me a *Psychic* Medium. It means I can communicate with people who have died and can also often feel things that are going to happen in the future. I'm also able to sense where a person is stuck or commonly self-diagnosed as "blocked" in their life.

I'm often asked what the difference is between a psychic and a medium, or if they are the same. While all mediums are psychic, not all psychics are also mediums. And trust me when I say, I absolutely hate the title Psychic/Medium/and/or Intuitive. They all creep me out and make me roll my own eyes at myself. What I really am is a curious human being, a person who doesn't busy herself in the latest trends. I used to, but it got exhausting and made me feel as if I never measured up.

I don't watch TV or put any effort into planning my meals for the week. I don't clip coupons, and I have no desire to do mundane tasks. I am forever grateful to the General Mills Company for creating cereal because to me, that is a full and balanced meal. I live on one-dollar coffee from McDonald's, and I'm partly embarrassed to say that and equally OK with it. I wish I had the ability to have a premeditated thought process to plan meals and mix ingredients together and create something yummy and nutritious, but I am just not that person. In fact, I'm not interested in the basic skills we all need to do to keep life moving forward in a natural direction. Daily human tasks seem to pile up and overwhelm me. I mean, I do them. I sometimes do cook simple stuff, I do pay bills, and I do laundry, and sometimes I even put it away. But that is not remotely from where I gain my joy in life. Unfortunately, I do always feel really super good when everything is organized and handled. Such is life: a balance between what we like to do and what we don't.

Well, my passion is understanding the Science of the Spirit, the Physics of the Soul! I want to know all about that which we as a species do not yet know for certain. I want to know what life is all about, why we are here, and how we got here. I want to understand our thought processes and how and *why* things happen the way they do. I want to know how to make things better and why I am not perceiving things in a positive light. I am obsessed with the human condition and more important, the role of our spirit in it. I want to teach you about and raise your awareness of the existence of an afterlife.

I'm enthralled with why we all often make things harder than they need to be and how, how, how we can remedy this—even a tiny bit—so we actually *enjoy* life. Why are we all so focused on what's ahead of us, and yet we continue to take what is already behind us as our fuel to get us to a new outcome? Why aren't we happy? Like truly, truly happy. We have more methods of automated conveniences in our lives, and yet we are still not happy—not constantly anyway. I've always wanted to know why we feel disconnected and alone here on earth? There are over seven billion of us here on the planet and we feel alone and DISconnected? Yikes! What is contributing to that and again? Can we fix it, and if so, how? Why are we so hard on ourselves just about the time? Why can't we just be?

What really happens when we die? Are the deceased OK and if so, how can that be? Don't they miss life here? Don't they miss us? I've wanted to know these things for as long as I can remember. It's kind of annoying for one's life goals and incentives to be driven by questions that truly remain the ultimate mystery of life. And if I can find peace, answers, and ways to improve my life, maybe, just maybe, I can help others find that, too.

This is what drives me. I'm beyond fortunate that I can do all that, and make a living, and I practice gratitude for that literally every single day of my life. I wish I was just content in any of the many roles I have—as a mother, daughter, girlfriend, sister, aunt, medium, and as a human. But I'm not. I'm driven to understand much of which is beyond our human experience. Not a really great career for a grounded Taurus who likes to experience earthly things.

I was always plugged into the larger picture. I didn't get too worked up sweating the small stuff, at least not when I was younger. I was never the teenage girl who was terribly obsessed with her appearance, nor did I think anything *should* revolve around me. I basically liked myself and yet was very shy around boys or new people. I never felt I fit in completely. I didn't feel like a complete outsider, but I've always kept my circles small.

I wasn't the girl who partied. I thought I wanted to be that girl, and I know I could have been that girl if that was what I really did want. But fitting in never motivated me enough to do things just for the sake of being popular. I liked *Teen Beat* magazine, adored Joey McIntyre from New Kids on the Block, read the *Babysitter's Club* series and ate raw cookie dough from the roll. (And I still do.) I had sleepovers and secret crushes. I had sticker books and loved the oil stickers. My favorite was the whale. I collected plastic charms for my "trendy" 80's necklace. My favorites were the lipstick and the roller skate. I was a regular girl with heavy thoughts. I felt and knew things, but I didn't know what it was I knew.

I learned to read very young, and so I turned to the books on my mother's shelves. On them, were Norman Vincent Peale's *Power of Positive Thinking*, books from Dr. Elizabeth Kubler Ross, Steven Levine, the Maharishisi, Ram Dass, Shirley MacLaine, yogi books, *Man's Search for Meaning*, and picture books celebrating the lives and cultures from around the world! Religion, philosophy, sweet little books that I thought were for children because they were illustrated beautifully, like *Flutterby*, *The Ice Queen* and *The Fall of Freddy the Leaf*, *Hope for the Flowers* by Trina Paulus, *The Velveteen Rabbit*, *The Little Prince*, and *The Clown of God* by Tomie DePaola. Those were really adult books with a simple message, and they were my early teachers.

I would sit and pull each book off the shelf and sometimes just stare. I smelled the pages and loved the sound they made when I turned them. I reread them all multiple times, for in those days, we didn't keep accumulating more. Instead, we reread and reused what we already had. I read and then understood something, then reread and gained a deeper understanding. This went on for years. There were no video games then. No cell phones. Only one phone with a very stretched-out cord in the kitchen, and one TV with rabbit ears that became too frustrating to deal with. Instead, I'd go play with my Barbies or dig in the dirt (if I could find a kitchen spoon) when I was bored. Those were the days of pure introspection and creative free thought via play. I lived in my thoughts and was constantly seeking to understand the big questions. Who am I? Why am I here? What is this all about? How can we be the only species in this Universe? What is real? What makes anything real? Gotta love that Velveteen Rabbit and in more recent years, the Toy Story movies. Why is life like this? What makes life like anything at all? Why do some people have certain things and others don't? What the heck is this all about?

In my teenage years, I craved to have a deeper intellectual concept of physics and neuro-psychology, theology, and philosophy. I set a goal for myself as a very young woman that I wanted to "revolutionize the way people think about science and spirituality." That's a hefty goal for someone, who at the time, dropped out of

Fordham University because of an issue at home and a growing inner depression. I remember telling my therapist how aggravated I was with *myself* for having my only passion which was to find out what happens when we die, and that is so stupid, because at that time, I believed I would have to die to really find that out and never get to share that with people. So, the irony of my life would be nothing short of torture. (And, yep, that's pretty much the mind of a person suffering from depression.) Yet, for some reason, that didn't deter me from continuing to pursue, learn, observe, feel, and process.

Then something did die in me, the old mindset, anyway. It died in me, and a new me emerged. I've learned a tremendous amount about life and death via my own personal ups and downs, my own deaths, and rebirths.

This is me—at least the me in human form who is currently taking up the space of my body and experiencing the world around me from pretty much a vantage point of never-ending seeking. It's *exhausting* to be me. At times, it's exhausting to be around me. There are very *few* moments that I don't question, rehash, look at differently, then question again. I'm intense. I have been insatiable. Until, well, the deceased got hold of me.

I have a story, as we all do, and it's the story of who we are. Some of those details for all of us are fascinating. We all have some really cool self stories, aspects of our experiences so far that make us say, "Wow, how did I survive that?" Or "Wow, imagine having to do *that* again?" Or "Wow, I am still so impressed and proud of myself for accomplishing that." And of course, we all have the "Why *didn't* I do that," or "Why did I?" Ha. Life is filled with all of this, and more.

My earliest clear and actual memory of my brother Christopher was long after he had passed. One day, a man showed up to my home with a gift that changed my life. The doorway to my future was blown open by old family home-movie footage he had taken years before. I can't recall how old I was, but I know my parents were already separated or divorced because I can remember that my father was not there with us. Although I have no idea who this man was, he rocked my world in a way that I believe was the beginning of my journey through grief I didn't even know I had until that day.

He spoke with my mother with great familiarity and care and set up a slide show, so they obviously knew each other. We removed the huge painting of a sailboat that had hung on my living room wall for as long as I can remember so we could use that scuffed wall to project our deepest and most emotional family memories. I can't remember if it was set to music or not. What I *do* remember, is lying on the floor on a pillow, completely unaware of the impact this would have on me. I was actually excited to see pictures of myself young. Because I was the youngest of four kids, I was included in only six of them. Seeing little Debbie was going to be very exciting for me. At least, that's what I thought.

And then there he was. There we *all* were. My early family in the middle of living with a young boy who was dying—was projected in silent moving pictures on my living room wall. The same living room in which my brother died. I then realized there was a time when I actually had an intact, "real," family—a mom and dad together, siblings, fun trips, family dinners, and a bedtime. And then, a terminally ill four-year-old brother who changed everything.

Christopher died of a rare childhood cancer, neuroblastoma, when I was three. He and I were the youngest of four children in a modest suburban family. My parents were city folks who moved to upstate New York so their children could grow up in their own home and with space. This day, as we watched the images projected on the wall, was the first time I recall seeing my brother running around as a normal, healthy little boy, and then of his growing illness. I watched images of us riding our three wheelers, wrestling our dog, visiting West Point, and then *celebrating* Chris's birthday in the hospital, where my oldest brother was overcome with grief. Now, however, many years later, through the eyes of a young pre-teen self, I could actually see what I *missed*. It was a sad visual, a Happy Birthday for an emaciated young boy who opened presents with IVs attached to his arms.

I also watched Chris taking a swing with his Yankees uniform on in our front yard. At this point, he was nothing more than skin and bones. Still, he was a skeleton with a lot of energy, especially considering that he died days later. There were movies of Chris riding his bicycle perfectly at three years old, and dribbling a basketball, again, perfectly. I even watch us destroying our kitchen by deciding not to wait for Daddy to wake up and feed us. My mom and siblings were away on a trip and we, the babies, were left behind, and made our own breakfast. When my father woke up, he grabbed the video camera just to have proof of our culinary skills.

Cereal, milk, and fruit punch were everywhere in the kitchen and I mean, everywhere! We also must have had some post-breakfast enjoyment, as we decided it was a good morning to paint each other. So yes, food, drink, and paint, everywhere in that kitchen. It looked like fun. It looked silly. I had a buddy, and then almost immediately, I missed him. For the first time in my memory, I *missed* my brother. I missed the antics. My buddy. My partner in crime. I realized, he and all that went along with our relationship *died*. No more playing. No more painting bodies. No more wrestling. No more big brother Chris. My identity changed because of his death, even before I was old enough to *have* an identity. That then became a part *of* my identity. I had a buddy, he died, and I'm still here carrying on.

Only eighteen months apart, Chris and I were inseparable. According to stories, he liked to wrestle me, and he always came to my rescue. He still does to this day, only differently.

All of these thoughts began to flood my mind, as I lay there on the floor. I remember the grief welling up inside me so very intensely, to the point that I had to excuse myself from the living room and go into the bathroom. I couldn't get there fast enough, and when I did, I closed the door and just sat and sobbed. Intense sobbing. The missing piece of my early history was just projected before my eyes. The hidden and unconscious memories came to the forefront. And that was it.

I sat in the bathroom for what felt like forever. I prayed and begged and pleaded. I spoke to anyone who would listen. I spoke to Christopher. I spoke to Jesus. I spoke to Mother Mary. (Isn't that who we Catholics pray to when we need help?) I didn't want my mom to know how deep to my core this hurt me. I felt foolish for having this reaction. It was like ten years later! I wished I had never opened up this Pandora's box of latent memories and grief.

I was desperate to find some comfort in this pain, desperate, for the first time, to know where my brother was, and if he still knew me. By dying, that little boy helped me—the earliest form of the me I am today—be born. My identity was born out of this experience. His death created my life's work. I had been searching for my brother's soul to heal my own grief since the day he died on May 31, 1979, and right there in that bathroom, I found him again. I missed him so much, asked him to come to me, and then suddenly, immediately, I knew he *was* there with me.

In that instant, I stopped crying. I felt him and knew he was there. I found a speck of peace, and I consumed it. I went back into the living room knowing I was changed forever. I was opened. My life was special. My experiences were extraordinary. There was grief inside me, but there was something greater than the separation. There was a *knowing* that there was a never-ending connection, and that death is not about a disconnect and an ending, but something much, much greater. I was connected, and I could hear them through my feeling them.

I was heard in that bathroom, and I heard them all. Yes, Jesus, Mary, Christopher. I felt at peace. It was the sort of peace one feels after a good cry—exhausted from carrying so much pain, only to feel the relief of that flooding out of me. It was a quiet, internal knowing. He was here. They all were here. They never left. I couldn't see them. I couldn't yet hear them. But I could know them and therefore feel them. And they knew me all along. They knew the me who woke up that day, long before I even knew she was missing. It made me feel better in that moment. I was opened and freed, changed forever and in peace. Everything made sense.

Then, almost as quickly as the Bright Light of Illumination and Personal Enlightenment came to me, my rational mind returned, and I started to doubt myself. I started to think I was nuts for thinking I was *heard* by Jesus, Mary, and Christopher! I started to tell myself I was self-centered for even thinking the dead *would make* time for me. I told myself I was only trying to answer my own pain with a brief, false knowing. I wanted my newly opened, oozing-out sideways grief to stop, so I must have resorted to mind games and self-trickery to close this gaping hole in my heart that was reopened that afternoon. I struggled with the conflict between knowing something for sure and wanting something to be true.

This was my first experience with what I have now coined as the "The asshole brain." What we think is what we *allow* to be true. Our mind is brilliant. It's recorded every event in our lives since conception, and really, I believe it holds the stories and memories and codes of all of life within each of us. When you use your mind to validate an experience, it's limited. It draws from previous experiences to understand and provide a framework, a *concept* if you will, of what is real. It's terribly shortsighted.

When we connect with the deceased, that connection goes against our minds' logic. It tells us immediately to kick this thought out simply because it typically doesn't have solid foundation to base its knowledge. There's no scientific evidence convincing enough to support it as fact. We were told, when we die, we *go* to Heaven (or Hell). We are no longer here, and we are certainly not in a space where we can communicate with each other.

Communicating with the deceased seems illogical to most of us. So does thinking the big hole in my neighbor's backyard dug out to remove a post was a tunnel to Satan and hell itself. But yet we still chose to play in it. You would think we would be afraid to get sucked down, but nah. We just continued to play fearlessly on the entrance to hell itself. We were bad asses.

The brain only believes what it's been programmed to know. Every bit of data is based on top of data that came before it. Up until that point, I didn't have a moving, living visual memory of Chris, and so when I saw him live and in action, I realized he was gone. Sounds silly, but it wasn't until I really saw him living that I knew that he was dead. Before this, he was just a story to me. My brother was a photograph and a bunch of stories told to me by family members. I didn't remember him from my own self and my own memories. I didn't remember him in the flesh. Nothing. I was too young.

I knew him through everyone else's memories of him. They weren't mine. These videos showed me with him. I got soap in his eyes while we shared a bath, and I wore his boots when he outgrew them. We shared mismatched mittens, hats, and coats so we could play outside. We fought over who got the Big Wheels and who got to pet our dog. We ate the same meals of ziti and pork chops. We both reached our grubby hands in the jar to find the last cookie in pieces at the bottom.

All this came flooding back to me. It became real and then unreal. I didn't know the difference between life and death. Real and imagined, truth and fake. I thought I was crazy for feeling something so intense, so real, and yet, I questioned whether that was all make believe. Then I further questioned the real life and living he and I shared that I could not remember at all. His spiritual visitation to me in the bathroom felt more real to me than any other experience with him I could remember. Yet, I was making myself feel crazy for thinking the unreal, was real, and the real wasn't. Three decades later, I have rectified this conundrum.

From this point on, I struggled with both my left and right brains, I straddled between logic and intuition, and I have fought hard to strike a balance. I needed to know for certain what happens when we die. If I could find proof of this, then I could satisfy the answer. I didn't even care what the answer was. I just wanted to know it so that I wouldn't be lured into believing in some fairytale.

I wanted to answer all the questions, and I did my research. I turned to science, religion, philosophy, psychology. Intuition and experiences led to wishful and magical thinking. Life after death, communicating with Saints and Sages, to me, were as illogical and mentally unstable as believing in fire-breathing dragons. And although I loved *Puff the Magic Dragon*, I wouldn't dare convince myself that dragons were for real simply because I felt it was true. I wanted proof of these things, not just a feeling.

I was rigid and bent on not believing in anything I couldn't see, feel, or touch. But there was always something inside of me that knew otherwise. The conflict was intense. There was something bigger and more real than what we can perceive to be real. What that was, I didn't know, but I *did* know it. I also remember that moment in the bathroom and how it brought back the innate knowing we all possess. I was brought directly to meet my core, and meet it I did! I got a massive insight into the nature of what we all really are. We are energy, and we do not die. Energy is real and infinite. I connected with it, strongly. It's there. I just didn't know where it was, or how I could reach it again. All because I struggled to prove it rather than be it. I wouldn't learn until decades later, that we cannot use our logical minds to solve or understand matters of the soul.

I now understand that my natural sense of knowing and my childlike curiosity in the unknown, life, death, and science originated from a great loss. It had to be this way. Christopher George died from a rare childhood cancer at the age of four. My three-year-old self didn't know how to express that I missed "Cricky." Yet that brilliant three-year-old self also stayed plugged into a knowing that death wasn't the final end. Little Debbie knew he was there all along. That knowing was reopened in that bathroom. I was reawakened.

Adolescent Debbie lost that understanding along the way through school, and the indoctrination of "dead is dead and that's it" that is so prevalent in our society. Again, I was conflicted with what I knew inside me, versus what logic and reason taught me. We live in a world that likes polarity, where what we think is real and what we feel is not. I've now learned it's the opposite. It's quite a feat to relearn this. But we must, and you will have a better grasp of that after reading this book.

I often had the opportunity to speak to my mother about almost anything, and I remember expressing my questions or sharing my "theories" of life. I remember knowing about light, space, and what I now know is called consciousness. I remember being obsessed with Einstein, and somehow having a broad understanding of his Theory of Relativity. He was looking for a Unifying Field of everything. I knew, as a child, what this Unifying Field was. I understood this and yet, I didn't have the vocabulary and conceptual framework to explain it. It was inside me. I didn't know how to get it out of me. Somehow, I felt I was trying to understand the same phenomena he so desperately wanted to figure out. Again, I knew I was onto something big, but my human self felt foolish and even arrogant for thinking little Debbie Hanlon could possibly know something Einstein *himself* couldn't fully grasp. I couldn't understand fractions or remember my times tables! And yet my insides wanted to delve into quantum physics? *Yeah. Crazy talk, Deb. Be quiet. You are an idiot. You are full of yourself.* But deep down, I knew I wasn't. There is something more to all of us and all of life itself. And it's quite simple. Ah, how the human ego loves to make our True Selves so, so, small. Sigh.

My mind never stopped questioning life. What is this thing called energy? What is our True Nature? Are we all really linked the way I feel we are? And if so, how? Is there time? What is perception? Why are our perceptions skewed as humans? If there is no time, how can there be death? How can we grow old if there is no time? How do we even know there is no time, when we are living in a conceptual framework of time? What the heck does no time even mean? How does the universe continuously grow if there is no time? Aren't growth and time related? If I could figure out how it all fits together, I could help millions of people. Help them do what? Not age? Never die? I still didn't even know what the point was or what this knowledge or proof could do for us. I had no clue! No conceptual framework of what to do with this. Still, my mind never, ever stopped dipping into these questions! (It still doesn't stop, but it's much more enjoyable to ponder it all today than back then!)

Other than this, I had a seemingly normal childhood on the outside, but on the inside, I was constantly trying to understand how my thoughts and feelings and my *knowings* were connected and how the heck I was going to explain all this to the world. I always knew within me, I would someday have an audience with whom to share everything, but who would even listen to me? Who was I to know anything about... well, anything? In my younger years, I was intense on the inside, and no one really knew it. Today, I'm intense on the outside, and everyone knows it. I like the current version of me much better.

I vacillated between what I *knew* and craved understanding of, and all that I didn't know. I thought I would never be smart enough to comprehend it all. It's funny how the mind of a child works. I was never good at math, and so I figured I'd never be able to fully understand the concept of physics without the math. This frustrated me. How could I understand it all if I couldn't understand algebra? Who was I to think I was smart when I couldn't grasp basic math? I acted as if the *only* intelligence measurement was knowledge of PEMDAS and formulas. That's because, then, as a school-aged kid in the 1980s, that *was* how intelligence was measured.

So, I had deep thoughts as a kid, and yet I still played Barbies, with matchbox cars, flashlight tag, joined sports teams, and attended sleepover parties. I was a kid, and yet, inside, so plugged into wanting to know something much larger. I definitely didn't share my insatiable thirst for quantum physics with my friends. I simply just assumed they didn't think of these things. Now, I wish I had shared more with more people. Only until my late thirties, did I realize the value of the thoughts, opinions, viewpoints, and philosophies of many people. Early on, I was exposed to great teachers, but after Chris died, I was isolated from this sort of intellectual sharing, and life got hard. Thank goodness for my mom and her library of books!

I knew, even as a kid, that eventually I would find a science behind it all that would someday make for a concrete and tangible explanation of all that was invisible, although I couldn't yet make sense of it. It's like we know what we know, but we just don't know how we know it, nor do we fully know what it is or what to do with it. This knowing would literally drive me crazy. I knew that I knew something important, and yet, I didn't know what that was, or how to even prove it. Oyyy.

As I said, I still have zero *actual* memories of my earliest years when Chris was alive, and yet I have some powerful yet fleeting memories that have to do *with* Christopher after he passed—all of which are of him post-death. One time is of being in the bedroom of family friends with my remaining siblings and friends Matthew and Kevin. There was a board on a small table in the middle of the bedroom, next to the bunk beds. They were all gathered around this board, excited, giggling, and nervous.

They were moving their hands, and asking questions. "Are you here? Chris, are you here? Chris if you are here, let us know."

I was like, what the heck? And then, I have a fleeting memory of *seeing* Christopher. I remember actually seeing him. But either my memory or my understanding of that moment gets confused. I begin to doubt what it was I saw as true or as a desire to want to see. Was it real or not? I don't know if I thought it was normal, or if I thought I was *just imagining* that I was seeing things. Was I thinking of him because they were talking about him? My sister later confirmed that I did know he was there, and I said it out loud.

At the time, I knew that I knew, but as soon as the moment passed, it felt as if I had played a game of cruel imagination with myself. I was unclear if that was real or not. But what I know now after all I have learned and experienced, is that Christopher *was* there. How do I know this? Because I feel it even now.

Years later, I learned that board was called a Ouija board, and it's used to contact the dead. Clearly, *something* happened because I saw it. And we all received messages from Chris that day. Are Ouija boards real? Are they portals for negative spirits and energy? I highly doubt so. No more so than that giant hole in my neighbor's backyard was the very entrance to hell itself. My logical mind fights me to remember it is just a piece of cardboard with eerie font marketed by a modern company called Milton Bradley. Hardly the tool I would expect the other side to request from beyond. But something happened that day. That's for sure. We all know it. But the logic of it messes with and then dulls the experience. The mind will not help us understand matters of the heart and spirit. My mind still tells me I was daydreaming or experiencing wishful thinking. My heart knows it connected to spirit.

I was home with Chris when he died. Oddly, there are varying stories of where and how Chris died, depending on whom you ask. I don't know which is true. He was either in my father's arms, or he was on his cot in the middle of the kitchen. No matter which way it happened, I was there when his spirit left his body. I was there when they placed him in a body bag and took him away. My father remembers that I was very upset about them taking Christopher away. My mother doesn't remember this moment at all. I can't imagine being a parent in this situation. Either way, I was three years old, and I had just experienced the death of my best buddy in the purest form one can.

They took him away. Years later, when I heard that I was very upset at that moment, I had another moment of grief well up within me. I was touching a part of myself, and the grief of that scene overtook me. I mourned for the little me whose brother was taken in a body bag. That realization and grief occurs over twenty and even thirty years later, though. At the time, I experienced his death as sad, I'm sure, but I believe that I also knew it was normal. It had to be normal because it happened. What we experience is what we consider normal, until we discover in life that, no, not everyone experiences having a four-year-old family member die in their home and be taken away in a bag. Usually, siblings of this age have a moment of separation when the sibling enters kindergarten and leaves behind the baby who anxiously waits for their return. Four-year-olds don't die, and they don't get taken away in a bag.

For us, it was normal because it was what happened. So, my little three-year-old mind believed this is just what happens to people. Today, I am grateful for that reality. Death was a natural part of life, no matter how too soon this death was. I carry this knowing today— after many years of struggling with it. Death is a natural part of life. And there is no order. It's not really supposed to make sense. It happens… and it happens to all of us. There is simply a time for us to die, a time for our spirits, our energies, to be released from our physical bodies. It's painful. But it's unavoidable. It's not convenient. And if logic were applied to the dying process, no one would ever die at a young age. Logically, we would think the purpose of life was to grow older, to gain experiences, and then die. But we all know that is not reality. People die every day from both horrific and peaceful causes. People of all ages. And it's normal. It's just as normal that we *all* really dislike this, immensely.

For years, I buried Chris' life. I never thought about him. I feel that I didn't even think he existed. I don't know if it was because my family was going through so many other traumas at the same time. My brother was dealing with depression and addiction. My parents divorced, money was tight, and my mom was just keeping her head above water. My father was grieving in ways I don't even know.

He left us and moved away. Even though my life was constantly in upheaval for one reason or another, I felt very much at peace in my core. I felt that I understood a bigger picture was at work for my family.

I knew, or I felt, there was something I needed to share with the world someday. I used to think I was just a kid, thinking kid thoughts, but today I know I really do have messages for the world. I believe I needed to understand trauma, dysfunction, and chaos. I had to realize that life isn't perfect. It's perfectly messy. And it's perfectly arranged. Chris had to die for my entire family to become who we all are. He gave me life and a way to express myself and have a sense of purpose. I now help thousands of people gain some insight around death and life. It wasn't ideal, and it most certainly isn't the way I would have preferred for it to go and planned accordingly! I was given an ability and that gift was to connect. *Not just connect the living to the deceased, but also to connect the living with the dead parts of themselves.* I've experienced a lot of my own human emotion because I've lived it, watched it, and felt it. Understanding gives me an advantage of nonjudgment. I also know *nothing* transforms us like experiencing a death. I believe I can help people not only to grieve the death of a loved one, but to also understand death from a much bigger perspective. We can have life after death, in both realms, spirit and earthly forms. We simply need to understand things in a broader way. Life and death operate in a cyclical way rather than a finite cessation of being. Once you get that down pat, the rest is smooth sailing, sort of. And I can help you help yourself.

Deborah Hanlon

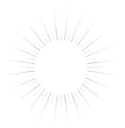

2
Mediumship and the Path

"And what do you do for a living?"

Just a few simple words stop me whenever I am asked this question, whether it is in a social setting or a professional one. How does one answer that when one's job is talking to dead people? How can I casually say, "I am a medium"? When I reply that way, people usually respond in with shock or silence. They try to hide their disbelief. Because my ability to feel a person is astute, I can't help but sense a high level of discomfort.

Some people are believers, and they get excited or sometimes even worried because they suddenly think I'm downloading all their earthly secrets into my brain and I know everything about them. (I'm not, and I don't.) Some people are not believers, and they think I'm some whacko who pretends to have knowledge I apparently found on Google. (Not accurate either.) Google would love to get hold of the information the way I do, but so far, it hasn't figured out how to contact the deceased.

Others have extreme religious beliefs that instantly place me as the devil him/herself and feel open enough to share that with me.

I read *The Devil Wears Prada*, and to date, I don't own anything Prada, so there.

Then, there are the regular people who are surprised, intrigued, and respectful. Although most of the people with whom I work are like that, let me tell you, the others leave a mark on my psyche. After all, I'm human, and I don't want to be incorrectly viewed by anyone. I'd like to be taken seriously because I have a lot to offer.

How do I not say what I do? It's a conundrum that I suppose you may not have thought about. I mean, let's be real here. "I talk to dead people" instantly makes us think of the famous line in the movie, *Sixth Sense*, which by the way, is one of the creepiest movies I've ever seen. No, mediumship for me is nothing like that movie, and yet I'm still dumbfounded that people didn't know Bruce Willis wasn't dead all along. *Hello?*

When filling out mortgage applications, I had to answer this dreaded question many times. I ended up just stating, "I'm in communications," a career to which people respond with a fake certainty of "Oh, cool." They think Verizon, or Google, when really, I'm in the "connection with the deceased business," which ultimately means I connect the living to their heartaches, and help lead them to a happier state. That description does not fit neatly on loan applications. Nor does it fit in our world *yet*. Sure, society has grown more open to talking about this topic, but it's still far enough outside the norm to be considered a bit taboo. John Edward created *Crossing Over*, which led to countless other radio shows and TV programming to educate ourselves about the deepest mystery ever known to man. And am I grateful to him for paving the way.

Mediumship has been around for centuries, but at some point in history, say, when religion got all scared of those who had an ability to connect with nonhuman entities, it was shut down. Our abilities didn't close up, but our comfort zone of being able to openly talk about the spiritual world did. Hundreds of years later, people were finally able to talk about the time they saw Uncle Peter right after he died, or the night when a bright light filled with messages appeared at the edge of the bed.

I always find it sad when we feel we can't be open. When we feel stupid or crazy for having unexplained human experiences, we're living in a human prison within our minds. Let's take paranormal activity out of the conversation for a moment. If you are a parent, I'm certain there have been times when you thought negatively about your parenting skills, but you didn't dare tell a soul out of fear you were the only one who had ever felt that way. Or remember as a kid, when you wouldn't dare raise your hand to express that you didn't have a clue what the teacher was talking about, again out of fear that you were the only one? Well, that's how these experiences work. We don't say a word because we are afraid that others will think we are crazy or stuck in wishful thinking patterns. I can't stand that.

We can't or don't share some of our most profound, unexplainable spiritual experiences out of fear of what others will think? Pure definition of insanity if you ask me. Add to that the intense emotional situation death places us in, along with this secrecy and fear. Quite frankly, that's a recipe for disaster when we don't openly express our thoughts, experiences, hopes, wishes, and fears. It's why we as humans feel we are separate and isolated, and we do it to ourselves. Back in primitive times, cultures shared and celebrated spiritual encounters. Paying homage and speaking to the deceased in many cultures were natural and normal events. That's one of the reasons I'm on this planet. The road needs some more paving.

Death leaves us blind and searching for answers. It leaves us feeling vulnerable and having no place to turn. Grief leaves us questioning and craving time to apologize, time to cherish moments we think we took for granted, time to process, time to be alone, time to try to redo things, time to make sense of it all, and time to, well, torture ourselves. Death opens the doorway for needing insight and clarity on not only the deceased, but it forces us to consider the aspects of our human selves that we may not have previously needed to understand. It pushes us over the edge. We are destroyed by sadness and anger, and then we are left to put our pieces back together—without a map, without a single place to turn. We usually turn to what is familiar to us at first, and often, the familiar simply no longer fits for us. That doesn't feel good and right either, which leads to feeling alone and lost.

The industry of death, if you will, is a tricky one because ultimately, no one knows a thing until, well—until we die. Until then, we are seeking for answers on a human level from a human perspective on a topic that is anything but human. We rely on our own logic and emotions to tell us the story of death, to help us figure out where our loved ones go and what and how they are feeling and thinking.

Our own minds and hearts turn on us. Nothing makes sense, and we work hard to figure it all out. *Where did they go? Do they see me? Do they know I loved them?* We seek to understand the all-time most frustrating question there is: *Why? Why did this happen? Why couldn't I have changed it? Why are we all even here in the first place? Why, why, why?* Our human selves seek to understand the spiritual and energetic side of nature. Yet, using human logic will not suffice in our searches. We are limited when we use our intellect. It simply isn't enough when dealing with matters of our souls.

Humanity has largely used religion to help guide us through the forest of the unknown. Religion has provided enough answers for many people through generations of civilization. Mainly those answers are: *Don't question death; don't wake the deceased; there is a room where we await our eternal fate based on our deeds here in physical form (so, be good),* and *don't anger your creator.* If you abide by those rules, all will work out swimmingly. Argh. Yes, I am putting strong theological principles in very watered-down, sarcastic terms, but that's because I have been exposed to thousands of people who are simply not satisfied with that any more. I've also been exposed to many more who haven't lived because of their fear of the unknown.

Those philosophies were never enough for me. I craved answers for as long as I can remember. I knew and felt things, not in a paranormal sense, but in a very inquisitive, astute sense where my logical mind simply could not explain. I *knew* things, and I had no clue what it was or how I knew it. I never really questioned my knowledge either. I never pointed out a dead person and said, "Oh look, there's Aunt so and so and hey what's up?" or "Thanks for the advice, man." I had a connection to a place where all is well and all will remain OK as long as we stay in a mindset where we remain open to a reality much greater than we can conceptualize. It is not as it is portrayed on TV, thank goodness. I'm not the only one who has been connected to this knowing state all along. So have you.

I remember feeling a sense of pure calm—a knowing all would be well in the world. I truly remember knowing to trust. When I say this, people reply, "Oh, that's because you were a carefree kid, and all kids feel that way."

I was anything but carefree. I had life smack me in my little face early on, and I was fully aware that life had difficulty, heartache, and stress. In fact, I did not know life as anything but stressful and depressing. I just didn't listen to it. I knew none of that was mine. They were the adults' issues, and sure, I was affected by them, but I was a child among chaos. I wasn't the cause of it, and yet I signed up for it cosmically.

The experiences I've had all led to writing this today. Even as a child, I was attached and detached at the same time. I work to apply this method to my current life, although I find it much more difficult when one is an adult, and I am often stuck in the mindset of figuring out all I should do. Ironically, our stress is found in our doing, and we lose our being in all of it. That's called accessing life only via our human states of consciousness and forgetting there is a much larger component to us, called our Spiritual Selves or Higher Selves.

What is a medium? Many people still understand it as "a

person who can talk to dead people" (blech). Really, though, a medium is someone who has an ability to suspend our own human senses. Before you think that sounds like some ability born in the movies, it is and it isn't. It doesn't mean we have a more direct connection or relationship to the disembodied than "regular" people. It doesn't mean we were chosen to connect. It really doesn't mean anything spectacular at all. What it does mean is we have an ability to temporarily suspend our own egos and our own beings in order to connect with the other side. It means we sense things, thoughts, emotions, memories, details, and locations that are not our own. *And we are aware we're doing it.*.

As you are reading these words, your senses have been providing you feedback of your current world. You may or may not have noticed scents around you. Perhaps someone is or was cooking nearby you or brewing coffee as you read this. Maybe you are in a park and can smell perfume or freshly cut grass. Maybe you have been aware of sounds and thoughts as you are reading these words. Maybe you have had flashbacks of certain loved ones or thoughts that are not pertaining to your current reality. As humans, we are constantly operating via our senses.

As mediums, we suspend all of our own beliefs and opinions of the world, and we somehow morph into or sense another's point of view. We are literally able to experience the world through the eyes of many who happen to be deceased. In the beginning of my work, I had constant thoughts that never made sense to me, none of which were negative in nature.

That's a crucial point I need to make. If, as you are reading this, you feel, hear, or sense information or messages from a source that you don't feel is yourself, and these voices or sensations are telling you to do negative things or are telling you bad things, then ignore them and seek mental emotional assistance. Mediumship is not about fear. It is the exact opposite of that.

Although they didn't make sense to me at the time, the

thoughts I had been thinking in my early years weren't elaborate enough for me to understand that what I was hearing were the voices of the other side. Instead, I thought I had an active imagination and just liked to think a lot. Whew. When I found out that wasn't the full picture, I didn't know whether to be relieved or upset. I believe we all have the ability to connect with our loved ones, but being aware of it is the key. Being able to get rid of your own thoughts is what you need in order to access them. Meditation is a key element here, but the ability is far beyond meditation.

Growth Opportunity

Get permission from and then think of a living person in your life. Say that person's full name in your head. Think about this person's characteristics. Imagine them in your mind's eye. Allow yourself to sweep their body. Starting at the top of their head, imagine energy just running down in through the crown of their head and filling their body. Notice how and where this energy lands in them. Is it the same all over? Are there "holes" in their body where the energy flows out of them? Do not make an interpretation of their energy field. Just observe this scene without making assumptions. If white light energy is leaking out of their shoulder, do not try to explain why. Imagine their personality. Get a full sense of the person—what they like, what they have experienced. Imagine you can leave your body and enter into theirs. What would it feel like to be inside their experiences? Inside their physical body. Recognize people they love and hobbies they enjoy. Notice their world through their own eyes. Try not to place a judgment on those characteristics and instead, just observe them. Feel them as them. At first, you will begin to see you are noticing and observing what you think of them. That's a definition of coming from ego. How do they feel in their own bodies? What is their world view? When you allow yourself to feel them as them, you gain a tremendous amount of insight into people. This is a skill. *It takes practice,* and the most difficult part is to not use your human judgments to creep in on the reality of who this person is. This exercise really helps understand how we are always coming from our own interpretations in life, and those perspectives can be incorrect or at the very least are skewed.

Now, do the meditation again, and this time imagine someone you do not admire, someone you either know, or have heard of. Choose a person who has wronged you or a figure in history; anyone you do not like will do. Imagine what it is like being this person, *as them.* Remember to realize there are people this person loves and who love them. See how they view their world. Realize everyone's perspective, no matter how twisted it may seem to you, is simply that, a perspective caused by conditioning. Work on understanding others without a lens to cloud you.

A medium does exactly this. We allow the energy of the person to be made known. We aren't placing judgments on this person's way of thinking. We are picking up on their thinking, memories, emotions, nuances, and habits, *as them* and not as ourselves. Once I can feel a person's energy, I can open up a conversation with that person. Every personality is different, and there is simply no cookie-cutter way of connecting with every energy. Why? Well, it's the same formula we have here on earth. I'm certain we connect differently to a judge while standing in front of him or her for a speeding ticket than we do our best friend at a party.

A trained medium also has a hefty responsibility. It's our job to sit with people, mostly in their darkest moments, to make a connection for them. The way we express things is key to a good session. Again, we can't make assumptions. We can't stereotype. We can only connect, feel, hear, and pay very close attention to our senses and thoughts. We must relay messages as precisely as they are given and not twist them to our own interpretation. We are humans who are making sense of a ton of data in seconds. We can see, feel, and hear so much information at a time, but are only able to truly process a small amount of it.

We must also make a disconnection with the person who has died as well as the clients we sit with. It's very difficult to give a message when we are emotionally charged. I call that getting too close. Sometimes, I'll relay information and messages to a client, feel tears well up and even cry. This means I, Debbie, got too involved in the interaction and, at that moment, only Deborah has been granted access to a connection. Deborah knows how to stay back and simply be the middle woman—the messenger, the medium. Debbie is a human who can't bear to see people in pain and can't stand to be in pain. Debbie is as sensitive as Deborah is cautious. I often half-joke to my close loved ones, "Whom do you want to show up today? Debbie or Deborah?" I'm happy when they say, "Debbie." Strangers are the ones who want to get to know Deborah.

Are all mediums the same? No. There are three main types or methods mediums may use: mental mediumship, physical mediumship, and trance mediumship. The most commonly practiced, and the type I experience, is mental mediumship. I am mostly a mental medium (which I jokingly say just means I am crazy), but I also use physical mediumship in my sessions.

A mental medium receives the communication and information through our thoughts, feelings, and senses. We pay close attention to our thoughts, and upon careful and focused attention, and we realize the thoughts behind our own, are actually the voices or messages from those who have passed on. This is an ability all humans possess when they take the time to slow down and pay attention. When you are thinking about someone, whether they are here in human form or deceased, you make an instant connection to their energy field.

You've probably had what you thought was a random thought about a person you haven't spoken to in a while, only to receive a phone call, text, or message from them a few minutes later.

That is not a coincidence. You were picking up on the thoughts from the other person before their physical ability to get you. All this happens on the level of the conscious, and it is mental mediumship—occurring in the mental or realm of our thoughts.

Physical mediumship is pretty amazing stuff. This is when the medium physically feels things as the person they are bringing through. Physical mediumship allows us to pick up the physical characteristics and nuances of the energy. For example, if someone was a double amputee, I will suddenly lose the feeling in my legs. Yikes. I've felt dentures or lack of them, tongue rings, scoliosis, people who are wheelchair bound, blind, deaf, and I have physically felt how someone passed. If the passing was sudden, it hits me quickly. With those who passed from long-term illnesses, I feel their relief. All this communication comes through as physical feelings, and let me tell you, it is exhausting. I often say, "I'm so tired," when I get home from work. My family teases me about how I can be so tired when all I have done all day is sit in a chair and talk.

"Are you kidding me?" I reply. "Today, I was shot, died of lung cancer, passed in 9/11, and had three heart attacks." No one really gets it.

Physical mediumship uses the sense of feelings to receive information. Perhaps you've heard of the Clairs. These are Clairvoyance, Clairaudience, Clairsentience, Clairgustance, and Clairagency. The word clair means *clear.*

Clairvoyance is the ability to see energy, either right out in front of us, or within our mind's eye, which is the way I see it. At the risk of seeming like a whack-o, there have been times, such as when I was in the hospital after giving birth to my son, where I have actually seen energy. It is rare for me, and I do not like it. I have made a deal of sorts with energies, and that is I do not want to physically see them. It simply creeps me out and leaves me feeling unstable. And so, I choose to only see them in ways in which I have the most control. So far, they seem to listen.

Clairaudience is when we can hear energy speaking to us. I like to describe that sense as this. Go ahead and repeat the alphabet in your mind right now: A, B, C... Did you physically hear anything, or did you simply know or understand what was being said? This is how clairaudience mainly works. It isn't an actual voice most of the time. I am sure you have had those moments when you could actually hear (outside your mind) the voice of someone calling your name, or calling out to you. This is also a form of clairaudience. When this happens infrequently and suddenly, and when those messages are of a kind and loving manner, it is energy communicating with us. Again, if you hear disembodied voices regularly, and if they tell you negative things, those are not coming from the other side. Someone trained in psychology could help you better understand and address them.

Clairsentience is when you simply feel the energy of the person speaking through you. It's a knowing via your emotions of what the person is trying to convey. Often in sessions, I am very picky with the words I use to convey messages. Why? Because words are powerful, and when they give me feelings, I am meticulous about choosing the proper words. It is my job to pass along messages as precisely as possible and to make sure the receiver of my messages understands their intentions. How things are said is just as important as what is being said.

Clairgustance is the communication via taste buds. It's often my least favorite way of communication, particularly when the tastes are pretty gross. Sometimes, I believe those on the other side get a huge kick out of making me sick. I've tasted favorite and distinct foods they used to eat. Most memorable was the fish-and-jelly taste I had while presenting a gallery (an open group forum where I bring messages to random audience members). I could describe it only as something like anchovies and jelly, and it was not pleasant. Turns out, a favorite snack of the deceased happened to be sardines with mint jelly.

Trance mediumship is rare. This is when the medium goes

into a trancelike state to literally act as a conduit for messages from the other side. I have doubts about this type of mediumship, and to be honest and fair, I have yet to witness a true trance medium at work firsthand.

Clairagency is the feeling of actually being touched or of witnessing physical evidence. Although this one is super rare for me, I have witnessed it. My most memorable proof of this was when a mother was coming through and telling her daughter that the reason her granddaughter had one patch of straight hair at the top of her head and the rest of her hair in ringlets was because that is where she rubs and soothes her at night. The young mother of this three-year-old child started to cry and pulled out a picture of her daughter. And wouldn't you know it, this little one had ringlets, except in one odd spot at the top her head going halfway down toward her ear, where it was perfectly straight. That was all the proof I needed. I could physically see there was a mark.

Let me once again remind you, I don't *see* dead people. At least not outside my mind. My mind's eye sees them. Over the years, I've learned there is a language of mediumship that one must study to understand. This language is filled with thoughts, imagery, emotions, and physical sensations. There is so much that needs to be personally deciphered for each medium. There isn't a one-size-fits-all for us. We receive information from the same source, and yet we all do it slightly differently. That's the cool part, and it's also the frustrating part. We can teach others how to get connected, but it's through personal practice where a medium can hone his or her skills. It takes intense skill in noticing everything, being plugged into our five senses, and becoming able to decipher messages in an instant. For example, I've learned that if I sense energy standing next to the right side of a person, slightly above their shoulder line, that is their father or a father figure (stepfather, father-in-law, etc.) On the left side, is a mother or mother figure. A grandparent or elderly generation energy is sensed slightly above the person, and sibling and peer energy is in line directly to a person's side.

Imagine a family tree. At the top of the tree, are our great grandparents, great uncles, aunts, etc. Below them, are our grandparents, then our aunts and uncles and parents. Below them, are our siblings, cousins, and then our children, and below them, the grandchildren. So, I have the other side organize themselves in this fashion to help me understand the relationship to a client.

Male energy mostly shows up on the right side, and female energy on the left, at least for me. At times, I still have an energy who pops over to the "wrong" side of a person, completely confusing my methods. Mediumship is not always precise—not a good career choice for a control freak. There is little we can do to make a connection happen in the way we want it to.

There are different types of intuitives and a variety of ways in which we pick up on information and energy. I personally do not like the word psychic because it reminds me of crystal balls, purple neon signs, and well frankly, creepy ill-intentioned people. I know that isn't accurate, but that has always been my perception, and it's still taking me time to erase or override this early belief. That is why I prefer the word intuitive. For me, everyone fits that word. We are all intuitive. However, not everyone decides to use their intuition and make it a career—much like singers. Technically, we can all sing, but we can't all win a Grammy for it.

We all have the ability to connect with our own loved ones who have passed, but we must learn what communicating is and isn't. Many people think mediums see, hear, and know everything clearly, but guess what? We don't. And guess what else? We aren't always right in our deciphering of messages because those messages are often far from clear.

In this book, I am going to share with you what I learned as a former skeptic turned unlikely medium, or as one of my friends calls me, "the medium next door." I'm going to share my view of the afterlife as it has been presented to me by those who know it best—

the deceased. I'm also going show you how we can create a sense of Heaven on Earth.

I wrote this book so you can adopt ways to feel better and become authentically connected to who you are while still living in the physical realm. The direct result of doing that will allow you to feel and be connected to not only your deceased loved ones, but to everyone, starting with both your human and your higher self.

3

Am I Crazy, or Can I Really Talk to Dead People?

I've had one visitation dream in my entire life, and it changed my life. I was 24.

It began with me in the backyard of the home I grew up in. I was somehow led to go inside the basement, but I had to enter though the small egress windows. I "flew" in, and was brought to an antique table with very few belongings on it: a wooden box filled with a coin or two, an antique map, a candle, and a photograph. Once there, I was greeted by my paternal grandfather, John Hanlon. I don't remember actually meeting him in real life because I was very young when he died.

The family stories of my grandfather didn't paint him in the kindest light. His legacy was that of an unkind alcoholic who had a passion for reading. For an Irish immigrant, he loved Shakespeare and could recite many of his lines. He was born to a middle-class family in Sligo Ireland, attended college for a short time, and then moved to New York City when he was in his early twenties. All we have left of him is a diploma or certificate from Black Rock College in Ireland. After that, what happened to him and what he did for a living are mysteries.

In my dream, my grandfather greets me with open and loving arms, yet he has a mission. He leads me through a recessed basement window into what was once called the workshop area of my childhood home. In the dream, the workshop is set up like a dry-cleaning establishment, with rows and rows of coats on hangers that go deep into the back of a seemingly never-ending room. My grandfather instructs me to "pick a coat" and to choose whichever one I want. I look at him and then at the rows of coats, and I spot the one I want in the back. As I start to move toward it, Grandpa pulls me back and says sternly, "No. Pick it with your mind. Choose it with your mind and allow it to come to you." I am confused, but then I feel a sense of trust come over me.

I nod, choose the same coat, and fixate my mind and eyes on it. To my surprise, it lifts off the rack and floats directly to me. It is then that I understand the Law of Attraction, without even fully knowing there is a formal law.

He puts his hands on my shoulders, and says, "Deborah, you have a gift. And I'm going to teach you how to use it."

Although I had no idea what he was talking about, yet I did. Something was about to happen, and I had to be prepared. I needed his help and guidance. For whatever reason, he was the one to give it to me, and I have used his wisdom every day during my journey. He is most certainly, a guide for me in this lifetime. Let me remind you that my using the word *guide* is like an atheist scientist using the word God. I never believed in them until this experience. Sure, I had this experience as a dream, and I have no empirical data to prove the presence of my guide, other than what I know in my own heart. For me, that is more than enough proof. It's indescribable proof, as always seems to be the case with everything I do. It's the Presence within me.

Two months after having this dream, while visiting Ireland, I had another experience. The home where we were staying had a foal that was born on the day before we arrived. I was told the mare would be very protective of her baby, and that I should not go anywhere near them. If she wanted us to meet her baby, she would bring it to us. Although not an animal person, I was enthralled and obsessed by the thought of seeing this mommy and baby. No sooner had we arrived than the mommy horse and I locked eyes. She began to prance toward me with her little one tagging right along. I petted the proud mommy and felt an intense connection between us. She was communicating with me, but I didn't get the memo! I felt something, but I had no idea what it was.

Three weeks later, after I returned home, after being sick and being terrified that I was suffering from the West Nile epidemic/scare going on at that time, I found out I was pregnant. That mommy horse knew it and was welcoming my little one into the world before I even had a clue. There was a connection and a knowing that I can never explain. Again, the former me would think I'm insane. I would laugh at the idea that I was communicating with a horse! I am getting a chuckle of out of how that sounds even as I write it. But again, I felt it. And I can't really explain it much beyond that.

This was my first pregnancy, and I wasn't planning it. I wasn't married, I didn't have my Master's degree. I wasn't prepared to have a baby, and yet, I knew this little energy needed to come to the planet, and I needed to be his mother. There was something magical for me and this baby. I was placed on a road, and although it wasn't the road I sought out at that time, the Universe is way smarter than we are, and this was now my journey. I'm so glad the Universe had different plans for me. Even though, at the time, I knew it was all meant to be, I didn't know the scope of how all these pieces would eventually fit together.

Sometimes our lives are like jigsaw puzzles. We have to create a frame to work within, and then the Universe fills in the rest. Eventually, we are left with a stunning piece of life and art that remains our legacy.

Jack's pregnancy was rough in the beginning with a lot of morning sickness, but when the morning sickness ended, his pregnancy was a dream. My mom would place her hand on my belly, and we would be in awe of the energy this little being was sending out into the world. We both felt it, this reverberation of pure vibration. We got to really know his intense, yet lighthearted way from the very, very beginning. While in my tummy, he was energetically the same young man he is today.

On March 6, 2001, my first thought as I felt his tiny being placed on my chest was, "Oh, I cannot ever die. I need to be here for him." I realized I was now responsible for the life of another. It was a magically intense moment. I was in love and yet intrigued that my first thought with a new life in my arms, turned instantly to death. Love, New Life, and Death were all wrapped up in the same instant. And they were all bundled up in the classic pink- and blue-striped newborn blanket with a head full of dark hair sticking out. He was definitely my baby. Talk about powerful.

Hours later, I was sitting in a rocking chair trying to nurse my new infant, still in awe and very unprepared for and unsure of it all but in complete love with this little person. As I looked down at this tiny baby, I saw a man walk into the room out of the corner of my eye. Startled by this person walking in on such an uncertain moment for me as a new mom, I saw his shoes and dress pants, and as I continued to look up, he disappeared. He was literally gone! I was shocked, stunned, and confused. But I wasn't scared.

Instead, I was a little worried that my blood sugar was low, or I was dehydrated from delivery. I calmed down quickly, and I immediately sensed it was my grandfather coming to visit us again. I just knew it. I hadn't thought about my dream before this moment, and I began to have some inkling there was a connection with my little boy and what was about to open up in me. Shortly after that, a Catholic priest came into my room and wanted to bless my little baby. This isn't a strange phenomenon, as it happens often in hospitals, except for the fact that I was listed as a Unitarian Universalist, not a Catholic.

My mom blurted out, "Deb, I know this is weird, but I really feel that is your grandfather's way of making sure Jack is blessed by a priest. He would flip if he wasn't!" I had never told anyone about feeling my grandfather's presence earlier or about the dream months before. My mom's inclination sealed the deal for me. Again, it was more intangible proof he was in fact surrounding us strongly.

Five months later, a family member's mother-in-law was very ill. I had met her a few times at family events, but I didn't know all that much about her. My family members were going out to Buffalo, New York, to visit her, but they didn't realize they needed to pack for a funeral. She passed away during their visit.

Unprepared, they called and asked me to get clothes they could wear to the funeral. I went to their house, and as I was going through the closets looking for a tie for my relative, an intense and ridiculously overwhelming sense of emotion came over me. I started to sob. I mean, really, really sob. I couldn't catch my breath.

At first, I felt I could feel where this woman was. I felt her as she experienced what we all call the Life Review. I could feel her peace, and then the flood of emotion. I thought I was going crazy. I thought I was having some delayed postpartum depression episode, as I just had my son five months prior to this. I sat on their bed sobbing. I couldn't stop it, and I felt ridiculous. What was wrong with me?

I went to Buffalo for the funeral, and during the few days while I was there, the feelings of the woman were getting stronger and stronger. There were so many instances where I just knew and had proof I could feel her around that I couldn't even deny it if I wanted to. I would overhear conversations of people asking, "Where did she keep her mother's blanket?" And I would hear in my mind, "Bottom drawer, left side." I'd mention that to my relative, who surprisingly didn't question me on any of this, and voila, there it was! Again, I wasn't rejoicing and feeling all calm and Zen. Instead, I was thinking *what is happening? This is stupid. This is weird. How did I know that?*

There was an entire weekend filled with these encounters. I received the final proof I needed when she showed me that she knew her son would kiss her face in a photograph every night before he went to sleep. Her son came into the room, pointed to the very picture she had just been telling me about, and announced to the entire room, "See that picture? I kiss her face every night before I go to bed!" After this message, I just knew I could hear and feel her. I just had no idea why, but I could. I wasn't just making this all up in my mind. I shared my experiences, and thankfully they were welcomed and encouraged by her daughter-in-law. I felt ridiculous and in awe at the same time.

This was the beginning of my practice. At times, it was incredible, silly, and amazing. I still didn't feel like a medium, at least not those in films who could clearly see the deceased. I couldn't see them. At least, I couldn't see them with my human eyes. I felt them. I heard them. I could imagine them. I was actually thrilled that I couldn't and didn't have to see them to communicate with them. (And I still am. That would freak me out!) But because of this misconception, I felt I must be doing something wrong, or there must be some other way for me to receive the information I was receiving other than it coming from "dead people."

I battled with the logic of it all. It didn't fit the mold I thought mediumship belonged in. And I certainly didn't fit the mold of a medium, or so I thought. I wasn't anything like Whoopi Goldberg! I wasn't creepy (at least I didn't think I was). I didn't own a thousand cats. I didn't have the same experiences as the kid in *The Sixth Sense*. I don't see dead people. I just know them.

I didn't wear caftans, and I had never even seen a crystal ball except in *the Wizard of Oz*. How could I explain this to anyone? It was ludicrous and pretty much against all the stories I had enjoyed reading about since I was a kid. Mediumship was for weirdos. I wanted to be a physicist, a neurologist, or have my Ph.D. in philosophy. I wanted to be a credentialed somebody, not a wackadoodle. Yet, here I was.

After this experience, I practiced giving messages to relatives and friends. Over time, I could see that this was an ability, something I could do for nearly everyone. I practiced by talking to people in malls, stores, restaurants, parks, and even Mommy and Me classes. Wherever I was, I practiced, and I was amazed (literally freaking amazed) when what I said made sense.

I tried to figure out what else it could be that I was picking up on rather than it being speaking to the deceased. I used to say, "Oh, I must be just reading this person's mind," as if that wasn't cool enough. But then, I'd say things that didn't mean anything to the person sitting in front of me, but when they spoke about it with others in their family, it made perfect sense. So, I couldn't be reading minds if the person in front of me had no clue what I was talking about. I tried to explain it all away. I worked so hard to make sense of this. It was so magical and yet insane at the same time. I loved it, and I hated it.

One day, I saw a man in a mall, and I instantly felt his mother around him. I was so apprehensive about saying anything. My sister, who was anything but shy, was with me that day.

"See that guy over there?" I said. "His mom died, and she's wishing him a happy birthday."

Next thing I knew, my sister was striking up a conversation with him, and she somehow got it out of him that his mom had died, and yes, this very day was, in fact, his birthday. I was standing a few feet away, listening in to this whole exchange and shaking. I was right. Wait. I was right? What? Why me? How did I know this, and how did his mom know I could hear her? I can't even see her. I can't even explain it. I just know stuff. I vacillated between, this is cool and this is crazy, and it's going to make me crazy. I didn't want to do it, and yet I couldn't stop it. I had a choice; that was always clear to me. I could turn it on or off as I wanted to. And I didn't have to make this my life's path. I was just intrigued. I was getting proof in a really weird way, but it felt so, so right, even when none of it made logical sense to me.

Many similar experiences kept me going in the beginning. No matter how uncomfortable I was at the time, I had to keep practicing. I had to keep giving messages. I had to perfect this "craft" and figure out this whole thing. The early years were awful. I had this deep sense and deep pull that I had to do this (to satisfy my own curiosity), but at the same time, I had a paralyzing fear of being wrong or looked upon as crazy.

I didn't want people to know, and yet, I wanted to yell it out everywhere I went! I tested myself every chance I got. I tried to use my logical mind. Tried to make it go away. Tried to not do it, but it was like my life force energy to do it and understand it more and more. I had a sense of purpose, a shaky one, but still a sense of purpose. I just wanted proof.

Years passed, and I had two more little boys. My life was busy raising these three little Caveboys, as I lovingly call them for their Neanderthal-like behaviors. I was fortunate to not have to work outside the home and was happy I could spend my days nurturing them.

In the beginning, I tried to open up and practice whenever possible. While using a mall bathroom one day, I was, of course, with my little Caveboys. As I walked in, I saw a young woman standing in front of the sink washing her hands and staring into the mirror. Instantly, I felt her grandmother with her, and I knew I had to give her a message. Well, if you have children, you know it's extremely unpleasant taking them into a public restroom. I had no intention of stopping to chat and open a potentially controversial/emotional conversation in this germ-infested place, while my baby Neanderthals ran amok. No way!

I squeezed us all into the stalls, stroller and all, did the whole "hurry up, let's use the bathroom, don't touch anything, and please aim properly" mommy speech to the boys, and told the grandmother in my mind, "OK. Listen. If she's still out there when we get out of here, then I'll tell her whatever you want," knowing full well there was no way she would still be at the sink. I had three little Caveboys to wrangle up. This was going to take a while! Well, I was wrong. She was. And she was noticeably upset. I made eye contact with her as we washed our hands, and I buckled the little ones back into the double stroller.

I told her I knew this was going to sound crazy, and I didn't want to scare her... and that I was really not some whacko, (it's the intro I always stated, which looking back, totally made me seem more like a whacko than not) but that her grandmother was with her and she wanted me to tell her that and to acknowledge the baby girl, whom she loved and adored.

The woman started to sob, and when she could catch her breath, she told me, "My grandmother died two months ago. I had a baby daughter after she died, and I was just begging her to talk to me. Today is my first day back to work since having the baby, and I just don't know what to do. I want to be home with my baby."

My mouth dropped... and for the first time, I really felt the impact of what mediumship can mean for a person. It was a remarkable moment for her and for me. I thanked her and her grandmother, and I was no longer worried about germy Caveboy hands. We both walked away crying. What a moment of validation!

It's rare these days for me to go up to anyone and just randomly give them a message. I've learned over the years that it isn't really respectful. Not everyone believes in this stuff. Not everyone has to. There are extremely varying degrees of understanding about mediumship, and I never feel it's my role to assume people want a message. Some people are highly frightened by it. Others are private and get very insecure to think anyone knows more about them than they choose to share. I respect that 100 percent, but it took me a few years and a few not-so-fun experiences to learn it.

My most memorable experience was when I was at the foot doctor. At one time, I suffered from plantar fasciitis so badly that I needed cortisone injections for the pain. While I was in those dreaded doctor office chairs—the ones with that crinkly paper that rips and makes you feel oh so great—as my palms were sweating from nerves about receiving this shot, I felt the nurse's father was there with us. He wouldn't go away, and it was driving me crazy. Quite frankly, I really didn't want to give any messages at this moment. I wanted my shot and to go home! This man wouldn't stop nudging me. I was resisting his presence so much... until she randomly out of the blue started a conversation with me that started with "when my father died..." and then proceeded to tell me all about her dad, and how close they were, and how much she missed him, and that he died tragically.

I figured this was my sign. This guy wanted a message to get to his daughter in the worst way, and she just happens to start talking about him? I had to listen now. I thought for a moment that perhaps she knew who I was and what I did, and this was her way of trying to get some information from me. But regardless, he had been chirping in my intuitive ear enough for me to concede.

I slowly nodded and shared some things her dad was telling me. I told her, "I am a medium, and I know it's weird, but he's been here since I got in the office and wouldn't go away until I told you these things."

What happened next was a scene straight out of one of those scary medium horror movies. (OK, slight exaggeration, but you get what I mean!) She slowly turned toward me, holding the huge shot in her hand, stared deeply into my eyes, in what I originally thought was appreciation and awe, and then said, "Well, you do know then that you do the work of the devil, right?"

The air came out of my body, and I was blindsided. The rest of that appointment didn't go so well. I was mortified. I felt terrible I had made an assumption that she wanted a message and I was so horrified to be reminded that what I do isn't openly acceptable for a lot of people. I was likened to the Devil. Ouch! I'm a mom! I do yell a lot, but I am not the devil! It was a lot to take in, and all right before a painful cortisone injection. Yikes. And yeah, "thanks a lot, man," was all I had left to say to her dad, who of course, had left the room. Or at least, my awareness of him left the room.

It was a lesson for me. Rather than stay upset or feel offended, I learned the hard way that not all people believe or even want to believe. Ironically, that was the last time I ever needed a cortisone injection, and I never went back. Divine intervention? Or slammed into total humility? Who knows? Lesson learned. Memo received. Move forward.

Deborah Hanlon

4

Gifts

A friend of mine had heard about a new reality TV show coming up. They were looking for everyday ordinary people who possessed an extraordinary psychic ability. My friend forwarded me the email, and at first, I thought there was no way I'd enter this competition. I wasn't confident about any of it, and was still trying to prove myself wrong. But the email continued to attract me. I felt I had to fill out this form and send it in.

My philosophy is to live with no regrets. I figured I'd always regret it if I didn't send it in, but I'd never regret it if I sent it in and never heard anything back. The deadline was midnight, March 6, and I knew that was my sign—my son Jack's birth date. I spent hours filling out the form and finally sent it off, only to receive an automatic reply that said, "Form cannot be submitted at this time." I was disappointed at first, but only because of the time I had invested. Then I let it go, telling myself it probably wasn't meant to be. Then I went to bed.

Two days later I received a call from producers in Los Angeles, asking me to come out. I was one of twenty finalists for their upcoming television show called, *The Gift*. I was in disbelief and at the same time, oddly confident.

The twenty finalists were flown in from all around the country. None of us was allowed to speak to anyone else. We were sequestered in hotel rooms until we were called for individual assessments and group tests. We took IQ and psychological tests, and we were interviewed for hours so the television people could explore our temperaments. I told them I curse a lot. They loved it. Finally, we had to read another well-known intuitive and the producers. Everything was filmed. It should have been a very intimidating process, but it wasn't. It felt normal and right to me, as if I had been prepping for this my entire life. The mother of three boys who lived in upstate nowhere NY, felt normal being filmed by a TV crew in LA? Yeah. That made no sense whatsoever!

I was called back to be one of eight on the show, only to find out a few weeks later the show was cancelled due to programming issues. I was bummed, and then I wasn't. This was my final validation that I really was onto something. That something really was, in fact, happening. I was tested. And I had "passed." Up until this point, I always felt deep down that what I was telling people wasn't really spot on, and instead people didn't want to hurt my feelings or make me feel foolish. I thought they just agreed with me because they felt bad for me, or they agreed out of trying to make what I was telling them make sense. Even if it didn't. Because of this show, I decided to go off and become a professional medium. I began the challenge of having to overcome my fear of actually charging people for this "skill." I started by asking for twenty-five dollars a session, which could last hours.

I started doing psychic house parties, but I hated calling myself a psychic. The term, intuitive medium, felt better to me. It's a matter of semantics, I know. But "psychic" is not even close to the identity I craved.

My first house party was held at my ex-husband's friend's

house with only three women present. It was a small house, and I was worried about where I would do these readings. This was the first time I was getting paid, and I was thrilled that I was going to make seventy-five dollars in one night. I walked in, and Lynda, Pat, and Isabelle were there, and so were Isabelle's husband and three kids. *Oh, no,* I thought. *I can't do this. I won't be able to focus.* I was so incredibly nervous. I have to be good at this. They are paying me to hear from their loved ones. I spent many hours preparing for this night, and it was now the moment of truth. I really felt incredibly pressured to perform. All the what-ifs popped into my head. *What if I really don't have this ability, and all those other times, I was just getting lucky guesses? What if they want someone to come through, and I can't hear them? What if they are disappointed?*

I meditated for hours that day to prepare. I mean, I sat quietly freaking out about how I was going to even handle this evening. It's amazing what the pressure of getting paid adds to one's passion. Now, I couldn't just enjoy this work. I had to be good at it. I sat down at the table, which was in an open room. The husband was watching TV (loud TV) to the left behind us, and kids were coming in and out of the dining room. In the midst of these distractions, everyone sat around the table, and it was basically like, "OK, Deborah. Go ahead. Tell us what you know." Gulp.

And I began. The night lasted for hours. I just kept giving messages as I heard them from whomever was "speaking." Although I gained some confidence, I was getting incredibly tired.

Then, Lynda asked, "Is my husband here?"

Instantly, I felt my heart sink. *How did I not feel him earlier? Ugh. I'm not perfect. This can't be real... if this were real... he would have come earlier... I should have heard him sooner.* These were my instant thoughts when Lynda asked about her husband. But instead of mentioning any of these things, I simply asked, "What is his name?"

"Mauro."

"Mauro?" I'm sure my eyes were wide. "Did he go to the

Unitarian Universalist Society?"

"Yes! Did he tell you that?" Lynda asked.

"Oh no! But.. but.. I know him!" I had my proof that this was all so incredibly real, and I couldn't make it up if I tried.

"Lynda! He came to me today, when I was in the car!" I still remembered where I was on the road when I felt his presence in my car next to me. It was as if he just appeared out of nowhere and was all of a sudden sitting with me. Before this moment, I had not thought of Mauro in years.

I began to tell her what happened. "I was driving right by the Newburgh Free Academy High School when I felt him." I hadn't seen him in years. I knew he had passed, but I heard about it long after the fact. I met him while I was teaching Religious Education at the Unitarian Universalist congregation in Rock Tavern, New York. His five-year-old daughter, Liz, was in my class. I spent many mornings talking to Mauro about how there was something amazing about his little girl. She always stood out to me, and she understood naturally the principles the UU was teaching. I adored her.

As I was driving, I felt his presence, and I said, "Mauro? Is that you? What are you doing here? How are you?"

It stunned me. But then, as soon as he came to me, he was gone, and I began to doubt myself. I tried to think of reasons why I would even think he was around. Maybe there was some unconscious reason I thought of him. Maybe something reminded me of him, and that's why I thought I felt him. It was just one of those incredibly real, yet surreal moments that my brain couldn't seem to catch up with it all. And as soon as my logical mind got involved with the experience, it was over. I let the whole thing go.

This conversation with Lynda was my proof. Mauro had come to me in the car! He was basically trying to let me know he was around for that night's gathering. I, like the best of us, try to explain things that we don't understand away as just being a coincidence or a figment of our imaginations. But this experience was so statistically impossible to have occurred that there was no way it was a coincidence. No way. And now, I knew. Again. There is consciousness after physical death. No doubts. I continued the night with a lot of messages from dear Mauro. And I left gaining many vital lessons I remind myself of every day.

The most important lesson is this, and I want to share it with you. Never, ever doubt yourself. Nothing is coincidence. Trust your feelings. Just go with them—especially the moments you can't explain.

Lynda Parisi ended up being one of the original people who followed me in my early years of mediumship. She filmed so much footage of my life and what it was like balancing being a mother, a wife, and a medium!

After the first house gathering, I started booking appointments every weekend. One person would have a party, and I'd read five, six, or seven of their friends, become exhausted, and then go home. I felt stupid every time. I wasn't confident. I felt like I was pimping myself out, but somewhere in me, something drove me to do it. Every time I wanted to quit, someone would book a "party," and I'd have to keep to my word and show up. Thank God, they did. It grew pretty fast. Westchester, Rockland, Orange, Dutchess counties in NY, and Danbury, Connecticut were my early stomping grounds. Person by person, I'd keep getting proof, and saw how people were getting happier and happier with the messages I delivered. I was still insecure, unsure, and slightly embarrassed by all of it. I'm pretty certain no one knew that because I didn't want to admit that to myself. It wasn't an easy beginning. The constant thoughts of self-doubt, feeling like a crazy person talking to the dead didn't feel right to me. Why couldn't I just be a fourth-grade teacher, live a "normal" life, earn a pension, and blend into the rest of society? But again. The Universe is way smarter than we are! I could never just blend in like that.

Time went on, and my husband at the time spoke to a friend

about doing a Gallery, an open forum, at his restaurant, for an audience. Again, I was sick with anticipation for this massive jumping out of my comfort zone. An audience? What? I hated reading a book report in front of my best friends, and now I was going to publicly claim that I speak with the dead in my small hometown? Was I insane? Was I was going to made fun of? I have to be good.

Thankfully, at that time, there were some great people around me who pushed me to do the Gallery. I was literally sick for days before this event. I hiked the entire Saturday before it in Black Rock Forest in Cornwall, New York, begging, praying, and pleading to my brother, my grandfather, and any energies who would listen, to either kill me so I wouldn't have to do it, or make sure someone showed up from the other side so I wouldn't look like a fool. And I do mean, I begged. I sat by a babbling stream, shaking at the thought of what I was going to do. I left my babies at home and tried to assume this identity of medium Deborah. I was a basket case. I had anxiety as never before. I tried to talk myself out of doing it. But again, I made a commitment to do it, and I wouldn't back out of an agreement.

Sunday afternoon came, and fifteen people showed up for the Gallery. I received ten dollars per person, and I was jumping head over heels for being able to make some money. They ate a buffet lunch beforehand while I hung out in a back room wanting to just die, and then the event turned to me. I was shaking. Mortified. Unsure. I wanted to cry. Felt like a loser. Felt like a fraud, because what if no one showed up? What was I going to do then? I hated every minute beforehand. And then no ordinary man showed up for my first public reading in front of an audience.

This man was a firefighter who died in the attacks on 9/11. His daughter was there in hopes of hearing from him. This beautiful pixie of a girl was listening to my words as I felt her father, Dennis, walking me through the entire thing. I feel no other person on the other side could have come through as strongly and taken away my fear, as powerfully as Dennis did. He has proven to me over and over since then. Anytime I need some help from the other side, I call on Dennis to release all fears and help me push forward. He is certainly still living on the other side as much a hero as he was to many here during his time on earth. I always feel fortunate to have met him. That day, he was my hero. He saved me from failing. He also saved me by once again giving tremendous proof that life and consciousness do, in fact, continue after physical death.

That experience began my public "galleries," which I still do today. After ten years and hundreds of galleries later, I am much more confident in myself, but I am always nervous before an event. I have the what-if-no-one-shows-up? fear, and I have to meditate and talk myself through it every time. I no longer have to sit by the water in the middle of the forest though, so I have made quite a bit of progress in the confidence department. When I first started out, I would run to my sister's house for her to check that my outfit was OK, and I didn't look frumpy. Today, GK texts me before each one to remind me, "Just have fun." He knows, when I am having fun, making people laugh and cry, the energy is good, and all is well. I've become dependent on his texts.

I spent a week at Omega in July 2007. This week changed everything for me. Not only was I in the room with two hundred other people who were interested in mediumship, and we could openly discuss hearing, feeling, and understanding energies, but we were in a safe place to give messages. There was a virgin, yet captive audience. It was a perfect place for me to jump into my new skin. I was pushed to do a large group audience reading by fellow classmates after reading them all during an intimate lunch break.

When we all got back into class, they volunteered me to do a group reading. Here I was, with James Van Praagh himself observing my reading. As you are probably aware, James is a gifted medium who created *The Ghost Whisperer* television series based on his own life, has appeared on numerous shows, written many books, and is basically one of the original modern-day mediums who have taken this gift to the mainstream—the pioneers who were brave enough to come out of the psychic closet and claim the impossible.

I was sick with nerves. This was it. This was the moment. All eyes were on me. I don't remember much about what I said, who received messages, or who came through. I remember feeling relieved when it was over. I remember what I was wearing and that I felt fat. I remember leaving the building that day, with my iPod playing Sinead O'Connor's *Heroine* song. It was a moment I will never forget. I did it. I faced a fear in a very public gallery, and I didn't make a fool of myself. I knew that from this moment on, I would be performing group readings regularly. I felt exonerated, as if completing my Ph.D. dissertation and not getting kicked out of the program. James Van Praagh, later during a group session on healing, whispered three words in my ear. They echo to me often: "Confidence. Love. Trust." When I am in doubt, I remember those words, his gift to me.

At this retreat, I learned the value of understanding the chakras. I knew about them from all those books on my mom's shelves. I had profound experiences in guided meditation that have me still trying to wrap my head around the power of meditation. In the most memorable meditation, I saw Mother Mary. Yes, I know, it's a cliché! I can hear the words of the famous Beatles song, *Let It Be*, but I really saw Mother Mary in my guided meditation—again! I remember even thinking while I was in the meditation, "Oh my God, Deb! No, please don't become one of those people who sees saints and remarkable religious and historical figures now." I was rolling my eyes at myself and was really kind of disgusted by this "fake" experience. And yet again, at the same time, this felt more real than anything else I have ever experienced.

While I was in this state, Mother Mary (I know, I know. Go ahead, roll your eyes... I did!) handed me something. It was a perfectly created crystal. She opened her hands, presented the crystal to me, and said, "When you receive this, you will know all of this was real." I received the crystal from her and had tears in my eyes. Then she left. I reentered the workshop space and needed a minute to regroup. What the heck? It was profound. It felt real, yet my mind was telling me I made up the whole thing.

Immediately after this moment, a woman I had become friends with all week long approached me with a gift. She told me not to open it until I got home, and that it was a little token gift for me to thank me for the week. All week long she kept telling me about her homemade soaps and that she was going to bring me some. Naturally, I thought that her gift to me was some of her homemade soaps. Of course, I opened it immediately. I nearly fainted when I saw it—literally the exact crystal "Mother Mary" presented to me during the meditation. It was, again, my proof. I am all about the proof! I need proof of everything; it's just how I'm wired. This crystal was major, major proof for me. Proof for myself that I was not making this up, and that I really did know something and have an ability—even if I didn't know everything about it yet. Mother Mary, was in fact there for me, again!

I started to study guided meditations and forced myself to lead more guided meditation workshops for my clients. I didn't know what I was doing at first, but as soon as I got into the meditation, I was channeling the entire experience. I never plan what is going to come through during a meditation. It simply comes to me. The response has been nothing short of amazing. I started out going to people's homes for psychic parties to give readings and lead small groups. My mediumship practice continued to grow.

Now, I have a fully booked calendar for private readings in my office, and I hold large gallery-style readings, where hundreds of people show up for dinner, drinks, and to listen as I share information from some of the attendees' loved ones who have passed. I am a regular on several radio shows taking callers live on air, and have also started a new show called, "In the Moment" with radio veteran Joe Daily, aka, The Morning Mayor. I'm in awe of how this has all grown, and yet, it all feels natural and normal to me. I've been prepping for this somehow my entire life, and I had no idea.

I flash back to those years before, when I sat and spoke to Mother Mary, and a small part of me thought I was foolish, and yet a smarter, more evolved sense of me knew to continue to reach out. Something was there. Someone was listening. And to this day, that feels more real than the doubts my mind can tell me. I know what I know. I know what I felt. I know what I experienced. And you do, too. That's the presence of proof.

I believe Jack's pregnancy and birth were all a huge part of my opening up to mediumship. I know he had to be on the planet for me to even entertain this ability. His birth made me aware of the cycle of life and death, as well as the process of time itself. I was once an individual, and then my DNA replicated and created a future aspect of me. It instantly made me realize the past, present, and future all at once, the "past Debbie," the present mom, who is needed for the survival of another helpless human, and the future me, that is all the DNA that will be created in the future because of my offspring. I do not feel the act of my son's birth woke me up to just the ability of mediumship. It's more that his birth woke me up to all of it—the past, present, and future. It woke me up to my emotional field of love, the purest love I had ever experienced up until that point.

Add to that experiences that were neither common for me nor sought after, such as my grandfather showing up and then disappearing in the hospital room! I knew I didn't make that up. Why would I have picked him? If I consciously wanted someone there, I would have chosen my brother Chris to show up, but he didn't. None of it made sense to me, not in the logical way or standard way, and yet it all felt right to me, and in that way, it all made perfect sense. Remember logic never applies to matters of the spirit.

It validated to me that proof is all around us. It's something we feel. It's not something we need hard evidence to understand. Proof can be a tangible thing, felt in the heart and not only seen in the hand. The light bulb that our feelings and thoughts are just as real as solid matter became a predominant awareness for me. Our thoughts and feelings are things. This opened the doorway for me to make serious connections later on. It also has opened me to no longer entertaining any thought or reality as "impossible."

The young girl in me was back. I can be, know, or do anything! We all can! My original three-year-old self was reborn, rediscovered, uncovered, and raring to embrace life again. Motivation, connection, and excitement for all positive possibilities surged through me. I had one of the most spiritual experiences we humans crave: I embodied a feeling of purpose and connection to everything. Furthermore, I had a path to go on to explore this. Pure human Nirvana.

As human experiences go, this feeling waxed and waned over the years. Ha! The constant back and forth of being a human while knowing there is more to our Being, is the root of all our desires, struggles and pain. It's what makes us grow and search, but it also leaves us feeling empty and alone at times, too. It's Yin to Yang. It's ebb to the flow. It's the back-and-forth movement that literally creates motion. This is the process of life. This is the vehicle for evolution. Awareness of the tangible and intangible, and how they work together—back and forth, in and out, human to spirit, enlightened to clueless, illuminated to darkness, and back again! Over and over and over. Exhausting, but necessary.

Time itself (and therefore forward movement or evolution) according to Deepak Chopra, is a "measurement of experiences," and I am a human being made of spirit/energy and matter. I am partially still bound to time and experiences while my spirit is housed in my body. We all are. Human beings have experiences. Spirits do not. They are all of the experiences connected. The totality of it all. The alpha and omega. The beginning and the end. Infinity and the vast summation of everything. Energy is the entire ocean, and humanity are the separate drops.

Individually, we are one drop. Together, we are an ocean.
~ Ryunosuke Satoro

There are two aspects or fields in creation. These experiences, or markers of time, are all an illusion when viewed from the spirit/ energy aspect of ourselves. It's the yin to the yang. The corporal to the ethereal. There is a constant vacillation occurring in all life between our physical and energetic selves. I believe it's what causes our desire, which I am defining here as "an emotion designed to keep us in motion yet unobserved; it often gets us stuck." Oh, the paradoxes! Desire is usually viewed as wanting something we do not have, or wanting something back that we once felt, or wanting something to happen. Meaning, it is a craving for something that isn't here already. Or isn't perceived to be here already.

Consciously and unconsciously, let's look at how desire really works in easier terms to fully grasp this.

Air. Most humans on the planet consume air effortlessly. We don't think about it much at all. How many times have you monitored your inhales and exhales while reading this book? Um... unless you have had an asthma attack or are on oxygen at this very moment, I'm guessing you haven't really given it much thought. In other words, you have not desired air. Why? Because you don't feel the need to. It's a given to your psyche and entire being that air exists, and you take it in, and exhale. It's a given in the typical human experience. You unconsciously believe and know with certainty that air is a vital foundation of which you are not in lack. There's no desire for it—except, deep down, there is. Your body knows it and handles it for you. Your body, in truth, does desire and indeed requires it. On your exhale, your body is saying in measurements of time we can't fathom, "Oh hey, we need to rev this back up and take in oxygen" and so, a chain reaction occurs within your body, and your inhale. And again, the body, as it inhales, says "OK, we need to release some CO2 now," and so it does. It's a vacillation of in and out, give and take, lack and abundance, and it's happening all the time. Thankfully, breathing is a necessary foundational function in order to get the rest of our bodies in alignment with living, and it's taken care of effortlessly. This is the state of Being, Knowing and Doing we need to be in. We don't allow our minds to interfere with our process of breathing, which is why it is always there!

Growth Opportunity

Allow your brain, your human self, to interfere with your breathing. Realize how deeply you do or do not inhale and exhale. Ask yourself, is it enough? Am I taking deep enough breaths for my lungs to be cleansed? Am I breathing slowly enough? Am I appreciating my inhales? Am I aware of everything I am releasing when I exhale? Am I exhaling at any given time? Do I need to release more? Am I doing this right? I can probably release more and I bet that would be better if I did... So, I'll take deeper inhales so I can exhale more... I wonder if so and so does this better than I do... I wonder why I can't seem to get my breathing under control. I'm not certain air exists... How can I know for certain?

Are you dizzy yet? Lightheaded from interrupting your natural flow of being? Once our mind engages and changes a perfectly natural occurrence, things get a little off kilter. I can take this example to an extreme and lead you down a path of hyperventilating, but we can stop here.

Of course, I exaggerated that exercise. But the point is to see how the more we over think that which is already coming naturally, the more we interfere with it. The more we try to see or experience it, it changes the experience and flow of it entirely. Then we work even harder to get back to the natural state. Only thing is, the natural state doesn't need to be worked on. It's already perfect and operating flawlessly in tune with every other aspect of nature at the same time.

Our energy and connection to it works the same. All we need to know, is that our connection to everything and everyone (spirit and otherwise) is a given. It's always right there, and we are experiencing it all the time, even when we think we aren't! (We are breathing even when we aren't placing our focus on it! It doesn't change the fact that we are in fact, still breathing. In other words, it's happening whether you realize it or not.) It's only when we stop, think about it, and try to experience it, that it gets confused. When the doctor asks you to "breathe normally" when he or she is listening to your chest, all of a sudden, you forget how to breathe.

We become more focused on the lack, and we get stuck there. Sound familiar? Can you think of a scenario in your life where you are now aware of your attention to the lack of something rather than the abundance, or at least focused on needing the answer and path to abundance?

The desire to feel the connection and awareness of the all-knowing one space within us, our spirit/energy selves, or our Higher Selves - to have a taste of it - leaves us always wanting more. That slams ourselves back into the reality of being separate identities again. Once we realize we want more of it (or of anything), we are coming from a perception that we don't have it, or don't have enough of it, and that is how we lose the connection to it. Again, we are sad, disconnected, and craving something to be back in our lives. This is why we feel we are doing it wrong, and by it, I mean life. We are doing something "wrong" in life if we aren't feeling happy all the time.

Figuring out how to balance the two is what makes us humans. We are little creators. Knowing we are spirit and form, we have quite the capability to create a reality through knowing we are already connected and consciously taking the steps (focusing) on that one reality to put it all into motion.

So, what is real? In physical form, nothing! Nothing, not one thing can be perceived as one absolute way in physical form. And yet, everything in energetic or spiritual form is real! That seems completely contradictory, right? You would think something we can all perceive and tangibly see, touch, taste, smell, and experience should be the object that is considered real. But it's not! Why? Because of the trillions of ways things in physical form are perceived. Objects can only be seen by the "seer," felt by the feeler, smelled by the smeller, tasted by the taster. And no two people have the exact same perceptions.

There are not even two people in the entire span of all of time, past, present, and future, who have ever been nor ever will be able to witness and experience life in exactly the same way. How magnificent is that thought? This is what makes us each as individuals unique and our perspective special, but not the end all be all. The observer is the creator, and all of creation is a sum total of all the perspectives together. That is what is known as the truth. That is our energetic/spiritual makeup of which we are all a part. That whole is also you. I call it The Collective Whole. And you are the whole, expressed separately through your experiences. There is no hierarchy in that system whatsoever. Everyone matters. Everyone is "right." Everyone is seen, heard, and expressed. It's a given, and that's that. The Collective Whole of which we always have been and always will be is Infinity itself. That is where we will all return when we leave our physical bodies. We return to the Collective Whole of it all. And yet, we can achieve the awareness of this state while we are still held in our physical bodies.

Cease trying to work everything out with your minds. It will get you nowhere. Live by intuition and inspiration and let your whole life be Revelation.
~ Eileen Caddy

Deborah Hanlon

5
The Endless Pursuit of Happiness

The Endless Pursuit of Happiness can be a dangerous path. How many classes, workshops, oils, meditation CDs, yoga poses, therapy sessions, moments of insights, books, psychics, astrologers, journal entries, emotions "dug up," uncovered, blamed on your parents, or lack of guidance, can you experience in search for the reason for your unhappiness? How many therapists have you spoken to endlessly about everything under the sun that bothers you, only to have more of it come up?

I've dug to China and back many times only to find myself right back where I left off. What's the deal with that? When does it end? How can we achieve a state of happiness and still actually live (not to mention, make a living), and never feel unworthy or not good enough? I have spent decades on self-discovery, on energy, on positive psychology, and discovering the so-called purpose of life. I've studied religion, ancient civilizations, philosophy, meditation. I've become familiar with energy, physics, and basic laws of dynamics to figure it all out. I've lamented over absolutely needing to understand why we are here. And if we really are divine and amazing bits of energy, then why do we all suffer so much at times? Why are some people seemingly so apparently fortunate and others not at all? What memo are a supremely large number of us simply not getting?

As I've already said, I've been obsessed with what happens when all of this "life" is over and with what comes next. I've wanted to know that if I put effort into this living thing, will it be rewarded? Will it be worth it, or will I even care when I'm dead? I've spent many a night awake with these thoughts. I've been spiraled into depression carrying them. When they seem so hopeless and that there is no specific purpose or reward for our trials and tribulations, I've been left in despair. I've wanted to give up more times than I care to mention. On a few occasions throughout my life, I've been treated for depression. These thoughts can still lead me down a path of feeling hopeless. I know you have been there, too. You wouldn't have picked this book up if you hadn't been. We are human, and it's those thoughts are sometimes a part of our journey here. But then, what do we do about this? How do we move into the flow and rhythm of living without all this fear and uncertainty? How can we actually be less human and more ... well... like the deceased?—all Zen-like and at peace with ourselves and our surroundings?

I teach people the stuff you're reading in this book every day. Sometimes, I throw all that I study, learn, and aspire to right out the window in a moment of frustration and anger! I'm assuming you have those moments too, because I highly doubt I'm going to appeal to an audience who is or believes themselves to be perfect. You may be seeking perfection, and that's fine. I believe "like attracts like" so if you have gotten this far, you are most likely a lot like me. Real. We are all real (OK, *really*) something—angry, sad, confused, happy, confident, insecure. Sometimes, I do want to find perfection, and other times, I'm perfectly OK with not achieving it. Sometimes I want it all, sometimes, I'm thrilled not to have to handle anything more.

What I do believe is that we are also alike in that we are working on being happy and authentic. We are obsessed with feeling better, and therefore doing and being better. You are a seeker of all things, tangible and invisible. If you are reaching for perfection, go put this book down and pick up something by Dr. Amazing Perfection someone or other. I don't need to control or create perfection. I gave that up a long time ago. Today, it's about awareness.

I did then what I knew how to do. Now that I know better, I do better.
~Maya Angelou

I love Maya, but I will tell you that I don't always do better. It's a process. I seek for knowing better, and therefore actually doing better, although so many times, even though I know better, I still don't do better! I know it isn't good to eat chocolate creme powdered doughnuts from Dunkin Donuts, and yet, I do. Often. Yet, I seek to find my own inner self and connect to what is already here right in front of me. I want to be at peace with what is and also know it can and will change.

I know you have turned to this book to learn more about life, death, our true nature, and how we can understand our own energy to live a more authentic and fulfilling life. I hope this book puts *being* rather than most *doing* at the forefront of your life. I'm constantly exhausted by what I plan to do, have to do, want to do, and wish I could do. All that puts us in a mindset of no presence, precisely the exact opposite state we need to be in to feel content. Wishing, wanting, and waiting are all states of either being in the past or looking toward a future. But all of our happiness lies in the present, which is created from our being.

This is the secret. This is the state of awareness and consciousness the deceased are in all the time. You can get there too.

The state of doing will come naturally when you finally understand the nature of your being. So, don't worry about it. This is the process of growth. It's an ebb and flow. A state of chaos and confusion leads to learning, and then we gradually move into a space of new living until something stirs it all up again, and the cycle repeats. We will feel settled and calm once we understand this. The more we learn, the more questions we ask.

The bottom line is, I often feel as if I am on an unending pursuit of happiness, in the name of balance. And I get exhausted from working on me. Can you relate? We go right back to the beginning and find more to work on. It's exhausting! I recognize there is a cause and effect to everything in life. I understand the law of opposites—for something to exist, the opposite must also exist—but I'm just seeking for peace and to end my suffering, which only leads me to put more light on it. But what am I trying to heal or fix, the past? I can't change that! The now? Aren't I OK right now? My future? There's nothing to worry about there; it hasn't happened yet.

We are constantly in a *doing* mode, and in that space, we can't find peace. Somewhere along the line, we feel "broken," and that something we do can actually fix us. But, ladies and gentlemen, we aren't broken. We don't need to be repaired. We need to be upgraded. We need to see we are in a flow of constant change, internally and externally. We need to let the ghosts of our past (our former selves) die when they no longer serve us. We need to see when it's time to let go and when it's time to create. We need to have a better comprehension of our True Nature, so we don't get caught up in the illusion of what it appears to be us.

Life ebbs and flows. Happiness comes and we think, "Oh, here it is, yes!" Only to see it leave again, which often makes me feel we've failed to maintain happiness. Sometimes, it lasts for moments at a time, and sometimes it lasts for weeks, even months. I don't think I've ever lived perfectly happy for a full and entire year. In fact, I'm positive I haven't. Have you?

For as much work as I have done, I still have so much to learn and so many things to discover. I get angry that I have exhausted myself and that I know better not to give energy to my anger, or to stop saying, "I should have done such and such." But guess what? I am human, and I've also finally learned that a person can be happy and still have negative emotions and circumstances. In fact, that's pretty much how it works for everyone. Well, for everyone who is brave enough to admit it, that is. When everything seems perfect all the time, something is up.

I am sure you feel or have felt the same way at some point. That's because we are all in this together. We are living in the physical, meaning, we are human. We are energy, housed in a body, and that body is dense. The sheer density brings the potential for heavy energy to be attracted to us. What is heavy energy? Life's experiences themselves! Feeling unloved, unappreciated, betrayed, worthless, not good enough, dealing with financial issues, family members, handling wanting to be free and open and having to juggle jobs, illness, families, and busy lives. Wanting to travel and see the world but not having the time or resources to do that, wanting to be chosen and wanting to have time alone. We are contradictory animals. We are complicated because we have these brilliant minds that create dreams, and yet, the same minds place a ton of emphasis on what we have and do not have, which can create some intense misery.

Being human is hard. We have a lot to handle most of the time. Unexpected moments can leave us feeling devastated and numb. People get sick, disabled, sad, hurt, and people around us die. We are often in a constant conflict with just wanting to be and having to make a living. I'm pretty sure most people think that if everyone could live exactly as they wished, feeling fully accepted within themselves and their communities, working at something they enjoyed and receiving gratification—and still providing a way of living that was safe and stable, we would all be happy, wars would end, and there would be peace on earth. Right? Well, I'm not certain about that. Why? Because we don't live in an airtight world where we can control everything and everyone. Besides, struggle can create the grandest opportunity for learning. If we all did exactly what we wanted to, would we even know it? Or would something else stir up inside us to cause internal chaos? It's part of our nature to be on a constant search for something else. That is how we grow.

The tiny seeds have to break through a shell before they can push into the soil around them and reach for the warmth of the sun. We are evolving; that's our nature here. We have an innate, possibly unconscious desire to keep learning and growing all in the name of survival. We are all operating in a cycle of birth, death, and rebirth. It's how everything flows. Because of this, we will always search for the "next thing." This keeps us alive, or so we think.

We have yet to understand that nothing is finite. We live in a very logical world, where we believe we have the ultimate say over everything. We make judgments and insert our small opinions all around us, based on what is happening in the now in hopes it will make things better. We try to fit ourselves into small lives and identities that aren't challenged or updated. We live constantly seeking something and reaching forward, and yet we do this through the most ridiculous system possible! We typically do it by reaching back into our past and continuing a cycle of habitual living, and we aren't even aware we're doing it. This creates the illusion of time being slow and unchanging, and it causes us deep frustration. We have simply been doing it all backward.

The mentality of what's next? also known as desire, is often the root cause of your suffering, but it doesn't have to be. The solution is actually quite simple. You must change your mindset.

According to Buddhism, there are three kinds of desire, or at least, three different aspects of desire. There is the type of desire that most of us easily understand and recognize. It's wanting to please your body or senses. Think about when you're eating something sweet or delicious. Imagine yourself taking a bite. When it tastes amazing, you desire more of it, right? When we have things that please us, we naturally desire more of them.

Another form of desire, and probably the one that causes most of our suffering, is the feeling of wanting to become something. The intense feeling of ambition, trying to become rich, trying to feel happiness, trying to have purpose, the desire to become more than, or different from what you are now.

When your desire is leading you to want to become something, then you can also experience a desire to get rid of something. If you're full of anger or jealousy or fear, you have an intense desire to be free from those emotions. So, when you desire to become happy, you may feel as if you need to get rid of your anger to achieve that.

Desire doesn't need to be a source of suffering. Recognize that feeling any form of desire can only cause suffering if you hold on to it and react to it. If you are consumed by your desire to become someone different, you will always feel that something is missing in your life. Instead, recognize the desire and let it go. Focus more on what you have, and feeling gratitude for all that you have. Gratitude brings joy, and with joy you create and connect to your true reality which ultimately attracts you to other people, experiences and thoughts that you are striving for.

We must learn how to use our constantly changing selves to ride the waves of change, rather than view life as intermittent surfing between tsunamis. We must develop a new way to think, and learn how to perceive and fully understand our nature, and to finally comprehend just how magnificent we all really are. We need to realize and teach how our beliefs have caused a neural pathway of thinking that has literally created everything around us.

It's all according to our beliefs, which are entirely based on our past conditioning. We move through life via our desires. Sometimes they propel us forward, and other times, they hold us back. It all depends on whether we perceive ourselves as achieving or obtaining our desires. When we do, we consider ourselves happy.

There is also the desire to have our physical needs met, sensual needs, the desire to be recognized, the desires to teach or help others, the desire to be enlightened, and the desires to be free of all negativity (jealousy, anger, sadness, lack). Instead, what is helpful is to observe your desires. The next time you are eating, notice your desire for your next bite. When you are recognized by someone, notice your feeling to replicate that over and over. When on social media, notice your desire for more likes, comments, opens, and shares. When you are uncomfortable, notice your desire to remedy the circumstances. Notice how you feel when you see something you want—a job, a material item, a relationship, a level of security. Or notice when you desire to be understood, heard, praised, or loved.

Desire truly is the emotion of our movement. The problem is that desire takes you out of the present and away from what currently is. Desire can leave you feeling frustrated when you are impatient for its results, and it can feel ugly. You do not need to seek to be free of desire (because that is a desire: to not have it!) Instead, you need to be in touch with it. Observe it. Sit with it. Feel it. Recognize the response and reaction you have to it. Notice if you automatically set yourself up, thinking nothing you want will be achieved, or obtained. Notice if you are fearless, or ruthless in obtaining your desires. Notice and embrace your ability to have desires, and then let them go so your being won't be attached to them.

Then what? Then you get present and don't allow your emotions to dictate your thinking, which creates your reality. Otherwise, you will stay stuck in your wanting and not living in the moment of being. In the past, when you set a goal, you stayed in a moment of wanting, and you carried out that desire to achieve it, rather than becoming the mindset of already having/being/doing it. If your conditioning, your basic and primitive beliefs have surrounded the "truth" that none of your desires are met, then your ability to achieve your goal naturally gets harder. We all know how past conditioning can cause you to set up a mental block that says, "My goals are not easily achieved." That's when you set yourself up to fail or fall short. This is why we get frustrated with diets, savings plans, self- improvement programs, and exercise regimens. Because our past often dictates our perception of what is going to happen in the future. It's the "monkey see, monkey do" phenomenon.

Instead, we must learn to create goals for ourselves, notice these goals as desire, and detach from the outcome—work forward, move forward by staying right here, in this moment. We can learn how to enjoy the process. Being in the now and realizing all of this, is the Human Struggle. You literally must become the changes that you seek. Create a mindset that only allows for thoughts that revolve around the Transformation and not around the process of change. We must open up our awareness to a much larger spectrum and enter into a state that goes far beyond our tiny egos.

All that I've just written, you have read 10,000 times by a slew of other authors throughout all of recorded history. And yet, we still think we aren't getting it. How do we do the above? Is it even in our human nature to comprehend it, and then live it out? I believe, yes. It wouldn't be able to be written if it wasn't possible to attain. We only know and see that which is possible. Otherwise, we couldn't conceptualize it yet. The question becomes, are you able to comprehend and transform yourself? Are you willing to do the work? Are you capable of getting brutally honest with yourself in a loving and non-judgmental way?

Of course, you are. You wouldn't have picked up this book if you weren't capable. How do you do it? By accessing the non-human aspect of your nature. Your spiritual self. Your Higher Self. Your soul. The pure energy of which we all are made. The unifying field of all existence. We can access this energy and create a world around us that is fluid and easy. That space is the mindset of perfection. It is the awareness of that which we think, is real. It's based on the presence of the current thought and not on the conditioned thoughts of the past.

And we can do this while we are right here in our human bodies. We can attain that while sitting in traffic, standing in line in an airport with our shoes off waiting to be patted down. We can do this while waiting for medical test results and while sitting at the funeral of a loved one. We can do this while nursing our babies or shooting hoops with our teenagers. We can do this when the bank account says a negative number, the car is repossessed, and divorce papers are served. We can do this hungry, tired, happy, and motivated. The Higher Self, your pure energy, is present within you, in this very moment, and it's been greatly untapped. Are you prepared for meeting the True Being you really are? Well, get prepared. Because you are huge. Immense. Powerful. Capable. And you are all that, in this very instant as you read this!

I've learned from a very unusual crowd today how to live a more authentic, productive, and well, basically a happier life, by examining how I perceive things. The dead talk to me—and newsflash, they talk to you, too! I'm telling you all right now, communication with energy is nothing like what you have been previously told, read about, or seen on television. You, we are all mediums. The ghosts? Those are the apparitions of your former self. What? Yeah. Those aren't Civil War heroes and old farm wives angry that you are occupying their former spaces. Those are former aspects of yourself. When you listen closely and feel their words, you will see it's a former you. We can all sense energy and understand it, if we 1. Have interest in understanding it; 2. Have figured out the art of detachment; and 3. Are able to be mindful and to pay attention to your entire mind, body, and spirit to receive these messages.

Somehow, by luck, by divine intervention, by the twists and turns of fate, I decided to listen. And they have changed the way I think and therefore how I live. How I perceive life, and what we think death is, has dramatically changed. The deceased are still with us. They are alive not because they possess a body, but because they have graduated to a higher awareness. They have perfected a state of being, and have finally reached heights of a Macroscopic Awareness of all that is, and one that we, too, can adopt, here in our microscopic worlds. They have done this simply by separating from their bodies, the dense physical selves that weigh down our energy and pull it all into a small self. When we lose the self-proclaimed "self," we expand into a much larger field of Potentiality. We can think differently. We can change our perception of death. We can expand our awareness enough so we can in fact live a meaningful life. And we can do this while we are still housed in our physical bodies.

Changing your mindset and reprogramming your belief systems take work. I'll be the first to admit that. Not many people are successful at living a "Zen-like" existence all the time while living with the stressors of everyday life, but there is no question that we can learn from those who have passed on to higher levels of being. Every step you take toward understanding the interconnectedness of the Universe, your mindset, and your role in it, is one step closer to living the life you've always dreamed of living. It isn't about being perfect, but rather, seeing the perfection in it all. Are you open and ready for it?

The more you focus on the stuff that is present in your life, the more those things increase. This is a book about human awareness. It's about changing mindsets and ending old paradigms of thinking of living that no longer work for you. It's about life, viewed from the consciousness of the deceased. Most of all, it's about how you, no matter what is going on in your life, are more connected and powerful than you think.

The Law of Attraction, if you are familiar with it, is often marketed or explained in a way that really makes the readers think that if they simply think good thoughts, then good things will happen. And while, yes, this is a small basic tenet of it, it is not what the entire law suggests at all. People often comment to me that I must be a good "manifestor" because of all I have in my life. Sometimes these comments are said with a genuine happiness for me, and other times, they are said with a slight touch of anger. I appreciate the sentiment that I am a good *manifestor* of my reality, and at times, I do believe that is true. However, I also know how hard I have worked toward my dreams and goals. I know what I have had to overcome to keep myself focused in a positive direction.

I never give up for good, even though there absolutely have been times when I have given up. There have been occasions where I just didn't see my life going in a direction I wanted, or I had lost people and opportunities that left me crushed. Nothing has been perfect. Nothing has been filled with complete ease, and yet in hindsight, it's truly all worked out perfectly. Yes, I work hard at it, and no, nothing has seemingly popped out of the ether and has been handed to me. I have been ridiculously fortunate and therefore immensely grateful for all opportunities that have come my way, or moments that have worked out and come together when I didn't know how it could ever be OK.

I have manifested a lot. Some of it was hard work, some was being in complete trust of the Universe, and other times I was simply surrounded by people who were wonderfully supportive and brilliant to guide me. The Universe truly does not make mistakes. The Law of Attraction is all about a mindset. Focus your thoughts on what you want and let go of all the rest. Let go of how you want things to work out. Just set the intention, let go, and then jump on every opportunity, interaction, and synchronicity that the Universe sends your way!

Recently, I cleaned out old goal books that I wrote when I was in my late twenties. At that time, I had three babies under the age of four. I was exhausted, stressed, and not living the life I always imagined. While I was grateful and in love with my babies, they weren't all that fulfilled me. There had to be more to life. Well, as I sat in the office shredding old papers, I read a description of the home of my dreams and had so desperately craved over thirteen years ago—as I was sitting in it. It took nearly fifteen years to "manifest" this house. I cried as I had the realization: I never gave up, and I never lost the full vision of this home I love.

I didn't wish for that house and then do nothing for it. I helped the vision. I made vision boards. I worked. I saved money. I made myself believe in my heart that, it would happen. All of this was created in my tiny bedroom of our teeny house in the ghetto, where there was truly no indication that I'd ever be able to have something like it. It never appeared possible, and yet, because I held my vision on the house, it was impossible for it to not be possible. So, intend, let go, take action. Learn to be patient. That's the recipe.

Growth Opportunity

Do you want to stay unhealthy? Keep focusing on your poor diet. Want to stay in debt? Stay focused on your lack of money. Of course, you don't want these things. Instead, right now, take a few moments to imagine your day without negativity, without limitations, or lack. There is no room for negativity. No room for excuses. You must only fill your vision of yourself with abundance and what feels good. If you know what you want, you can have it. To experience more of the good things in life and have what you want, you have to change your mindset so that you only focus on the things and experiences you have and your gratitude for it all.

Think about it. What do you do when you want a glass of water? You get your glass and stick it under the faucet, and turn the water on to get what you want. All right. It's the millennium, so imagine yourself grabbing a water bottle. Either way, you probably pretty much always assume the water will be there, and so it is. You don't think twice about it. Your life is like this constantly flowing faucet (or unending supply of water bottles). You just need to stick your cup out and grab it! Don't assume what you want isn't there.

Instead, assume that everything you want and need is right there, and you can just reach out for it, the same way you do your glass of water.

How often do you set up a roadblock over brushing your teeth? Or showering? Seriously, have you ever suggested to yourself that you can't brush your teeth? Or that you don't have access to a shower? No! Why? Because you live in a mindset that automatically assumes those things will be present for you. But guess what? Those aren't Universal truths. There are millions of people in the world who do not have access to water for brushing their teeth and showering on a weekly basis, let alone a daily one! It isn't a given in the world. It's a given in your world because you automatically assume it is there. You probably never question being able to do it or to have access to it. You have it because you give no attention to not having it.

Begin to imagine that your life consists of all the components of happiness that you require or desire. To do this, you must train your mindset to focus only on the parts of your life you like. Your mindset needs to be on what you have and your gratitude for all of it. There is no room for negativity. No room for excuses. No room for lack. Expand your awareness to encompass a much larger terrain than just your physical body. You must only fill your vision with only abundance and what feels good. This includes being able to connect with your loved ones who have passed! There is a connection among all of us that never dies. It's impossible to be severed. The communication lines stay open forever. They have been there all along.

Become aware of your thoughts. You'll probably notice recurring themes. They probably cause you to worry whenever they pop up. Do you wonder if you'll have enough money to pay the rent this month or get a new dress for your friend's wedding? Are you sitting in front of the TV snacking on a bag of chips while simultaneously thinking you'll never get rid of the feeling of your belly hanging over your pants?! People have between 50,000 and 70,000 thoughts each and every day. Become more aware of what your thoughts are, so you can start focusing on the positive thoughts and begin releasing the negative ones.

Deborah Hanlon

6

Head vs. Heart; Human vs. Higher Self

Tony, a friend of my parents from long ago, passed suddenly on his motorcycle on a gorgeous October day. He had taken some time to stop and see his son during his lunch hour, asked for a picture of him to be taken with his bike, and then drove off and met his fate. The night before, he was casually talking about what should be done in case he should pass away. The entire situation, from every "outsider" just seemed so crazy. Did he know he was going to die? Did his human self actually know? No, I don't think so. But, did his spiritual self know? I believe, yes, absolutely. His Higher Self was preparing him for his return to the Source.

Connecting with Tony shed light on this very phenomenal fact: No one dies when it *isn't* their time. We often hear that when a life is saved in the final moments, it is called a *miracle*. And it is. But the true miracle is that our Life Force determines when we leave and when we stay. Our Life Force is the Ultimate Knower, and it follows the one path it has been given. That path is interconnected with the trillions of other Life Source energies present with it. It's our egoic self, or our human self that has an agenda, a timeline of what should be. That agenda is very small minded, concerned only with itself and perhaps a few other family members and friends.

Our human self says, "I don't want to die because I have so and so to care about," or "I don't want so and so to die because I want him/her here with me." Our human self has absolutely no concept of how far reaching and interconnected our Higher Self's purpose is. The Higher Self knows precisely its purpose and knows exactly whose lives we touch without even physically meeting. Every *moment* in our lives is in tune with every other moment in every other person's and every other living organism in the entire universe. The human self, which I'll now reference as the *hs*, is teeny, isolated, and wrought with limitations. The Higher Self, from now on referenced as the HS, is all-knowing and connected to the bigger picture, the entire Universe. The HS has the hs's best interest at hand but is mostly concerned with it for the good of the whole, rather than the good of the one individual. The hs is our logic, and the HS is our intuition.

In that space, when we connect to our HS, we are operating out of the Goodness for the Whole, and not just for our own limited (selfish) motives. Limited is a much better word for selfish because we are spirit in human form. Our bodies house our spirit (yet another reason to take really good care of our bodies). As you are reading this, you do have desires and wants and needs that are born purely out of your own small and limited experiences because that is generally all you think you know, and that is all you connect to, the here and now.

We sell ourselves short with our thoughts of what is possible for us because of our habitual patterned way of living. If the people surrounding you are living in a particular way, chances are you are too. It's rare to see a bungalow right next to a twelve-thousand-square foot home. Right? Living in this way is normal and OK. It's part of our journey here as human beings, but is it what you want, or are you just lured into believing that your highest potential is relative to what others around you have accomplished?

We, as these upright balls of information and energy, are really just trained to think and behave as those who surround us. We take cues from our culture, whatever that is, and we live that out. Not many think much more about it. Life is what it is. What is right in front of us is often what we experience as truth. And, when coming from that perspective, that is true. We make truth exactly as what we can perceive, but it's not the whole picture. It's a teeny tiny fraction of the Full Truth. The Higher Self is your connection to a much broader and brighter existence. This is what I want you to remember.

When we lift ourselves up and operate out of our Higher Selves, we can see there is a much bigger picture and a much better organized Power in charge of it all. Only then can we sit back and relax, knowing the best interests of *all* are being tended to. We all like to get in the way of that and think we know what is best. But again, we are only considering a limited set of circumstances and drawing from a very teeny tiny set of possibilities that we lay out for ourselves.

The Universe and our Higher Selves are much smarter than we are—every time. Can you surrender to that? Can you let go just a bit of what you want and how you want it and allow for a much larger source to handle it for you? If you are entering a car race you want to win, and you have the option of choosing a professional driver for the car or to drive it yourself, which would you choose? If you were planning a wedding or huge event that needed an elaborately decorated cake, would you decide to do it yourself or choose a professional baker? If your child broke a bone that needed to be reset, would you do it yourself, or would you seek out a doctor who specializes in that?

It sounds silly, but that is exactly what we do every day. We keep deciding that we are the smartest knowers of everything in our lives, and that we can handle it all ourselves or that we must be the one and only in charge. Instead, defer to the power of your Higher Self to handle things for you. Defer all major decisions to your Higher Self, and I promise you, all will go just as it needs to with least effort. This is energy.

There is clearly a Life Force present in the Universe. This force is what keeps everything in order and synchronicity. Are you capable of keeping all of Nature in order? No way. Leave that up for the Collective Whole, that field of potentiality where nothing and everything exists. It's a major relief to know you really are supported by a loving and all-inclusive force. When you get your ego out of the way, you can see and experience life in an entirely new way. You can see you have purpose at every single corner. Every breath you take is in synchronicity with everyone else's. You do your small parts for the good of the whole and leave it at that. You—we—are connected, supported, and loved. Be a part of that mindset, and you become more and more aware of what is in alignment in your life, rather than what is not working, unfair, or flat-out lies.

There are two aspects of ourselves that are activated within every one of us. The *head* and the *heart*. The **head** (brain) is a pre-programmed machine that has recorded every little bit of information through your five senses and has organized all that data into patterns. You learn something, it's stored in the brain, and is used as a reference point for learning from that moment forward. It's very linear in its design. Neurologists still do not understand how our memory works. There is *order,* and things "make sense." It's predictable, concrete, and tangible. It has form. The head *can* evolve and grow, but it doesn't always. It's enabled through conditioning and learning.

The typical child who learns to turn over eventually learns

how to sit up, and then crawl, and then walk. So, progress is seen and made, but only some patterns get upgraded in the head (brain), not all.

Some patterns are simply easier to upgrade than others. The brain, is arguably different than the mind. Scientists are still stumped as to what the mind is because we cannot locate where the mind is. What or who is the thinker that causes the brain to fire off neurons? After a person dies and is declared brain dead, there has been scientific evidence that activity is still occurring in the brain. Is that the mind? Is the mind the connection? The Eternal Ether that connects all living things? Or is the mind the shadowy figure on the walls of Plato's cave?

> *We are products of our past, but we don't have to be prisoners of it.*
> ~*Rick Warren*, "The Purpose Driven Life:
> What on Earth Am I Here for?"

The Allegory of the Cave is a theory presented by Plato to compare the effects of education to the lack of education on human thinking, feeling, and actions. It's about human perception, and the belief that knowledge gained through our senses is opinion—and if we are to have real knowledge, it must be gained through philosophical reasoning.

Imagine people being imprisoned in a cave from childhood, and they have never seen the outside of the cave. The people are chained by their hands and legs, so they can see only the wall of the cave directly in front of them, each other, and themselves. But behind the prisoners, is a fire, and between the fire and the prisoners, is a raised walkway behind a partial wall that people walk on carrying objects and puppets on their heads. The shadows of the puppets and objects being carried are cast on the wall in front of the prisoners, but the people carrying the objects do not cast a shadow. The prisoners cannot see anything behind them and can only see the shadows on the wall in front of them and hear the sounds of people talking. The prisoners mistakenly believe that the sounds are coming from the shadows, and that the shadows are real. (Remember, they are completely unaware that there are people behind them.)

For the prisoners, the shadows are the reality. They have never seen anything else and therefore do not realize that what they're seeing are only the shadows of objects. They have no concept that the objects casting shadows are inspired by real things living outside the cave, either. To the prisoners, there is nothing else beyond their cave, each other, or the wall in front of them.

If one prisoner is freed from the chains holding him in the cave, when he first turns around and sees the fire, the light from it will hurt his eyes because he has never seen it before. The prisoner used to the dark will have a difficult time seeing the objects casting shadows.

Someone could explain to this prisoner that what he viewed on the walls all that time was not real but just the shadows cast by the objects he is now viewing, and the prisoner won't believe it. Instead, the prisoner will turn his back to the fire, so his eyes can return to what they know and what they are used to, which are the shadows of the objects. The shadows will be clearer to him than the real objects in the light of the fire.

If the prisoner is dragged out of the cave and into the sunlight, he will be pained and blinded by the bright light. The new reality of the sunlight gives the prisoner the knowledge that there is a whole different world beyond the cave. As his eyes adjust to the brightness, he first sees just shadows and then eventually, reflections of objects or people in water, and gradually, his eyes adjust until he can see the people and things around him.

It isn't until he is freed from the cave and able to see reality in the sunlight that he is able to reason and understand it exists. It is then that the prisoner realizes his previous view of reality was wrong. Plato continues the story, saying that once the prisoner has learned this new reality, he will find it superior to the reality inside the cave, and he will want to bring the other prisoners out of the cave and into the sunlight as well.

When the freed prisoner is returned to the darkness of the cave with eyes that have now become acclimated to sunlight, he will be blind upon entering. The prisoners in the cave will assume the freed prisoner was hurt by leaving and decide they should not leave and should put up a fight to prevent being freed. I love this because what happens to us then is astounding. Those around us feel we are up to no good or "changing" in ways they may not like or appreciate.

The mind gets programmed and used to this setpoint, and anything too different from that setpoint is challenged as "not right." We have all lived in the cave of our experiences. We have all thought the way things have been are the way things are. We have taken our personal experiences and made assumptions that they are universal. This all happens when we are completely unaware, and there's no blame for it.

How can you know something that you do not know? Many times, pain is a motivator. When your world view no longer fits, you turn your head around and learn a new perspective. This naturally causes change, and change leads to evolution. People around you may not like this.

We cannot unlearn things (without drastic interceptions like accidents or illnesses that cause us to lose an intellectual facet). Once we learned how to walk as babies, we didn't continue to only crawl. In fact, we crawled less and less because we learned a better way to move around. Life is like this. When we learn a new way, and this way works for us, we rarely go back to life as we knew it before. We are all in the caves until we leave. Then, once we leave, we seek more light. Grieving one's death provides the greatest vehicle for your personal growth. Trust me on that.

If we should ever return to the cave for a visit, it seems unbearable. We wonder, *how did I ever survive in that environment?*

Have you ever been in a relationship (or a job or a friendship) that wasn't good for you, but you stayed in it? Then one day, usually over time, you realize you can no longer stay in this space, and you move on. You start living a new life, accustomed to a new way of living because the old way no longer fits. The next time you encounter the person or the dynamics you had with him or her before, you think to yourself, *how did I ever put up with that? How could I have lived that way?*

This happens when you leave your parents' home. It was once comfortable and what you knew, and then at some point, you moved out on your own. Visits back home, under the old dynamics often send people over the edge. They can't stand to be under the old rules and energetic dynamics. Although leaving the cave is the scariest thing we can do, it's crazy making when we try to reenter it after learning a better, brighter way.

When we return from the light, those still in the cave cannot relate to us. We can't go back into the darkness of what previously used to be perfectly fine for us. People still in the cave often think something bad happened. Or that you are "wrong" in your new beliefs and ways. Those who aren't growing as you are, in the directions for the reasons and purposes as you, just can't understand, and that is OK. We all aren't supposed to be growing in the same ways with same interests and beliefs, but we are capable of being aware of whether a change is a good one for someone. Often, the cave dwellers are so stuck in their experiences that they can't even see if your changes are good for you. More often, they see these changes as blasphemous or an attack on their way of life. Personal transformation and growth is not an easy thing to do in the social realms. In fact, those closest to you often have the hardest time with your changes. This is normal and very confusing.

So, imagine being in a cave of thinking this is all there is: that humans are born, and then humans die. And that's it. Then suddenly, an experience leads you to find out there is, in fact, consciousness and awareness of the physically deceased after they leave their physical bodies. You have proof. You have experienced it. You have felt it. You want to share this experience so badly with those around you but are afraid. Once you have seen the light of awareness, it's impossible to go back to the dark. Those who don't believe as you now do, will most likely think you are "off" or not telling the truth. As I said, this is not an easy path. Welcome to my world. You are most certainly not alone in it.

The great news is you can get yourself out of the Cave of Darkness, and you can walk into the light. You can take a look at your life and see what darkness you are living in. You may have made an unconscious decision to keep yourself in the dark about things—ranging from small changes to huge ones—that you aren't even aware are possible.

Some learned behaviors don't change until something *forces* change on them. If we don't constantly challenge what we think is true, real, and right, then we will never give ourselves the opportunity to learn otherwise. We stay limited in our thinking and therefore in our being. We stay small and do not come close to living out our full potential.

Remember, the head/brain is limited to what we have learned and what we challenge ourselves to learn. It dips back into the past to retrieve old, possibly outdated information from ourselves all the time. Think of it as an old operating system. It works, but oh, is it limited. This is your **head**, and this is exactly how humans are wired.

The **heart**, however, is completely opposite. It operates on what it *feels* intuitively *knows*. Almost nothing ever makes "sense" in the domain of the heart. It operates in a non-linear, unpredictable manner. It has no form, to support its reasoning. It's formless, intangible, the *knowing* within you, your gut instincts. The heart just receives inspiration out of the blue. It responds to the nurturing of yourself. It's connected through meditation, prayer, and is often enabled accidently in moments of intense need. It's creative, exciting, spontaneous, and refreshing. Boundless and formless, it is sometimes scary to listen to but hard to ignore.

Sometimes we only use it because nothing else is available to us at that time, and sometimes we use it for a reason we call faith. We believe and know something that is unknown to our core. The real and true is the *unseen,* and yet we still have more confidence in it.

In the domain of the heart, everything is possible. It is the field of potentiality itself, and it goes against the mindset of humans completely. *The Heart is the mind of the Higher Self.* This is how spirit/energy/divinity works. It creates and flows. There is not a lot of effort involved in using the heart. It simply is as it is, and will be as it will be. And it's perfect and in synchronicity with all of life.

Our human self, (hs) is just like the brain. It wants predictability. It wants certainty. It usually hates the "what will be, will be" mentality and is extremely impatient. It wants what it wants, and it wants it now. It's materialistic and believes heavily in the concepts of lack, death, and endings. You have something only if you literally have it. You can't pretend to have it. It's a very black/white mentality, extremely preoccupied with the outcome and obsessed with all things temporary.

The hs wants to control and think it's creating and is only happy, albeit temporarily when it's sees or attains a particular outcome. It's not necessarily pleased with or satisfied with the process of creating. The brain measures in terms of time and space. The hs doesn't understand the concept of time as an illusion. We typically focus on what is right in front of us, make idle plans for our future, all based on our behaviors from our past. It's quite caveman-like if you ask me. How do you explain infinity and your part in it when we are really preoccupied with sales fliers and keeping up with the Joneses?

How can we ever understand the shadows on our walls are not the real truth? How can we understand that which is real? By leaving the cave and by realizing the lens of the human mind will limit us at best. But we do have another resource to turn to for our connection. We can turn to the Sun, leave the cave, become temporarily blinded, and overwhelmed with all there really is, and then struggle with the changes, and finally grow accustomed to the light. A whole new world opens up. We see and understand things from an entirely different perspective. This happens right after our physical death for sure. Oh, how everything is abundantly possible when we leave our bodies, but we have the potential and ability to open ourselves up to this Grander Reality while we are still in our bodies. We must *think* like the deceased.

The human self (hs) alone, taken at face value, is like observing a small seed in the palm of your hand. You technically know its potential of growing into something, but when you look at it directly, it's a small seemingly "dead" object. It's tangible, and there is an expectation to it, the expectation that if we provide the seed with all the right conditions, it will grow into something larger that we can observe. An apple seed is one tiny object that is really responsible for the potential of creating an infinite number of apple trees. One seed may grow into one tree, but that one tree creates hundreds of apples with more seeds in each one that grow into how many more trees?

An infinite number of seeds came before the one that grew into a tree, and an infinite number came after it. Wrap your head around that for a moment and ponder on that seed. In one tiny seed, you are able to see, feel, and touch infinity. It can be expressed in physical form but can only be understood when felt in this way, and when you think of it in these terms, you can literally hold infinity in your hand.

When taken into context of yourself, you too are an expression of infinity itself in human form. You are a particle in a wave of potential. You are a physical temporary manifestation, a vehicle if you will, of infinity itself. All the DNA that came before you and all that comes after you is boundless. Understand this now as a flow of energy, rather than as us being a parade of drones doing and behaving in ways in which we always have, with no purpose or connection. The flow of this energy, the infinity flow, is akin to our Higher Selves. The HS is effortless. It is the mind of God, the heart energy within us. It's connected to everything on the planet and has the awareness of all beings and the flow of life itself. It creates simply because that is what it does. It does not seek to control, for it has no need for that. There is no specific or desired outcome for its creation. It knows that every aspect of it is in perfect divine order with everything else. It simply follows the flow. It's patient. It is enthralled with the process of presence, and it isn't fixed on outcomes. It's infinite, never-ending, and it resonates with abundance, flow, and creation. It has the entire cosmos in check and balanced.

We need both aspects of ourselves to exist. We do need to be logical when we are operating in the physical world, and we desperately need to remember to "let go and let God." Life is a balance between all opposing forces. Thing is, we do not need to operate these two aspects *against* each other. We can marry them and create a relationship where both are heard, followed, and understood. Both are in charge of their own domains, and both can work with the other.

You can keep your human self (hs) busy by allowing that aspect of you to make basic, logical decisions, such as should you shower with clothes on or off? Should you stick your hand on the hot stove over and over? (Probably not. Just sayin'.) Should you stop at a red light?

Allow the smaller self to find the stamp to go on that piece of mail that needs to go to your mortgage company or landlord. The smaller self is OK with the small tasks. It thrives on connecting the dots of ordinary linear life. It wants things to *make sense*. It has its place in the Universe and is valuable and unique, and yet, it's limited when it comes to transformation and changes. It's built on a foundation of safety and security and only likes to experience what it knows rather than to be challenged and expanded. It's indecisive when it comes to change, and it's extremely convincing of why not to do something that is out of its comfort zone. It's not good at challenging you. It doesn't particularly care for a constant upgrade. If it had a mantra, it would be, "Stick with the old. It's what we know." Could that be any more boring?

The Higher Self, (HS) operates on the Goodness for the Whole. It has the big picture in your best interests all the time. The HS knows what is in its right timing, and what needs to wait. HS knows all the details, and works to choreograph all aspects of life for everyone's best interests. The HS is only interested in creating the best possible scenario for you and all those who are a reflection of you, which is ultimately everyone, everywhere.

It is expansion itself. It has no concept of limitations because it is the whole of everything. It can include what is best for you as well as put into order what is best for all because it knows they are one and the same. Although it does not need to restrict your identity, it doesn't operate off your limited beliefs. It's much more magical and precise. Its eyes are on evolution and forward movement. It works using the law of least effort, making change an effortless occurrence. Change happens. It doesn't get stuck on indecision but rather flows like a river moving with the terrain knowing its final destination and not paying much attention at all to anything that is in its way.

It simply flows around, through, or over everything and keeps the final and ultimate goal of reconnecting to the Source. It doesn't put any one thing or person over precedence of another. It's like the coach who knows which players to put out on the basketball court at any particular time. It knows the best way to get what needs to get done, accomplished. It doesn't play favorites. It does listen to the program of the human self.

The Law of Forced Efficiency says, "There is never enough time to do everything, but there is always enough time to do the most important thing." We're all overwhelmed with life, aren't we? Our jobs and family responsibilities are always piling up. You probably have a stack of reading material you're hoping to get through and a list of places you hope to visit. The reality is, you'll probably never really get caught up. As soon as you do, more tasks and desires pop up. What you can do, however, is stay on top of the most important things. You can always find time to do the things you absolutely must complete. Your Higher Self operates under the Law of Forced Efficiency. It's always prioritizing your life and ensuring the right "things" are taking place, even if you aren't clear why. You are almost never clear on the why. That's where Trust and Faith come in. Build a relationship with your Higher Self, and the trust and faith will naturally follow.

Arianna Huffington says, "Complete a task by abandoning it." That has become one of my favorite quotes of all time. I am constantly thinking of new things I want to learn, do, or create. The Law of Efficiency allows for what is truly important to occur. Everything else is just byproducts of any other given moment. Sometimes, things just need to be dropped so what really matters can occur. Be OK with that. Get present with it. There is a ton of peace in the present.

Always trust that the Higher Self has a much clearer understanding and picture of the entire cosmos at all times. The difference between the human self (hs) and the Higher Self (HS) can be explained in the following analogy.

Imagine you are in a car stuck in a traffic jam. Directly in front of you, is a huge Mack Truck that you cannot see around. There you are, stuck in traffic with no idea of what is ahead. Is this jam caused by something just in front of the truck, or is this backed up for miles? Your thoughts will begin to run wild. *How much longer is this going to take? I have to get to work. What if I am fired because I'm late? I hope I don't know anyone involved in the mess ahead.* You may even bang on your steering wheel out of the stress. It is very rare when you surrender to moments like that and say, "*Oh that's OK. This is all working out for my Highest Good."* No. You want your plan to go according to what you planned. You want to move constantly, in your own way, as determined by you.

Now, your Higher Self operates like a traffic helicopter hovering over the scene. It knows precisely what is wrong, how far down the road it is, where there are valuable detours, who is on the scene, and how long it will take to clear up everything. It can merely report the situation and can understand and appreciate the needs and purposes this one accident caused for so many. It understands the people who are directly involved, as well as those who aren't even there on that road with you, such as all those in your office waiting for you. The Higher Self isn't stressed at all.

It knows that the jam ahead is/was preventing all those stuck behind it to slow down. They were meant to stop and stay stopped for a while. Everyone is exactly where they are meant to be in the order of the entire cosmos. The accident that occurred ahead was precisely what was supposed to happen to the unfortunate people in it without blame or fault. Those responding to that scene also are all a part of the bigger plan. The hospital staff (if needed), the insurance companies, tow trucks, repair trucks needed later, the news reporters, the traffic helicopter, all of it, were all part of a much larger network.

In that moment, we are all connected on a deeper level. Why did that accident have to happen? For connections' sake. For the sake of everyone's purposes. It's so widespread that it's not even traceable with our computers and data trackers. I suspect we will never be able to create technology that can monitor this level of constant connection.

Perhaps there was someone waiting in the traffic who was supposed to catch a plane. Now they have missed it, but that allowed someone else far away at some airport to actually get on the plane, in that seat, so they could get to say goodbye to a dying loved one in time. Or get to a job interview they desperately needed to continue to support their family. Or to simply get to their vacation spot on time so that plan goes well. Who knows? The possibilities are literally endless. Every single action we have going on here on earth, has multiple reactions and interconnected relations to everything else all the time. It's all a part of a beautifully complicated and yet simplistic flow of reality. We are not operating separately, not ever. We are all the particles that make up the wave, the continuum. They are one and the same, operating out of different Sources. The human self operates out of its limited beliefs, while the Higher Self, operates out of the potential for growth and expansion for all.

Do you often come and think about life from that awareness? Of course not. All you do is think *Oh, no. I'm going to be late,* and on and on you go. You and we are coming from our egoic small, limited self. We are the center of our universe, and we have stuff to do and places to be.

So often we all feel we aren't living a life of meaning and purpose. But tell that to the first responders to that scene. Tell that to the insurance companies and the car dealerships who now have to fix or replace those vehicles. All of those people have been given jobs to do. That has meaning and brings purpose into everyone's lives. Getting ourselves out of the "I want it that way" mentality and being able to realize how important we all are in each other's lives is critical. You might not know or like your purpose at any given time, but that that doesn't mean you don't have one.

Somehow, we think our purpose has to be something grand if we are to be validated. We feel we need to cure cancer, save villages, or do some sort of ongoing amazing superhuman feat to serve others. Quite the opposite is true. We serve and live out our purpose trillions of ways, millions of times within our one lifetime. Most of it is unknown. Like the example above, the person stuck in traffic who missed her flight has no way of knowing how perfect it was that she missed it.

Stuck in her human self, she's most likely complaining about how inconvenienced she was, while she may have opened the door from one of the greatest gifts to another human being. The person who got on that flight will have no idea why she or he was afforded the opportunity. Our Higher Selves, know all this. It's the greatest air traffic control center ever known, and for some reason, it is always perfect, and it always operates flawlessly.

We will never be able to duplicate the efficiency and perfection of our Higher Selves' vibration in Human Form. But we can be made aware of it, and we can go back to trusting it when we are stuck or feeling as if everything is going wrong. We can stop our brains and give gratitude for where we are. When we can do this, we can really understand and see the broader picture at hand. We aren't self-centered, and we become a part of a grand whole rather than feeling as if we are operating as lone individuals.

When we die, we leave our hs and become our fully-actualized HS. We realize the HS has been here all along. The spirit part of us is infinitely connected to everyone and everything, but our human aspect prevents us from remembering that.

One of the most frequent questions people ask me has to do with spirits, and what it's like after we die. But to explain how the spirit operates or the nature of spirit in a way that will make sense to you, we need to first examine the concept of what it means to be human.

Deborah Hanlon

7

What it Means to be Human & How Our Beliefs Shape Us

A belief is nothing more than a chronic pattern of thought, and you have the ability—if you try even a little bit—to begin a new pattern, to tell a new story, to achieve a different vibration, to change your point of attraction. The Law of Attraction is responding to your vibration, and you can easily change your vibrational point of attraction by visualizing the lifestyle you desire and holding your attention upon those images until you begin to feel relief, which will indicate that a true vibrational shift has occurred. ~Abraham Hicks

Yes, we're born, and our identities begin with our family of origin. From day one, the way we are raised begins to create neural patterns in our minds, and from there, we form our belief systems. The depth of these beliefs is astounding once you delve into them. For example, if you're raised in a vegetarian family, your first experience meeting someone who eats meat can be a transformative experience. It changes your core, changes a basic former facet of life you believed was simply a given. Seems silly, but think of all the *givens* you thought everyone did, only to find out the astonishing truth that there are millions of ways of being and living in this world. Think about the rules of life in your family of origin and how many of those you kept going. Traditions, ways to celebrate holidays and events, beliefs about how to raise children, to teach or not to teach religion: These rules formed your earliest beliefs. As we develop, we naturally begin to challenge a lot of these rules and create some of our own. However, a lot of the rules are unconscious, and we haven't thought of alternatives for them.

When I was in first grade, I attended a Catholic school. One day when we were brought into the gymnasium to get measured for our uniforms, we had to give our addresses to the seamstress, so our uniforms could be delivered. I answered "3 Helene Terrace," as proudly as I could, because I had just learned my address. I watched her write down "Helene Terrace" on a line on her piece of paper, and then she wrote a numeral three in a different box. In that moment, I learned not everyone on my street lived at 3 Helene Terrace. That day was the first one that I noticed different house numbers on my street. Such a small and simple awareness, and it was life-changing for me at that time.

Every day at lunch, I sat with Kim, whom I had known since kindergarten. I ate peanut butter and jelly sandwiches every day without fail, and so did she, only Kim's sandwich was always "wrong" to me. I actually felt sorry for Kim having to eat a whole sandwich crust and all—not cut in half like mine. Of course, there was nothing wrong with Kim's sandwich. It was just different from what I was used to.

We experience thousands of learned moments like those when we realize not everyone thinks, behaves, or believes as we do. When things are done differently than what we are used to, we often perceive it as wrong. We learn what we learn, and we believe those things we've learned are facts until something or someone comes along and shows us a different belief. Many of these are mundane, and in the grand scope of life, they mean absolutely nothing. But in the formative years, they all add up, and from there, we create an identity, which we hold onto strongly until something or someone shakes it up.

Think back to a few truths you had until you got older. Perhaps when you married, you discovered your spouse had different holiday traditions. As kids, we woke up to our Easter baskets laid out on the kitchen table for us to run to. As an adult, I learned that many families hid the baskets, sending the kids on a hunt Easter morning. What a concept. When I created Easter for my children, guess what I naturally did? Yup, I set up their baskets on the kitchen table. Monkey see, monkey do. Their cousins have a basket hunt on Easter, which is what made them ask me to do the same. So now, my forty-year Easter tradition has changed to basket hunts. Silly moments like this add up. It's no wonder wars are started because of different perspectives, and it's easy to understand why so much miscommunication occurs in the world. We are all unconsciously defending our own truths. Creatures of habit, we literally train our brains to behave in one way, and that way becomes The Way.

This is the process of identity—learning who we are and how we live. It's realizing we have a choice to believe and abide by certain morals, traditions, and values. There are trillions of these beliefs— from the simplistic, un-cut sandwich issue, to larger religious, financial, social, personal, and familial beliefs that form our understanding of ourselves and our world. These belief systems begin to crowd our Collective Whole Energy Field, the infinite and Holder of all Beliefs and all Truths, making us feel smaller and less empowered.

We get so attached to our human identities that our Spirit, or Higher Selves suffer. We become focused on our small, human selves, which are riddled with limitation and lack compared to the

Collective Whole. Who we are is so large and expansive and all-inclusive of It All, that when we take on one facet of It, we shrink our expansiveness. This is why we understand ourselves as right or wrong. It's all based on how we were raised and what we have chosen to continue to believe to be as absolute truths, rather than preferences. We are all sitting in our own dark caves.

As we get older, we begin to see and experience more and more of these different preferences in the world. Hopefully, as we grow, we begin to think less of something as being wrong and have more understanding of things being different. We can then choose to open ourselves up to new experiences and new patterns, habits, and possibilities, or continue to live small and stick with only the beliefs we were raised on. We need to open up our curiosity.

Which thought patterns do you fit into? If you are reading this book, you are probably in the group of those who choose to challenge some of what you were taught, and you are on your way to opening yourself up to a larger reality. You are on your way to being empowered and to learn how to use your energy field (which is directed and fueled by your thoughts and beliefs) into creating a better reality for yourself. That includes feeling more connected to not only those around you who have passed on, but to your Higher Power and God (The Collective Whole/The Universe). It's pretty huge. This process allows you to learn how to trust your gut, how to know the difference between intuition and fear, and how to experience life as it is manifested with you as the Creator, rather than always being a victim to what happens.

As humans, we are very shortsighted. We can only understand so much about anyone or anything. We draw from our collective experiences to make assumptions about well, everything. We aren't even aware we are doing this! Our beliefs that were formed since the moment of our birth have created reality for us. We believe what we know. We reenact what we know. We are comfortable with, what we know. The problem is what we know is really only based upon events that have happened before—that is, moments we have experienced, read about, or heard another discuss. We dip back into old wells all the time, which oftentimes causes us to act and react as we did in the past, regardless that we are in a new moment and in a new scenario. This is especially true in scenarios of trauma. We seem to continue to replay the responses to traumatic events each and every day with absolutely no awareness of this. If we felt financially unsafe as children, there is no doubt we will grow up to be adults who feel financially unstable. It doesn't even matter if it's true. We could grow up and become millionaires, but if we haven't updated our reality to "I am financially secure," then it doesn't matter whatsoever. We live out of the beliefs and feelings that were surrounding us as children. Our beliefs about everything get created and locked into our cellular memory by the time we are nine years old. Everything after that, is a huge reenactment. Stay with me here. Am I saying that we are all little kids running around as adults with all these feelings of unresolved insecurities and inadequacies? Yep. I am. These soft spots in our lives begin to solidify the more we identify with them. The overweight child becomes the overweight adult, even if he or she has mastered a fitness and nutrition program and is physically fit. If felt as a child, the mindset "I am fat and unattractive" will remain the old well the adult mindset will draw from unless some sort of personal development and awareness shifts take place. The consciousness of the overweight child will run the show—until it doesn't—until you finally recognize the underlying belief that you have identified yourself with and have unconsciously replayed that old tape.

Some of our old tapes are good. I have one where I truly feel I will be successful at anything I really put my mind to and love. I do not let the fear of *what if this doesn't work out?* ever enter my mind. I also have a belief that I will only gravitate toward things I enjoy and therefore I want to get better at. It is rarely a struggle for me. Things come effortlessly to me. Now, please don't confuse this. I also work very hard, and I have a not-always-good belief that if I want something done right, I have to do it all myself. This can be isolating and well, extremely inefficient, lonely, and just plain stupid.

The awareness of both beliefs has helped me dramatically. I can now identify when I am slipping into my old rigid mindsets of "If it's going to be, it's all up to me," and "If you want something done right, you have to do it yourself." Now, I can change the thoughts and redirect them into new beliefs. The more I become aware, the faster I change the behavior, and therefore I create a new neural pathway toward success or at least more ease in my inner life. The former way had me handling everything while this new thought helps me connect with those around me and not carry it all on my shoulders. This has definitely been an upgrade of living for me.

If you grow up believing you don't have any limitations, then you realize anything is possible. ~ Jennifer Bricker

The person raised in any extreme religion grows up to believing that way is the only way. They are usually quite shocked to even learn that other religions exist. The child who is taught all Christians are "bad" believes that to be truth. It's sad, but how can they know any differently? We learn through repetition and the behaviors of the "big" people around us. We watch and we simply replicate what we see. These are called learned behaviors. Sometimes, oftentimes, especially as very young children, we can feel there is something wrong about a rigid mindset, but we can't understand how our feelings don't match what is being taught to us. We have all witnessed the purity of a child just being themselves and fully accepting others. That is because our logical minds haven't developed fully, and we are still mainly operating out of our hearts and intuition. Something may not feel right, but we just don't know what because we are trusting the big people around us to show us the way. When logic and intuition clash in our early years, there is a huge potential of learning not to trust one's intuition and to challenge what we feel over what is told to us.

Some people have been raised on the words "Money doesn't grow on trees," which implies there is never enough. So, what does this little person grow up to feel? That there is never enough money. There is fear around money. A person with this belief will either work harder and save it all and rarely spend it, or this person will never have it because their mindset is focused on there never being enough.

The child who is told they will never amount to anything grows up believing that. They either work harder to prove everyone wrong, or they simply take everyone else's word for it, and what happens to their life? They feel they never amount to anything. This person can grow up to be a Nobel Peace Prize winner and still feel that they have amounted to nothing. The tangible result of our beliefs means nothing. The mindset and feeling the mind creates around our beliefs create our true identity and purpose.

Success truly comes through finally recalibrating yourself with who you are in this moment and loving that person with all your might. How? By living like a dead person. By raising your consciousness to supersede your ego. You must understand what happens when we die. And then, we can figure out how to adopt the principles of awareness the deceased have and live that out in our daily lives.

People don't realize what's normal or not normal. We often don't even know what it is we are doing or believing and how or why it limits us. You don't even question it most of the time. We experience things and believe "that's just the way life is." Our belief becomes our reality. Our reality is a direct manifestation of our core beliefs. Some people say your reality creates your belief. What you believe and think is what becomes real.

The Law of Attraction explains that when you align yourself or agree to something subconsciously, that's what becomes your life and your reality. If your parents taught you there isn't enough money, or that members of a particular religion are terrorists, then that's what you'll experience for the rest of your life unless you change your thought patterns. We believe what we are told, until something hopefully intercepts these former realities. We always find what we are looking for as well. When a person believes all Muslims are terrorists, then he or she automatically and unconsciously aligns with the reality that it is true. So, what happens? Then they only see, read, and hear about "those Muslims" who engaged in acts of terrorism. Somehow, they don't meet, or learn about the complete opposite reality. They haven't wired or attuned their mindset to even hear otherwise.

If you think your spouse is cheating on you, trust me, you will find reasons that will back this up, even if it isn't true. People can make up and twist things to align with their beliefs. We all do this all the time. When you have something set in your mind, the universe will bounce back the false truth to you. You won't even be open to seeing, hearing, or believing any other way. It'll get filtered out of your awareness until (if) your awareness shifts just a little. The hs doesn't like to be wrong, so it will always find anything to back up its beliefs.

Growth Opportunity

Here's a small-scale experiment to test this theory. Seeing kangaroos in the wild in North America on a regular day is not a common experience for Americans/Canadians, but for the next forty-eight hours, align your thoughts and beliefs that you will in fact see a kangaroo during the next two days. Just continue to hold the image and experience of seeing a kangaroo and watch what happens. At some point, over the next two days, when you truly have deliberately placed your focus on this image, you will absolutely see one. Now, will it be sitting outside your house? Will you see one running across the road? Who knows? You just might see one on a piece of paper or look up at the TV and happen to notice one during a commercial. There may be mention of a kangaroo, or even talk about Roo from *Winnie the Pooh* that you might have easily filtered out had you not placed your focus on this. What you focus on, is what you will experience. What you believe is true, you will manifest. It's a pretty cool notion, but one that can be quite empowering or quite devastating. Keep this in mind through the rest of this book. It's key.

You have to first recognize that your beliefs are not necessarily the whole story. It's your story thus far, but it doesn't necessarily have to be the way things will be. How do you recognize what your beliefs are? If you don't know what your beliefs are about relationships, take a look at what your relationships are like right now. If people in your life are present and warm and caring, then that's what you believe about relationships. If your relationships feel like you're always picking up the pieces or people always betray you, that's who you will attract. Do you have money in the bank? Do you feel secure in your financial future? If so, you probably have a belief system that you always have enough money. If you don't, you may have a feeling of lack. Whatever you believe is what you attract. If you want to know what your beliefs are, just look at all the aspects of your current life. They will reflect positively and/ or negatively what your deep core beliefs are.

How can you do this? Start recognizing your thoughts. Just sit and write everything your brain thinks for a period of time. Learn to become aware of your thoughts. Step back and look at it as if you are an outsider observing the thoughts so you can be aware of what they are. See what judgments or assumptions you make of others instantly. Look at each aspect of your life. What are your beliefs (your truths) about money? Career? Men? Women? Children? Parents? Housing? Members of a different ethnic race, relationships, friendships, family, politics, religions? Assess what your beliefs are about all aspects of your life. Break them into categories to help you organize them. I do mine on a large poster board, or you can do them on individual sheets of paper. Make it large and noticeable for you to begin to see some threads. Take note of what is working in your life and what doesn't seem to be working. Then take note at your beliefs surrounding those areas of your life.

If you recognize that your thoughts are always worried about whether or not you can pay a bill, there isn't enough in your bank account, you can stop that thought itself and replace it with *It's going to be all right. There is always enough. Something is going to happen, and it will be paid.* Bring in empowering thoughts of *I got this. I can handle it.* When your old thoughts come creeping back, you have to be aware of them so you can start replacing those thoughts with the new ones again. You can't erase your subconscious tapes. You just need to overlay them with the new thoughts. It is very normal for those bad/old thoughts to come back. Know that is what happens in this process and be less hard on yourself. Just recognize when it's happening and realign your thoughts to create your new reality.

Many of your beliefs aren't even accurate, and they don't have to become your reality. You might think all rich people have easy lives because they have money, but people with money still experience death, hardships, divorce, and other problems that interfere with their ability to be happy. So, if you believe rich people are jerks, you could also be preventing yourself from making more money because you don't want to be that way. I know a lot of people who hold the belief that if you are going to have money, you have to lie, cheat and/or steal from others. If you are not in alignment with lying, cheating, and stealing, then you just might naturally create a block from your having money. We can't want to be one thing and yet believe if we have that one thing, we have to be a certain way to get it. Our beliefs and our desire must be in alignment.

Through our identity, we attract both negative and positive experiences. If someone insults me for being very tall, for example, then I can choose to take that offensively or not, and I use that experience to create my response to the world. We all do this every day, twenty-four hours a day, seven days a week, throughout our entire lives. If someone hurts us or takes something from us as a human, it is our egos—or our identities as humans—that get offended and angered. We feel we are attacked by another when we ourselves believe there is some truth to the attack. If you were to tell me you did not like my purple hair, and you thought it made me look ugly, I most likely will not get upset because I know I don't have purple hair. I might get annoyed that I do not see what you see. But I will be so firm in the fact that I don't have purple hair, and therefore I can't look ugly because of it. However, if you told me you thought I was lazy, and that the reason my website wasn't finished quickly was because I waste too much time on Candy Crush, I just might be offended because it's a truth about myself that I don't like to admit. We all crave validation of our worth. It's sad and absolute madness, and it's what I believe is the main cause of human suffering. Yet it is easily remedied, if you will take the time and discipline to change it. It requires you to face the truth and forces you to see where you were limited in your thinking.

When we die, we lose the physical body and the identity that was created around that body, as well as the things we believed to be true based on our time in the human form. We are no longer attached to the body or more important, to the human identity and beliefs held by that body. It is the body in the dense form that created that identity that attracted all of our experiences to us through that energy. When we die, the human identity is released, and our spirit, that essence that has been there inside us all along, that thing that is present in everything, everywhere – remains. We are freed. We are no longer contained in a teeny tiny limited vessel. We lose our human identity, and we no longer feel tied into what we are or aren't and instead– we become everything and nothing at the same time. We are simply connected to everything. We are the energy that binds it all.

Our human selves operate quite opposite of the way we operate as spirit. But we can learn from spirit and retrain our thoughts and beliefs to understand we have no limitations, that there need not be so much focus on negativity, and that we can fully embrace who we are. It is when we figure out how to do this that we really create our own heaven on earth.

Growth Opportunity

What are some of your beliefs? Do you believe you are lucky and always win prizes? Or do you believe you never win anything? Were you told people of different ethnic/religious backgrounds were in fact, very different from you? Were you taught that all single moms struggle? Have you heard things from your parents such as "Get a safe job with a pension, and then you will be happy"? Were you taught there is no such thing as the afterlife? Do you believe all men/women are cheaters because that has been your experience? Or that making a certain amount of money per year is impossible? There are literally thousands of core beliefs that you have, and these little thoughts are literally creating your reality. You are creating your life with every thought and belief. We are all in the cave of our past experiences, and little do we know we need to turn around and see life from a different perspective and mindset in order to change it. Write out what it is you know to be true about your world, yourself, and how you operate in it. This will literally create a map for you to finally see the areas of your thinking that you need to upgrade, and what can stay the same.

You're not a victim of your heredity. In biology class, most of us learn that our DNA determines who we become. Things like our eye and hair color, our susceptibility to diseases, addictions, or disorders are all predetermined by our DNA. In some cases, this belief causes you to become a victim of your heredity. If both of your parents are alcoholics or drug addicts, you might grow up thinking you're destined to become an addict, and since there is nothing you can do about your heredity; you just accept it as truth and give up. This belief that DNA determines all the details about your looks and health says you are less powerful than your chemical makeup (your genes), but it is actually your perception and beliefs that select your genes and cause the behavior which brings out the reality.

Your body is made of over fifty trillion cells. The body's cells function independently from your DNA, while environmental stimuli can affect DNA. The power of our own belief systems and our thoughts have control over our DNA. If you believe your genetics will result in your getting cancer because it runs in your family, your thoughts are more likely to cause cancer in your body.

Bruce Lipton, Ph.D., is a renowned cell biologist and author of *The Biology of Belief*[2]. In his book, he explains the power of perception over DNA, stating scientific discoveries that show the cells of your body are affected by your thought patterns and describes the molecular pathways that this process occurs.

Will you be more careful with your thoughts about your DNA, knowing your genes will express the beliefs you have for them? Will you empower yourself or shrink your energy into a limited space and literally create havoc for yourself?

Knowledge and awareness are spread and shared in the ether. Perhaps evolution itself is fueled by an energy of progress. The expansion of ideas creates the expansion of more ideas. The understanding of one becomes the understanding of all. What would happen if collectively half the world started changing their beliefs about who we are and how we operate? What would happen if there were a massive shift of awareness about our beliefs and how limited we are when we use our past conditioning to determine our future? What about how that will change how we view death and transformation itself. What if we finally realized we are all working together simultaneously and are all co-creating the entire globe and everything that happens on it? What if we realized it's our evolution that is actually causing the expansion of the Universe itself. Can we all get out of our caves? I imagine it would be a world operating on a vibration of empowerment, for the individual and for the Whole. Sure, this sounds like a great line in John Lennon's *Imagine*, but... what IF?

As I see it right now, we are instead collectively overly focused on super ridiculous celebrity gossip and hearing, seeing, and being exposed to the horrific acts that occur on the globe daily. Mainstream media has gotten a strong hold on our consciousness. And well, when we understand that our thoughts are connected, and we understand the magnitude of this connection, we need to take a look at all the negative imagery and occurrences we witness on TV and the internet. Yes, it's wise to be cautious, but not so much that we can't trust a single soul. This divides us. It encourages the stagnation of non-growth. It encourages the world to stop changing and shifting paradigms. It keeps things the same. The absence of life, is stagnation. It's non-change. The only things that lose out in that model are everyone and everything. Something will have to force a shift if we aren't allowing it to happen organically. Something will end the travesty of stagnation, wipe it all out, and start again. For that is the process itself. When the resistance to change hits a tipping point, change wins. Every single time.

Since change is inevitable, what side of it do you want to be on? The creative side, where you get to be a part of the consciousness to propel it forward, or on the side that says no to it, and finding yourself resistant and subsequently in the middle of a tsunami of change, feeling helpless and powerless? The coolest thing in life is that you get to choose. This is your human self, working alongside your Higher Self in a balance. Begin to know this: your beliefs in your ability and how to think is your choice. It's your free will, which will change how you create your destiny. Choose wisely.

8

Death: Transformation for Everyone Involved = the Afterlife

We experience death in every aspect of our lives—in our relationships, our jobs, our health, our friendships, in the cells of our bodies, in our identities, and in our own stages of growing. Death occurs all the time. It is simply the releasing of something for something new to emerge. You are continuously dying in various stages all the time. Trillions of cells in your own body have died since you started reading this book. New cells emerged since then and have kept your body, the human being whose eyes are scanning over these words, intact. Your existence didn't skip a beat at all when this process occurred. Instead, there was a smooth transition of one state to another where everything within your body seamlessly allowed one aspect of you, the tangible pieces of evidence that you exist (your cell), to die while a new you emerged. If this were not the case, your entire system would have to reboot every second for life to stop and then go.

If death were a final stage, then it would constantly interrupt every single process with a very clear beginning, a middle, and an ending point. That is not how life operates, not in the grand large scale. This is very easy to accept when we are talking about life on a microscopic level. What we don't see, we don't miss. What we don't have conscious attachment to, we don't notice when it's gone. So yes, life operates in this manner, but when we talk about the death of a loved one or a pet, our emotions and our very identity get rocked to the core. It isn't as easy to accept death in the macro aspect as easily. That's for sure.

Nothing is harder to bear than the death of a loved one. There are so many stages one must go through and so many opportunities that open up (while others close) afterward. Physical death causes deep emotional, mental, and spiritual transformation in those left behind. At the beginning of the journey, we all resist it. We are sad, angry, and lonely. We feel guilt and always lament over the would-a, could-a, should-a's.

"If only we went to the doctor sooner, so and so wouldn't have passed." "If only we took a different route to school that day, so and so would still be here." "If only we made him stay home that night." It's pure torture for the living to experience. Then we panic, thinking "Did they know I loved them?" "Why didn't I tell them how much I appreciated them?" I wish, I wish, I wish becomes a permanent state of mind.

This is a view into hell on Earth, and it is also an important part of the grieving process. No matter what, I do not foresee this will change much, regardless of how brilliantly aligned with our nature of who we are becomes. Although I know about the other side and how we never really die, I will be the first to state that I hate it when people I love die. I don't care if they are here in the spiritual or energetic realms. It's sad. We miss them. We live in the realm where we rely on our five senses, all tangible ways of experiential living and being. When those are challenged or taken away, we do not know how to react or respond. That is normal. As long as I am existing in the physical, materialistic world, then I want everyone I love to be there in the physical plane as well. I prefer to see, hear, feel, and touch those I love dearly.

However, I have come to the realization that when we can understand the nature of death, we can understand how we can live more authentically. It won't solve the fact that we have grief. Only grieving solves grief. However understanding death and the concept of the afterlife will help us to have a deeper sense of peace as to the timeline and synchronicity all life has. It can somehow release us from some of our own guilt and torture. No matter what, though, we will always miss our loved ones after they have passed. We are still here in the physical, so we want them to be here in that way as well. Ultimately, we want to know they are OK with us. John Edward always says, "We must appreciate, validate, and communicate with our loved ones while they are still living," so a medium like him doesn't have to do it for you. I love that. Yes, that is what we all should do, and this is what we all wish we did do when we had the chance. Sometimes we do. Sometimes we don't. It's all part of the learning curve. It's all perfectly arranged. So, let it be.

I wasn't a medium my entire life, not in the way I think people think anyway. I always knew stuff. I always had a sense of calm about me. People mentioned it all the time to my mom. People would say they could sense that I had a "knowing" about me, "a presence." No matter what was going on in my life, deep down, I really knew it was only temporary, that it was only my human self having experiences. I knew nothing was my fault, and all this was temporary. I knew it because I felt it. I knew it because I read it in my mother's books. I knew it because the Maharishi said, "The goal of the Transcendental Meditation technique is the state of enlightenment. This means we experience that inner calmness, that quiet state of least excitation, even when we are dynamically busy." I knew it because *The Autobiography of a Yogi* by Paramahansa Yogananda had pictures in his book that spoke to me. The words, although I didn't understand what they said back then, filled me. I knew it because of the illustrations in *Clown of God*[3] by Tomie De Paola. That book showed me we all have gifts to offer the world by the juggler in it offering his act to the Christ Child. I knew it because it was popping up everywhere in my life; my environment showed it to me. I knew it because the lyrics to *Puff the Magic Dragon* reminded me that little boys did not live forever the way dragons did. That song, I felt was meant for me. I literally thought I watched and loved that movie because my parents wanted me to remember Chris, my deceased brother. It resonated with me to my core. To this day, I think of Chris as Jackie Paper, and me, the Dragon, maybe because I was born in the year of the dragon. I really believed the song was about Chris and me. I knew about life because life was happening all around me and within me. I observed it. I listened to it. I studied it. Questioned it. Experienced it. Observed it. I knew stuff because I felt it. I witnessed it, and I paid close attention to it. That's all I knew to do. It was my escapism, I suppose.

In Malcom Gladwell's book, *The Outliers*[4], he coined the "10,000 Hours Rule." This suggests that for a person to be considered an expert at anything, there needs to be a foundation of 10,000 hours of doing that particular thing. There is an advantage to the amount of time spent doing something over and over to help a person become extraordinary. He discusses in the book how the Beatles performed live over 1,200 times within a four-year period resulting in more than 10,000 hours of practice. This set them apart from all other musicians. He also explains how Bill Gates had more than 10,000 hours of computer programming under his belt, starting as young as thirteen years old. This gave him quite the advantage of experience, leading him to his success. I had well over 10,000 hours spent being around grieving individuals whose emotions varied between states of doing "well," to being seriously disturbed by the time I was ten or eleven years old.

I had to develop a skill of empathy and being able to "feel" a room out. I had to exercise my intuition of when it was the right time to talk and when it wasn't. I was around grief, chaos, loss, sadness, fear, and insecurity in my younger years. Thankfully, I did always feel tremendously loved by my mom and siblings. This also resulted in a traumatic loss in my late thirties when those relationships were severed . . . the worst death I ever experienced. I've had a rich background of having to make sense of what is happening around me and how to continue to focus on the future while remaining present. Today, I am grateful and in much better understanding of how beneficial even the worst of my circumstances have been to me in the big picture of my life. This very deeply rooted sense of self trust and introspection have kept me sane and truly alive all these decades. My concept of the afterlife saved me. I have discovered I am not perfect, and my viewpoint on matters is only a portion of the truth. However, while they are only a small part of a much larger picture, doing what feels best and right for ourselves is critical at any given time in life.

People who lie to others, or worse, to themselves, have a much harder climb up the mountain of life. I never have to keep my stories straight, nor do I have to defend myself and my choices. They are fairly simple and clear cut, even the confusing moments. The truth truly does set you free. Truth itself can be tricky though.

What I see as true from my perspective, is viewed differently from another's point of view. The key is to always be open to listen and also know when listening is getting you nowhere, and parties may have to agree to disagree. I can hold on to my human self, have a voice, understanding my voice isn't the final say in all of life, but ultimately it is the final say in my life. This balance isn't easy and is best meandered by attracting people in your life who hold you accountable. Having people who call you out when your actions aren't matching your words, and vice versa, is key. Being able to accept healthy criticism is a skill. No one likes it at first, but man. How freeing when someone's perspective sheds light on all of it.

We are here to awaken from our illusion of separateness.
~Thich Nhat Hanh

Looking back, I didn't really know there were levels of our selves. I mean, I think I knew it deep down, just as everyone knows it, but I wasn't aware of chakras, and I didn't yet know anything about the existence of our physical, mental, emotional, and spiritual bodies. I just thought there was just one me. I figured I was a separate body with a separate energy field. I sensed we were made and connected by something, but I wasn't aware of how it all worked yet, at least not in scientific terms. So, I wasn't aware which part of me understood things.

I do feel, because of a lot of life stress, and the fact that I never wanted to add more stress to my family, I was good. I behaved. I did what I was told (as a kid). I didn't want to create waves, and I wanted to be known for being a good kid. My reputation was important to me. I was fortunate, though. Things came relatively easy to me. I wasn't a high-maintenance child. I did my homework, learned easily, followed rules, helped others, was mostly thoughtful and kind. Those times I wasn't haunt me to this day. I played sports and was fairly good at them on my first try. I applied myself to a degree and was an above-average learner. I think all that made me create a very positive energy field that helped me along. I thought was just me, yet it was a deep knowing of what was truth for me. I believe this knowing is what kept me at peace during the tumultuous times. I now know I had a deep connection to my spiritual body that houses all this understanding and ethereal knowledge. Clearly, I always intuitively understood the afterlife.

I never thought I was ordinary or mediocre. Yet oddly, in those formative and adolescent years, I had a chaotic life. My parents were divorced, my brother put stress on my family, my mother was having all sorts of emotional and financial issues, and my father was three thousand miles away. We had very little money, stuff was broken in the house, no oven, showers constantly clogged, unkempt yard, messy curtains, and a ripped-up couch. I was constantly doing without and yet, I already felt a deeper knowing in me that all of this is temporary, and that I shouldn't sweat it.

Growth Opportunity

Think about aspects of your life that do not feel right or good for you. Write them down. Ask yourself why you are choosing to continue to behave or react in certain ways that don't work for you. Why have you not changed your approach? Is there a perceived belief or conditioned response you've learned from your parents, family, or society that makes you feel you must do or be such and such? Are you willing to admit to yourself and get brave to find out what works for you rather than doing what you have been told? Do you keep doing the same thing simply because that's how it's always been done? At heart, we are still children who were programmed to listen to our parents and to live out our lives in the ways they taught us. Problem is, if you have grown, evolved, or changed in any way through your adulthood, chances are, you have found other ways that work better for the person you are today. Now, can you give yourself permission to make these changes and upgrades? You have more power to make the changes to your life than you probably give yourself credit for. It takes a lot to change. The first step is the awareness of what isn't working for you and the courage to make those changes even when you must go against your previously known norm.

I often had to appease or calm my mom, who was in constant turmoil or experiencing a manic high. She mismanaged her life, money, and everything from day one, and at ten years old, I'd be the one explaining to her why she should do such and such.

If it hadn't had this upbringing, I'd be an entirely different person. There is positive and negative polarity in every aspect in life, and lord knows, I've had enough therapy to make all the connections. I can honestly say that as dysfunctional as my early childhood was, that's life, and it happens daily. It gave me an early start on my ten thousand hours. My mom would talk to me about pretty much everything. At times, she was so stressed that I would tell her, "Mom, if you got yourself into this, you can get yourself out of it."

Since I was three, I've had hours and hours and hours of having to be calm, level headed, and introspective, and I believe this has helped me understand the human condition and more important, our emotional and mental aspects of ourselves. This is my conditioning.

How much turmoil are you experiencing in your life simply because you're doing things that are expected of you or because you've been conditioned to do them? I'm certain the awareness I had saved my life from a very early age. That's why I'm so driven to share with you. I want to save you and many others from excess turmoil. If you are alive, chances are you are going to have some turmoil. You might as well learn from it. Get real, get honest, get brave. You got yourself into this, you can get yourself out!

So how did I get to the point where I could communicate with the deceased to deliver messages? I wasn't hit by lightning or dropped on my head as a baby, nor did I have a near-death experience, as many have asked me. I wasn't born with superpowers or with the knowledge that I could do this. It developed over time, although looking back on my life now, I guess you could say there were signs that I was connected and guided by the deceased from a young age.

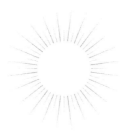

9

Human or Spirit? Particle or Wave?

One of the most common questions people ask me has to do with spirits, and what it's like after we die. But to explain how the spirit operates, or the nature of spirit in a way that will make sense, I had to first explain the concept of what it means to be human, and then how we are energy disguised as humans.

When we are living, we are really spirits, or energy, taking on the human form. Our spirit and soul are our essence. That essence is the same in everyone; it's energy. We're all energy, but we're just a different variation of the same essence expressed differently. For example, think about salt water in the ocean. Countless billions of drops make up the ocean. If you take a pitcher and fill it with salt water and fill a pool, a plastic bag, or any container that will hold the water, it's all the same water, but it takes on different forms depending on what you put it in.

Just as your spirit lives within your body, whatever container you place the water in becomes the "body," but the essence or core inside that container is the same. The spirit inside us is all the same. We correlate size with importance, but is the water in the ocean more significant than the water in a glass? No. The magnitude, the quantity of all this water is what makes it powerful. Think about how powerful we really are when we are no longer contained in anything. That is what many call God, Brahman, Source, The Universe, YHWH, The Light, The Father, Supreme Being, Alpha Omega, Allah, Spirit, The Almighty, Creator, and countless others across all traditions. It is no wonder that we all seem to think less of ourselves than we should. We are stuck in the illusion that we are separate from the Source and not a part of it. We believe we are here, and God or some larger force is over there, when in fact, we are it, altogether. When we band together, both in the physical sense, and through our consciousness, we can collectively understand our magnificence and power.

Unlike your finite mind, your infinite mind is not bound by the rules of time and space. It has ten thousand states of mind to view and examine experience through. ~Zen Koan

There is more to your mind and your being than your conscious thoughts. The conscious, (the Ego or human self hs) subconscious (our beliefs and early conditioning) and superconscious (The Higher Self or HS) minds go much deeper and have more influence on your belief systems than you may understand. Learning how to connect with the superconscious mind opens the door to accessing your "Higher Self."

Have you ever been driving home from someplace you travel frequently, and you become so lost in your thoughts that you find you've driven all the way home with no real memory of the trip? This is an example of your subconscious mind taking over. In many situations, the subconscious mind is great and helps us do what we need to do on a daily basis, while leaving our conscious mind free to come up with new ideas and thoughts.

The superconscious mind is a little harder to grasp. It exists beyond our space-time continuum. It's been called many different things, depending on whom you ask. I've been referring to it as the "Higher Self" throughout this book. The superconscious mind is the foundation that most metaphysical and religious teachings are based on. Carl Jung, an Australian psychoanalyst, was one of the first people to refer to this "thing" as the superconscious mind. He said that the knowledge and wisdom of all the ages was stored in the superconscious mind, and every single person has access to it. Imagine what you would be capable of if you had access to all the knowledge of people from all time?

Ralph Waldo Emerson referred to it as the *oversoul* and wrote that when we access this immense intelligence, we realize it's far beyond what our own human minds are capable of.

Napoleon Hill, in *Think and Grow Rich* referred to it as the "infinite intelligence." Hill interviewed five hundred of America's most successful men and women over twenty years and decided that the ability of these successful people to tap into this infinite intelligence was the reason they experienced such great success[5].

So, what do we do with the superconscious, the oversoul, or the infinite intelligence, anyway? Connecting to our superconscious mind opens our abilities for connecting to our Higher Selves, and the aspects of our being that existed before we were born. Through the superconscious mind, it is possible to connect to every other mind on the planet. On a conscious level, you may not believe in God, or you may feel there is no part of your being that extends before your birth or after your death. The superconscious mind contains the blueprint for your life. Think about all the times when you felt like you were in the right place at the right time. Or all the times when something happened that was devastating to you, or you felt like it was the worst thing that could possibly happen to you, only to find out later that the particular event had to happen in order for something great to happen later on? These are no coincidences. This is your superconscious making sure you are changing direction to follow your life's path and experience things that are beneficial to you.

I want to live without an ego, meaning, without an absolute identity. Is that possible? And if so, how can we realistically stay connected to the flow of everything, including time itself, while still in a body? Of course, it is possible, although it takes a tremendous amount of constant awareness and presence. Do you live this way, always aware that you are more than just this body who is busy doing, doing, doing? Do you take the time to stop and remember your connection to everything?

Let me answer that for you. If you are reading this book, no, you don't. We are born with this innate knowing and understanding of our true natures, and then we begin to grow and take on an identity, which creates even more pain while we are in the physical form. Our original selves know the truth, and from the moment of our birth, we try to find it again. We know better. We all really do know not to make mountains out of molehills. We all already know the secret, the answer that we are all OK. That we are all connected, and that all of life is happening around us just because. We know this from our core, our deep spiritual space within. Look how children are. They, who are closest to the state of the purity of being-ness. They just are who they are, until we undo that in them. (Guilty mommies, don't worry. It's OK. Creating an identity within our kids is also part of a later process necessary to undo that identity in a growing adult. It's all perfect when we allow it to be.) What happens to this purity, this innate knowledge? It becomes confused with "attaining" it, reaching it. We confuse a particular moment as all moments, a certain circumstance as being forever rather than temporary. WE have confused that state of being in Spirit/Energy form with the physical form. We become conditioned to have that which we can see, hear, touch, taste, and smell. Yet, what we really need to do while in physical form, is to remember that we can return to that space of quiet and connectedness when we are still and nonjudgmental.

A few years ago, I attended a retreat at The Omega Institute with Panache Desai. At that retreat, I learned precisely how to "have it all" by using everyone's experiences as my own. I was able to tap into my ego and the collective whole (my hs and my HS) simultaneously. In the workshop, he played his self-created, mixed, fast-paced dance music and told us we had three choices of how to experience this music. We could stay in our chairs, eyes opened or closed. We could sit on meditation pillows and mediate through it. Or we could get up and dance. Now, I've always loved to dance, but I'm sometimes shy, and the thought of dancing with a bunch of hippies, usually wasn't what I would choose.

In the past, I would have played it safe and stayed in my seat. I would have wished I could be up dancing, or happily meditating, but I would have stayed stuck in my seat, not enjoying my present because I was wishing it was something different. On this hot summer day, I found myself getting up and dancing, and the more I danced, the more I felt alive. The move alive I felt, the more I was able to appreciate my fellow dancers. I wasn't alone at all. Then I looked toward the chairs in the room, and I could feel myself as those who decided to stay seated. They remained in their chairs, for whatever reasons, and I was also experiencing the music through them. I then looked over to the part of the room where people were meditating though the music, and again, I felt that they were allowing me to also meditate as them. I didn't have to choose anything; I could be a part of all of it. I chose a path for myself, but the paths I didn't choose were also mine. I experienced the room in all scenarios. When the music stopped (hours later), I felt invigorated. I finally understood abundance and the ability to have it all. We need each other to choose different paths, so those journeys become a part of our own. This happens when we open up to the moment.

After this class, I also felt I could grasp Jesus' words of, "I will suffer so they do not have to." He was taking that path, so no one else had to choose it. So, through Him, we all suffer, but we are also saved. When we stop seeking it, and start seeing it, we will have it. And of course, once we have finished our journeys and physical lives here, we will absolutely return to this place that will reconnect us to what it is we thought was missing. We will finally understand what we failed to see all along. We already have the missing piece. It's hidden within us, buried deeply.

The search is on to go back to the state of pure peace, but sadly many of us do not find it until we are no longer contained within a human body. However, we do not have to wait until then. It's the stillness and the attitude of "All is well" that is deeply needed here on earth. We need not panic, need not be lured in by our fears. As we develop a sense of nothingness and let go of who we need to be, want to be, and who we think we are, we get closer to our core. Just by realizing we don't know everything, and everything we do currently know is simply a reflection of all that we have already learned, but isn't necessarily the truth, we get closer to our core. The less tightly we hold on to our small truth and open ourselves up to the larger Universe, the closer to Self we get. This is where the deceased reside, in the collective whole.

Know thyself. ~ Plato

To know thyself is key. Plato hinted that when we know ourselves, we have a greater potential to understand what is the nature of being human. And when we have this foundation, we are able to understand one another more deeply as well. Yes. When we understand our true nature, we then recognize each other as the same spirit. We lose our rigidity and the need to be right. We can still honor what we feel is right for ourselves, as long as we understand our right may not be another's. And when we truly know ourselves, we realize we are nothing like what we previously thought. There is great freedom in this wisdom. Can you let go of yourself enough to comprehend it? Can you open yourself up to the fact that you are exactly the same as your best and most loyal of friends as well as your most feared or hated enemies? (Chew on that.)

How is it possible that nearly everyone on the planet feels this feeling of something missing or that there has to be something more? Why are we all so disconnected? It's because we do know our True Nature. We do know we are bigger and all knowing. If we didn't know it, we wouldn't miss it. Do you know what a thrill it is to jump out of an airplane? If you haven't done it, then no, you don't. Do you know how wonderful chocolate lava cake or a juicy orange fresh off the tree taste? Do you know how devastating losing a loved one is? If you haven't experienced something directly, you will not truly know it, and therefore you won't miss it and unconsciously seek it out.

It's because we know our source that we miss it. We remember being Source. The connection and knowledge of it is there. We know how peaceful and connected we all are, and yet, when we aren't in that mindset, we miss it. We miss ourselves. We miss each other. We crave that connection, that feeling. We know it's there, and that's what drives us crazy. But where is it, and how do we access it? When we try to experience it through our ego, or hs, or we will always come up short.

We know at a subatomic, quantum level, that all of life as we experience it is just a reflection of what is actually real and true. There is the observer effect in physics that is so mind boggling it's still difficult to fully comprehend. The observer effect states that nothing can be purely experienced in its true state when being observed. The mere act of observing a particle changes its behavior according to the observer. An observer sees with limited and anticipated consciousness, which has an effect on whatever is being seen. So literally, we only see and experience something to a degree of which we can comprehend and understand. Anything we don't understand is changed or filtered out by the observer's experiences.

Are you getting the implications of this yet? If we can only experience life through a filtered lens, then we must be able to recognize we are merely filters of reality, and our filter changes according to our beliefs and conditioned of what is true. Anything foreign to what we know isn't even experienced. So, under these circumstances, nothing can be 100 percent pure, real, or true. It's only that according to your own personal filter (also known as your ego, hs, identity, or you). That's your small self, unclear and biased at best. It's OK to have your view. We are here in human form; however, when we only believe that to be our full and true selves, that causes a problem.

The observer effect states that particles can only be observed when they are interacting with other particles. So out of an abyss or a space called Zero Point, where nothing and yet the potential for everything exists, only in our interactions can we manifest and create something. "Like attracts like" in this space. We see and connect with others who are closely similar to ourselves, making the illusion of our reality even more real. When others around us are wired with similar beliefs, those beliefs become even more cemented as truths. Again, it's false and downright dangerous. This is how disagreements, wars, and a refusal to see another's point of view begin—when large groups of people cluster with the same, limited mindsets, when everyone operates only through their ego.

The starvation problem around the world isn't ours. It's someone else's problem. Wars are because of "those people," guns in the classroom, ignorance, and the debate over transgenders is for others. That isn't true. We are all collectively contributing to the mindset of the Universe. Where do you stand? In the shadows of your own ignorance? Or at the forefront of innovation and connectedness? Are you plugged into the fear? Or into the love? Do you want progress? Do you want to be empowered? Then connect. That is the only way to have power—as a group, not an individual. Sure, individuals gain power, but how long do they last? Not for infinity. Singularly, we gain power by being part of a group, a collective consciousness.

So, are we supposed to live miserable existences? Well. Maybe sometimes, yes. Maybe sometimes in life, there are misery and pain and sadness. This doesn't mean we live in misery. It doesn't mean there is anything deficient within us. It is simply that part of the flow we are in. Humans don't like that part. None of us do. Is it wrong to be sad, angry, intolerant, and all of the above? No. It's not wrong, but when we get to the root of why we feel those things, it's because we are attached to a particular outcome and desire things to be a certain way. We have experienced something we don't want, and that leaves us with negative feelings.

It's because our truths are trying to get challenged, and we are either not letting them be decoded, or they become crushed, and we lose our way in a world that was at one time so much more predictable and reliable—or at least we thought.

This refers to when we live in dysfunction and chaos too. If that's all you've known, dysfunction and chaos are safe because they are familiar. Do they feel good, though? Probably not. Familiar? Yes. Good? No. When things aren't going as we want or know or expect them to, we are usually crushed. Our identity is threatened. Who we are and what we have thought until that moment become threatened. When something was a given before, and it changes on you, you are thrown off. No one really likes that, not even when it's a positive experience. We either blame ourselves, others, the system, government, or someone or something to justify why our lives aren't going exactly as they should. We aren't wrong; we are simply operating out of our hs, that small, disconnected identity that forgets our True Nature.

The part of our brains that need to be developed for sociability in order to increase our feelings of connectedness to one another and of being part of a bigger picture is diminishing. People are spending more time alone, consumed with electronics. Ironically, people are spending more and more time on so-called social media activities, like Facebook and Instagram but spending less time face-to-face enjoying the company of others. As a result, people are feeling lonelier, and our human selves are forgetting something our true selves know—that we are all the same, that we are all connected, and that we are all part of the bigger picture. The constant perception that everything is always wonderful in others' lives throws us into despair. The disconnection from each other contributes to the collective mindset that we are alone.

We used to be able to see what those around us were doing to help us find our own little place in the world. Sometimes that can hurt us too. Again, it goes back to our conditioning. If we are raised around others who aren't motivated or taught that learning and self-growth aren't important and critical to being healthy, then we atrophy our ability to be healthy. We have an opportunity to gain insight and a sense of belonging, and even a sense of not belonging, from our environment, our families, peer groups, co-workers, our community. A sense of not belonging often leads us to search for our tribe, which ultimately gives us a sense of purpose.

We gain a lot of knowledge about ourselves via the mirrors of ourselves around us. This is even more detrimental now that we falsely appear to have thousands around us. The internet makes us think we are connected, when in fact, we aren't. We are falsely connecting. We are sharing only what we want others to see. We are comparing ourselves to others' non-truths. Intonation and intent are not easily understood in text, print, or a Facebook post. People lose friendships and family members over a misunderstood status. We continue to look at social media, celebrities, and biased television programming for a comparison of self. We can never measure up to the photo-shopped, perfect-bodied, wealthy lives of celebrities. Reality TV is anything but reality, yet millions of people are believing it is. People are now measuring their self-worth and ability to achieve hopes and dreams from the facade of computer and phone screens. No wonder we often feel hopeless and disconnected. Now, people equally love to watch said celebrities fail and fall from grace. In those moments, we unconsciously feel some level of relief, perhaps even grandiose and superior. We feel better about ourselves when we realize "the advantaged" are actually human and just like us.

I've actually heard people say they are happy to not have so much because then they have so much less to lose. It's all a game of skewed "See, that's why I wouldn't want what so and so has." Or "I would never fall so far." Or, "That is just a dumb human. How could that happen?" It's all ridiculous voyeurism that isn't helping anyone feel good about anything. No one is connected to the true joys and pains of celebrities or each other at all. Where is the compassion? The empathy? Why are we able to sit in judgment of one another when we haven't been in another's shoes? Why does everyone think their opinion and their version of reality is the final truth? Because we are allowing that to continue. No one sees the truth anywhere. When we don't see it around us, we don't want to express it within ourselves and in our own private lives.

We can often feel we aren't measuring up, or that there is something wrong with us, rather than realizing we are all fundamentally the same. We are all surviving and figuring out life as we go. Some people have more material items and financial opportunities, some have better guidance, but no one has more Spirit, soul, energy, atman, than anyone else. We are all truly the same at the core. How does comparing ourselves to others help or hurt us? How often do you compare yourself to those around you? How often do you spend time either wishing you had what so and so has, or making yourself feel superior based on what you do have? That's all a sham, a lie you keep telling yourself. That's an identity that will wear you out. Mark my words. That's your hs/ego/small self trying to be bigger.

If you want to feel better about yourself and your current situation, you need to recognize that we are way more than our small selves/our egoic selves/the hs. The no appetite, the non-desire to work out, the aches and pains, all of it will fade away and/or transform into something else. That's the nature of life; it ebbs and flows. Somehow, I think we humans think things in life should be a constant, and there should be a natural daily consistency to everything we do—all the time. But absolutely nothing, nothing, nothing in nature operates that way. So, whatever you are feeling in any moment is where you are. It's like rain in the morning, sunshine in the afternoon. We never try to explain why rain happens, right? So why do we try to explain to ourselves why sadness happens? It's all the same stuff. Just be in the rain, and then you will be present to witness the sunshine. Ebb and flow.

As we live our lives as humans, we create and fulfill our physical identity. The identity starts with the name we are given when we are born, what we look like, our jobs, our different titles or roles, such as mother, sister, brother, father. All these different aspects make up our identity and who we are in our physical form. This is what most of humanity believes is their truth and who they think they are. And that is the great illusion. This is the hardest part and the best part about being human. If we can take ourselves less seriously and realize that we are just fulfilling these roles right now, while understanding that particular human identity is not all there is to us, we would experience much more peace while in our human form. The core of us, our essence, is that pure, pristine, loving, and powerful energy that lives within each of us, and is far greater than our current identities. We are so much more than what we see in our physical form but we all have thoughts and beliefs that which hold us back from reaching our goals or living a larger life.

The deceased have shed their limited, egoic, human identities (hs) and have been reconnected to their grander, higher selves (HS.) They have released the illusion of separateness and have become aware of the collective whole. We can do that and get closer to it while we are in human form by knowing the difference between the two.

10
The Collective Whole

I mentioned earlier that the Collective Whole of Consciousness is the term I use for what we commonly hear as The Source, the Universe, God. It's the space or State of Awareness that has everything and nothing present in it at the same time. It is everything. All thoughts. All objects. All events. All beings. It contains all the details, data and knowledge of everything for everyone. It is a source that works off the parts of the Whole into the teeniest of details. And it's all in perfect synchronicity throughout time and space itself. It's infinity expressed as words.

The Collective Whole is what I call the space where all our energies combine together. There is nothing that it isn't. The Collective Whole is the space of all infinite intelligence, of All Knowing-ness, of Omnipotence. It's the connection and tandem cosmic dance of which we are all a part. It's more intricate than anyone can ever understand with our human, limited minds. And it is available to all of us, as it moves through us all. It is not a place, it is not a singular person, and yet, it is present in all places and within all persons. It's the knowing energy awareness or Force that causes our hearts to beat, keeps our tides in place, and the planets in perfect synchronicity with every blade of grass on earth. It's the fluid motion of Being, to which we are all connected. It is this space, this Force, this awareness, where there are no rights and no wrongs. Everything is understood as being precisely in its right place. Every action has a reaction, and all of that is in perfect Harmony. Everything is working together for the Good of the Whole. There is no such thing as "I", and yet, it cares for the individual parts—large or small—equally.

Sometimes we don't understand why, but there is no one reason for why anything happens. The answer is because—being the "cause" so that everything else is in sync. It's all happening for the same Collective Reason—Be Cause. The Collective Whole understands that everyone and everything has its own personal relationship with the rest of the Universe around it and the personal works with the Collective.

The entire Universe is represented in the Collective. Everything is on par to it. Nothing is wrong. There are deserts, there are swamps, there are rivers, and there are mountains. There are quarks, atoms, micro and macro organisms. There are varieties of people, expressions, interactions, thoughts, beliefs, and all are working in tandem for the Greater purpose of the Entire Whole. Nothing operates alone. Not one moment is a singular event. It is all interconnected with a pristine order that will most likely never be measured or understood. One person's high is another's low, and yet it's all in harmony according to our destiny and how we think and believe. We hold a place for one another. Do you want to continue to hold the space you are currently living? If you are enjoying your life and your space in it, then yes, you do. If you aren't... then no, you don't. That goes back to changing our beliefs and our thoughts to upgrade and change our realities.

This Collective Whole is creative, expansive and all inclusive. It's intuitive and operates via communication only. It's what inspires artists, writers, musicians, dancers. It's what keeps us going when we don't think we have anything else left in us. It's the saved-by-the bell, just-in-time moments that occur. It's mysterious and yet powerful. It's hidden and yet present everywhere. It's the inspiration within us, as it is also the depression within us all. Wherever you are is what is running through you. But it contains every possibility, everything that has already occurred and that which is already manifested and everything infinitely possible. It's the connection to everyone and everything, all the time. It is what levels the playing field. It is the interface between ourselves and the rest of the Universe. A duality exists throughout our Universe that has literally trillions of molecules and atoms, each having their own very unique experience and interactions with the Universe, and it's all done simultaneously. There is a connectivity so extreme and so precise it's difficult to comprehend. It's why nature is able to be both flexible and strong at the same time. It's the energy of give and take, inhale and exhale, contraction, and expansion. It's the drop in every ocean and the ocean in every drop. It's a vibration, a harmonious ether that collectively makes up one body: the Universe.

Our bodies operate like a micro Universe and can easily help explain this thought. Every part of your body's physiology is working with every other part. There is no part that operates for the sole purpose of existing on its own. The stomach cells have their own identity and purpose and yet they do not seek to overtake or perform better than, say, your blood cells. The lungs aren't trying to out-breathe the heart's rate. Instead, they work together. Every part of your body knows the ultimate goal is for the good of the entire body. Imagine if humans operated entirely on this theory, with awareness that everything we do as individuals is contributing to the health and wellbeing of the entire cosmos. Each individual human need not operate selfishly. We need to understand that our roles are perfect. We can upgrade our personal experiences, but we don't need to override the whole.

The weight of the world is literally on our shoulders, each of us, individually. We can contribute to a healthier, more mindful existence, knowing we are a significant part of a much larger system. This is where we would understand on a deep level that our mere being is our purpose and therefore, we do not need to find purpose. We simply need to be it—which we already are, just not consciously. We are operating as a duality with our environment.

It's the hologram. Understanding the hologram effect in terms of understanding the universe requires some background information in physics. Modern physics is based on two leading theories, quantum mechanics and the relativity theory. The problem with the theories is that they completely contradict each other. The contradiction is not just an issue with minor details, but rather a contradiction to the vital information that make up the theories. Quantum mechanics says reality must be discontinuous, non-local, and non-causal, and the relativity theory says reality must be continuous, local, and causal. Basically, in human terms, this means either life or phenomena are completely random, or they are connected and based on prior phenomena. How can it be both?

David Bohm, a physicist fascinated by the concepts of cosmic forces and the space that lies beyond our understanding, was troubled by the contradicting theories and the fact that leading physicists weren't paying enough attention to the discrepancy between them. Physicists share the understanding that modern physics is self-contradictory, and that it isn't even close to a finished model to explain reality. Bohm wasn't satisfied with this explanation and set out to resolve the issue by trying to find out what the two theories of modern physics have in common.

Bohm discovered "undivided wholeness," a concept that became the foundation of his research and contribution to physics. This is similar to what I call, The Collective Whole. Quantum physics show us that no matter the distance traveled between two beings of light (photons), when measured, they will always have identical angles of polarization. What does this even mean? It means that the two particles must communicate with one another instantaneously so they can agree how and where and how they are moving and changing. They make these changes at precisely the same exact time, no matter how far apart they are. They are communicating instantly, not back and forth, but instantly. This means there is a speed faster than the speed of light. When technology was developed to perform the two-particle experiment, physicists were unable to produce results to make the hypothesis conclusive—until 1982.

In 1982, physicist Alain Aspect at the University of Paris conducted an experiment[6] that led to a discovery that some people feel could change everything we know and believe in science. The team discovered that in some situations, subatomic particles communicate with each other instantly, regardless of the distance that separates them. The subatomic particles may be ten-feet apart or 100 billion miles; it doesn't matter. Each particle is somehow aware of what the other particle is doing. Didn't I tell you that we're all continuously connected to all other matter in the Universe? This helps prove that. If every particle in the Universe has the ability to connect with any other particle, how can we say communicating with the energy of the deceased is impossible? In fact, it's more than possible; it's what we do. It's a very facet of our nature to be able to connect and develop significant relationships. We are all doing this together, right now as you are reading this.

The result of this discovery means that either the two particles are connected, non-locally, or that Einstein's theory (the theory that says nothing may travel faster than the speed of light) is inaccurate. Most physicists don't want to admit any faster-than-light processes into the world of physics, and so some attempt to prove Alain Aspect's findings with other explanations. Talk about staying in a cave. Of course, there are movements that are faster than light. Mothers know the theory of instantaneous connection when their newborn cries at precisely the exact time their milk is coming in.

How many times have you thought of someone completely

out of the blue, and they suddenly call you? Our bodies' regulation systems itself already have proven there are instantaneous connections with our environments. Instantaneous connection. Faster than light. But we are talking on subatomic levels (of which we are giant manifestations of this light/photon energy).

David Bohm doesn't believe subatomic particles have some sort of mysterious communication method of talking to one another across space. He believes the reason they are in contact with one another regardless of their distance is because their separateness is an illusion. Like a hologram, he said, what we're seeing isn't really what is taking place. Finally, science, or rather physics, is catching up with the information sages have intuited for thousands of years.

Bohm's hypothesis is that physical reality is not how it appears to us, as a collection of individual, separate objects. Instead, it is an undivided whole that is always changing. His explanation of the contradictions between quantum mechanics and relativity theory is that the universe is one, united, undivided entity in which all the parts merge together. The undivided whole is in a constant state of change, an invisible atmosphere where everything is and everything eventually dissolves, including mind and matter. Bohm calls his theory the holomovement. The "movement" refers to reality being in a constant state of change, and "holo" indicates that reality is similar to holography. The universe is like a hologram. This describes, in scientific terms, the Collective Whole. Perhaps I should call it the Collective Whologram!

So how do we take Bohm's theory that the universe is like a hologram and apply it to understanding how we are all interconnected and part of the collective whole? Why should we even care about this information? Because to me, it explains it all, scientifically. We are infinity expressed in both particle and wave form.

The repeating patterns of everything inside everything else build upon themselves to create larger and larger forms of the same energy. It means that you are everything, and everything is you. Everything. Every tree, every blade of grass, every electronic device, every good deed, every bad one. It's all you, expressed in everything, and everything expressed through you. It's magnificent. It's unbelievable and inconceivably powerful. It means you are not alone, for you cannot be alone when you are everything and everyone. There is more proof and truth to Thich Nhat Hanh's quote, "We are here to awake from the illusion of our separateness." We really are "here," in the physical to understand our connectivity, our Wholeness. We are here to recognize both our significance and our individual purpose as it applies to the Collective Whole.

The Collective Universe, hologram, or Whole is moving and evolving, constantly in forward motion, gathering momentum from everything within itself. It's poetic. It's expressed brand new in each and every single moment, for all it knows is the moment. The volcano erupting is the same sort of energy release as your neighbor's anger that their laundry was left on the line in the rain. The forest fire can be likened to the grief of a mother whose child has died. The serene lake is the peace of the meditator on retreat. The sun is the expression of the job accomplished by the athlete who attained first place. The rain is the venting of a scorned lover; it releases and then blows away, to appear again another day. The autumn leaf hanging on a tree clinging to its last bits of life is the elderly person in the hospital bed, waiting to die. The trillions of seeds of the earth are all the unborn children in their pregnant mommies' bellies. The stripping away of all the trees in the rainforest, leaving nothing for the future is the murder of a man for his sneakers. The avalanche is the feeling of isolation and exclusion after not being invited to a fifth-grade birthday party. The extraction of oil from the earth to pollute our planet is the eating of processed poisonous foods. The wind is the laughter of those sitting in the comedy club. The stealing or swindling for one's own benefit is the cancer present in millions of bodies. The thunder in the sky is the frantic cry of the father whose child's life was spared from a horrific accident. The tsunamis are the overwhelmed feelings of the depressed person who wants to feel normal. The sprout pushing through the soil toward sunlight is the student working toward graduating. Lightning is the instantaneous divine thought and resolution to a problem for the scientist working for years to solve it.

You see. We are IT, all of it. It is all of us. It's incredible—the Collective Whole of the Universe, and we ought to slow down to see and really experience it—to appreciate and stand in awe of it. We need to understand it. Nothing operates as a singularity. We are all experiencing different facets of the same energy, the wave of existence.

Unfortunately, life is perceived by most humans as a singularity. Many of us perceive ourselves as being separate and different, alone, and misunderstood. We believe in only the smallest fraction of the reality of all that is us. We make ourselves so small that it's impossible to even see or feel the connectivity to the rest of it.

When we shrink down into our Human Identity, our human self, we understand the world as only a singular strand of events. Things are finite. Things are deemed wrong. Experiences are seen as different. Things don't feel right. We are over here, and everyone is over there. We are different. Separated. Alone. Only a small few these days even notice nature around us, and that we are a part of an organic, living, vibrating world. Even fewer people feel the connection between our environment and ourselves. Fewer still experience the connectivity to the whales in the ocean and connect their migrations to our daily lives.

I love to think that as I sit here to write this, and you sit here to read it, there are families of whales swimming depths of the oceans we will never see, and trillions of species moving around the rainforest floors creating micro communities that ultimately lead to *our* survival. There are bees pollinating trees so fruit can be born and winds blowing all over the earth keeping a sense of movement and change in the air, literally. It's all happening at this precise moment. I'm not alone in this world, and neither are you. You aren't operating as a separate being, but rather, an integral part of the Collective Whole. Your energy is present on this planet at precisely this moment, because the planet needs it. For what? We will be unable to answer some questions until we leave our physical bodies. When we lose that illusion of our separateness and finally realize we have been a part of a whole—and that whole is a loving force that seeks to support potential and change in all of its entities.

We are humans. We need to know something, be something, or do something really great, or else we think, be, know, and do—and therefore are nothing. This is so far from the truth. When we die, we finally grasp the magnitude of our existence. We literally see and understand our place in the Universe. We also understand all of life from everyone's and everything else's vantage points. As brilliant and powerful as we all may be, we are also incredulously limited in understanding anything when we see the world from our shortsighted lenses. Ironically, it's through our "death" where we finally understand all of life.

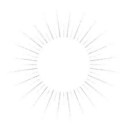

11
What Does Death Have to Do With it?

We are not human beings having a spiritual experience.
We are spiritual beings having a human experience.
~Pierre Teilhard de Chardin

There are many definitions of death, and all really depend on who is defining it. Religions define it one way, and most vary according to their dogmas. Scientists have a very clinical and specific definition of what death is, yet they argue about how to measure it.

Some say death is when the brain functions cease. Others say it's when the heart stops beating. Other scientists have recorded brain activity occurring even when the brain is no longer functioning. This has led the scientific community to question the difference between the mind and the brain. Clearly, the mind is something separate.

All right, I'll say it. I'm obsessed with death. The good news is that I am also obsessed with life and living. Spiritualists, Theosophists, and atheists all have their own version of what death is. My most recent favorite definition was stated by Dr. Amit

Goswami in his book *Physics of the Soul*[7]. He says, "the science within consciousness gives a clear definition of death; death occurs when consciousness withdraws its self-referential supervention (transcendent intervention) from living matter."

What does that mean? It means, death occurs when the observer or the human stops identifying itself as the human it was in accordance to all the past beliefs, conditioning, and experiences. It is the cessation of being the "you" you thought you were, and the entry way of being one with all.

Oh, how I love this definition of death. We finally become aware of our connectedness and who we truly are. We finally *die* to the notion that we are singular and small. We no longer carry our limitations and identify with the mundane things we allowed to define us for all of our physical years. We return to the Source, which happened to be buried deep within us all along. Not only is this a definition for death, but it's also an explanation for who we are.

It's hidden within us—our true nature, our connection to everything everywhere, through all of time, past, present, and future. What does our true nature have to do with death? Well, when we understand what and who we really are, we can finally believe that death is actually an impossibility. If who we are is "infinity" ourselves, a part of an Infinite Source, how can that ever cease? Infinity is. It doesn't end. So again, who or what is observing this notion of death? The notion that we die and cease to be? A limited self, a limited awareness is observing that, one who doesn't truly understand their true nature. A seed has no awareness of all the trees it creates after it.

Now, let me also tell you, that death is not a concept that only applies to those whose remains are either put in a coffin or an urn. It isn't just what you see when the flowers have shriveled up or all the leaves have fallen off the trees. It is not a final destination or a cessation of being. It's the end of an old, but yet, it's not instant, and it's not finite. It's not a black or white experience. Death is a transition period or process of change.

For anything to progress, there must be some movement, energy, or spark that is the final stage of a circumstance right before a new one begins. It's the bell in the high school hallway between classes. It's the space between the inhale before the exhale. It's the draining of the tub after a bath. It's the empty space right before you fill your coffee mug. It's the intention before manifestation. It's a transitory moment in time, where matter changes from one state of being, manifestation, or awareness into another. It's happening all the time. It creates the illusion of time by allowing each observable moment to move to the next. Death is the opening of a new doorway. It isn't as scary and unknown as many of us fear. It's not the final end.

Where is the "other side?" The other side of what? The afterlife. Why is it even called that? From the very start, the concept of death is limited by our choice and use of words. Semantics. Words don't always mean the same things to everyone. So, from our literal use of language, defining, explaining, or understanding death begins with a massive set of limitations and miscommunications. And of course, the other excruciatingly difficult task of discussing anything that has to do with physical death, is that while we can talk and study it, it's one of those things that can't be completely understood unless we go through it.

We are so focused on "the other side" being a *place*, or on learning what we will do once we get there, and who we will meet there, and what our job will be when we get there. Where is this place we will go when we die? Are we going to have purpose or desire there as well? Will we see and meet or miss our loved ones? Will we be thin? Fit? Wealthy? Will we be loved and accepted? Will our potential be reached? Will we be clear on what our purpose is? These are the human questions about death I've been asked a *thousand* times.

No wonder we live in fear of an afterlife if we believe our afterlife mirrors our human lives. Don't we want to be done with this stuff? Where is the peace in that paradigm? Whether you have it really good or not so good here on earth, the thought of an afterlife that operates like physical life is exhausting and daunting. If life is good here for you, having to possibly change that is scary, and if life is rough here for you, having a place to end up for eternity that might be equally as difficult is beyond draining to say the least. Talk about paralyzing.

Personally, I want the super deluxe French Riviera with perfect weather, perfect company, complete relaxation, perfect balance of foods, and a *vacation* after this lifetime, thank you very much. I don't want any more of this thinking, wishing, waiting, and doing stuff. I don't want more human interactions and potential for disappointment. I'd like to finally just be. Wouldn't you?

Yet, when we do conceptualize the afterlife in this way, we basically just recreate the material world and try to fit it into the spiritual world. That's like trying to make a dime equal to ten dollars instead of an infinite amount. Why would we limit the possibilities in such a way? Because we simply just don't know any better. We must learn to be dead to understand what death is. We can access our HS, and not come from our hs.

Can we think like the living and understand death? No. We must assume the consciousness of the deceased to be able to even remotely grasp it. When a student asked his master, "Master, what happens when we die? Is there an afterlife?" The master swiftly responded, "I don't know."

The student, baffled, responded, "But you are a master. How do you not know this?"

"I am a master, yes. But I am not a dead master, so I don't know."

Brilliant. Only the deceased have a full concept of death and afterlife. What survives after our bodies die? What remains when our ego is eliminated from the world? What comes after the busyness of our lives ceases? Can we even fathom not Being? Not having someplace to be or something to do? Who are we when our needs are fully met and all our desires are complete? Who are you at your core? How would you be if your only awareness was to be just that? You. In pure essence. You in perfect synchronicity with all of life over all of time? Yeah. Sit with that for a moment. Who is that?

I have the unique experiences and opportunity to be in the Presence of Proof every, single day of my life. I literally see the proof, through those with whom I work, and it's a game changer, a life-altering paradigm that can free us in the here and now, so we can create heaven on earth. If you can stop being who you are as you are for even a brief moment, then you can get closer to being "dead," which if you've been following along, you now understand really isn't being dead at all. Instead, it's being alive and fully conscious. It's the experience of connection. Your programming of everything needs to shift, even temporarily, to experience Heaven on Earth. But it's possible when you are willing to let go of what you think is familiar and jump into what you think is the great unknown.

Instead, the "unknown" becomes the all-known, and the familiar becomes a Unified Truth. Who needs roles and titles? That need limits us. Reach bigger for the transformation of Self, and see what happens.

In physics, the Law of Conservation of Energy says that energy cannot be created or destroyed. It always exists, but it simply changes form. For example, the kinetic energy of motion can be converted to heat energy, like what happens when you use your car's brakes to slow down. Everything is always changing. Change is inevitable.

Every time we learn something new that causes progress, we let our old thoughts and beliefs "die" as we give birth to new ones. It's a simplistic process that is happening all the time within each of us, and when we understand that, we can start to let go of the fear of death. There is always a life after death or transition and change happening all around us and to us.

When death is experienced from the vantage point of the deceased, the concept of death as being the "end" is the exact opposite of what it really is. Death is NOT a *disconnection* from life and everyone we love here. It is NOT a cessation of being. In fact, it is the direct opposite experience. When we die, we will become fully aware of the *connection* we have had and will always have with everyone (in the universe) and why.

When we die, we are more connected to those we love (and those we don't. Ha.) than ever before. Everything becomes clear. Desire kills us, but only when we are experiencing ourselves in the physical world. When we are alive, we often live like dogs chained to a tree in a small, fenced-in yard that is limited to the area we can see and reach from our chains. But when we die, we become more like soaring birds with the freedom to roam and experience so much more from a variety of vantage points. We see there are mountains, jungles, deserts, rivers, beaches, and so much more areas to roam freely. We can perch on a tree branch or glide through the air. From the vantage point of the flying bird, when we have died, we can finally understand our limited view of living when we were on earth.

When we die, we are no longer wishing or lamenting over the things we didn't or couldn't do. We are no longer holding grief, anger, resentment, sadness, defeat, envy for anyone. We no longer feel inadequate, or guilty. We no longer feel small and disconnected, separate and alone. We are more than enough. Finally. And we have been all along, although we didn't realize this during our human experience.

When talking about it with people, I'm always surprised that no one realizes that it is something we have all experienced a trillion times already. And we survive it every day, so why is there so much fear of it?

There is so much life and activity, movement, and change happening all over the Universe. People have died, babies have been born, stars have collided, astronauts are floating around in space.

There is so much life happening, all the time. There have been interactions, moments, experiences, that have died so something new can emerge. Plants have died, and new ones just pushed through the seeds. We are totally accustomed to what death really is, but we fail to describe it *as it is*. It is a word to describe the continuum of life. Somehow, we confused it with the end of life—because it's the end of what we have previously known, causing something new to be born.

We talk about our deceased loved ones as having "crossed over to the other side," but the reality is we are the ones on the other side. We are the ones experiencing death as the opposite of what it really is.

Death is the process by which something new emerges.

Every new beginning is another beginning's end.
~Enya

Does the caterpillar experience fear in that cocoon while it's transforming into a butterfly? Does it even know what is about to occur? Or does it think it's dying? A part of it is dying—the limited part, the part that is only capable of crawling on branches and the ground. The limited caterpillar self may fear the end, while the reality is, he is about to expand and blossom. He/she is about to be freed, to soar and to have even more movement and freedom. Life and "death" for humans operate exactly as that cocoon. If they did feel fear of the cocoon, then not all caterpillars would ever try it. The fear would prevent them from metamorphosis, the ultimate step in their freedom. Do you see fear's role in the change? Where are you afraid of moving forward? Notice that now, so you can make a choice to override it.

As humans, we hold fast to all the unknown parts of death and fear rather than embrace it. We resist even the mention of it as much as possible. It's a necessary function for our survival and evolution. We experience this all the time and have experienced it since the moment of our conception. As our cells were dividing to create our new bodies, old cells died off so new ones could emerge. Think about how you operate throughout your day. Surely you transition from one task to another all-day long. It's the end of one task to begin another, right? But we don't think of our days like that. Instead, it's a flow. Everything blends into the next moment. Life and death are a lot like that—a continuum, not a beginning and end.

As a result of this continuum, people die all the time, even while they are still living. You have had many deaths in your lifetime, and you will continue to experience death repeatedly. Can you stop, just for a moment, being terrified of it? Think of death as a beginning. Think of death as a moment of letting go. The ebb and flow; the inhale, pause, and exhale process.

In the big picture, it's good, *especially* from the vantage point of the deceased… and it will change everything as you know life to be here on earth from the vantage point of the living. There is a difference. This is the doorway into heaven.

The key to opening your mind to this new perception of death is to not confuse your human knowledge and experiences for what "the other side" is going to be like. It's nothing like this. Nothing. The process of death, or how people feel when things change or seem to come to an end doesn't always feel so great, though. You aren't expected to like it, even as you allow yourself to see death differently from how you've seen it previously.

I just want you to begin to look at it differently. Open yourself to the awareness there is so much more than our small human selves allow us to believe. The more we do this, the less stressed we get over the little things. We see life as experiences and not just one moment or circumstance. We are able to relax, breathe, and remain centered. When we are centered, we are in a space of connection to it all, instead of being prisoners of our brains, which have been telling us what's wrong with us and the world for as long as we can remember. When we are centered, we are calm. We may not be "happy," but we can at least see the next step of our journey. When we are quiet enough, we can hear that still small voice that tells us what is next. We stay in the flow, rather than going against, around, or through it. We are able to ride the continuum like a wave. When you do this, you can clearly see that everyone and everything around you are in perfect harmony, and we are all working for each other's highest and best good. The afterlife is present in every new moment.

Sometimes, we have to be the one who receives less so another can receive more. But if that is the case, then sometimes, you also receive more because someone received less. There is a law of efficiency in nature, and collectively, as a whole, we are all sitting, living, and being in abundance. If we can hold the intention of the earth in this way, we rapidly enter into the space where we can truly shout, "One for all, and all for one."

As Bohm's experiment proves, there is a connectivity among all particles of life. As I sit here and write this paragraph in my incense-filled office, pygmies in Africa are working in their villages, natives in South America are making bread, stockbrokers in NYC are making money, college students everywhere are stressing out about papers that are due, and a lonely single mom in Kansas is working hard as a chambermaid in a local hotel. Together, no matter how separate it may seem we are, we are not at all. It takes just one thought of each other, across thousands of miles to lift (or harm) another's energy field. I often think of all the "others" out there. I thank those truck drivers delivering my breakfast cereal to the store, that chambermaid, and those college students for existing. I imagine sending good energy to complete strangers, who most likely will remain strangers to me while I am living in physical form. However, when I leave here, I will be re-connected with them and we will each know what we have done for one another in this lifetime.

Growth Opportunity

Want to expand your circle? Your tribe? Your energy field? Send loving thoughts and energy to strangers across your town, state, country, and globe. Think of your food. Imagine that it had to be grown, or created by someone. Think about the processes it took that person/people to bring it to you. They had to grow, pick, and transport it. It had to be labeled, stocked on shelves, and rung up, all by people who are existing to support you. Thank each and every energy who took part in your food. The energy comes back to you, especially when you aren't looking for it. The Collective Consciousness/Whole works together, and the more people who do this simple exercise, expands not only their own energy fields, but the energy fields of those they are holding in high regard. We will all feel it; subtle changes make massive impacts.

Quantum physics has changed the way we understand matter and our relationship to it. We understand, or misunderstand, energy in a whole new way than in times of Newtonian physics. The "old physics" is able to define matter into protons, electrons, and atoms, but we know beneath matter, there is also vibration. Energy. We have discovered the universe is largely made up of empty space. And within that space, there is *something*. That *something* is as powerful as it is elusive. This nothingness creates everything. From nothing *everything* emerges. Emptiness creates a manifested reality. Consciousness is the stuff that somehow binds together and creates a perception of reality. Or a Truth. Life exists because of our awareness of this stuff. Consciousness is the stuff matter is made of. In other words, matter is here because our consciousness created it. How? Who is in charge of this? Whose consciousness is in charge? How did this all begin? What is the origin of it all?

Everyone from the beginning of time ponders the greatest question of all time: **What happens when we die?** It has stumped inquisitive children and wise sages alike for thousands of years. Scientists have loved to prove the non-existence of life after death (with no conclusive definitive answers on it) for centuries. How do you measure something that is contained in everything and yet isn't tangible? There is no "stuff" to observe, so therefore something doesn't exist.

Mediums come in handy for science (if only science would use us more). Religions have posed the question and have sought to comfort the masses with promises of an afterlife experience that is the direct correlation of how you lived your life on earth. If you are good, generous, and kind, you will be in heaven. If you are bad, mean, and dishonest, you will burn in hell. Does that allow room for us to expand our awareness of ourselves, the universe, and our place and everyone else's in it? Does it force us to go inward to get close to this experience of life and death? Does it make us challenge our own immortality and way of life? No. It doesn't. It causes us to fall in line and to not question any of this too much. It forces us to see life in our limited terms, rather than in the larger framework. When we don't question or challenge, we don't expand, grow, and find amazement with all that is possible. Death becomes a progression of a lamely lived life that eventually ends.

I love to think my place and space here on this earth is holding the space and place for everyone else, as everyone else is holding space for me at this exact moment. We are all interconnected in ways that truly cannot and most likely *will not* be fully comprehended through a human lens. If my life just ends, that leaves me to feel I end and my life had no impact. To me, that feels dead while living. No thank you. And yet, how many of us are living this way?

Are you among the living dead? Are you in fear of what is or isn't next? Do the thoughts of death—whether it's your own or other's—paralyze you? Are you so petrified of the unknown that you stand still in your own current existence? Bravo. That's not death.

That's worse than death. It's demented and dysfunctional. It's safe, lonely, and stagnant. And sadly, it's an extremely common way of thinking and living. Yet, it literally goes against the way nature works. Nature doesn't do stagnation. It's constantly looking to operate with the Laws of Least Effort.

According to Deepak Chopra, The Law of Least Effort states that: *Nature's intelligence functions with effortless ease. There is rhythm and balance in the natural world, and when we are in harmony with nature, we can make use of the Law of Least effort by minimizing our effort and maximizing our effect. We let go of the need to struggle and accept the present moment as it is, putting us in the best position to influence the flow life in the most evolutionary direction.*

The Universe thrives on efficiency and has the totality of everything in its best interest. There is no selfish agenda here. The relationship of one affects the other, and the Highest good of all will prevail. Our bodies do this all the time. Cells experience spontaneous death, or apoptosis, when it's in the best interest of the overall body to die. The purpose of their formation, productivity, and then death is in conjunction with the rest of the entire body. There is a synchronistic goal of keeping the main source—the body—healthy and whole at any cost. This reminds me of the purpose of military and armed forces, police, and firefighters. Individual soldiers put their own lives on the line for the benefit and health of the larger community, the globe, their country, or city/town in which they serve.

As humans, we fail to recognize this because we are so clogged up with habitual living, thinking, and being. We rarely access the spiritual part of ourselves and rarely get in tune with the part of ourselves that we do not know or understand. The truth of who we are and what we are is Our Energy. Our Core, Our Spirit. The Infinity of all of life within. We no longer feel attuned to the phases of the moon and no longer feel a true connection to our seasons or each other on real terms. It seems we only enjoy that first spring day after a long winter, or that one week of peak fall foliage and the first snowfall, but we rarely witness and flow with the *process* it takes to get to those moments. Instead, we get stuck in whatever is going on with us right now and it's caused by our habitual thinking.

We are the harried soccer mom late to practice because we had to wait for the uniform jersey to dry at the last possible second. Every time. We are the father who is stressed and feeling inadequate because he doesn't make "enough" money so his wife can stay home comfortably to raise the children. We are the grandparent whose body aches too much to be able to venture too far from home to travel and see the family. We are the teenager who is mortified over the pimple on his or her face. We are the young child who feels dumb in school because our grades aren't in the eighties. We are the fatherless child who never felt loved. We are the nurse who works overnights so he or she can be home when the kids go to school. We are the fat kid who was teased, the unathletic kid who wasn't included. Or so we still think and believe. And we live out these old selves every day. Then we wonder why nothing ever changes. Yes, of course, we have times of joy (hopefully), and yes, there are times we can and do see our own evolution. But, day in and day out, we are really living from our past concepts of self. When we do this, we are the walking dead. Those old selves are never relevant and current. They are ghosts of who we are in each and every new moment.

Something in the Universe occurs when we can no longer hold onto an old, outlived identity. This is death. We transform. Something old is over, and something new emerges. When we continuously and habitually bring up past aspects of ourselves, we are bringing the dead back to life. To *not* change is death. We are giving our former identities energy. By resisting the concept of death, we learn to hold onto our identities, the roles we have outworn. Life becomes precisely what we fear, a stagnant Groundhog Day of thoughts, events, and feelings we have always known. Because our consciousness believes in death as a finality, and we generally fear the unknown and cling to what we think is certain, we literally recreate our same lives as our early years. We resist death so much that we ultimately live as the walking dead. Ironic, right?

Instead, it's time to get brave and shed your old concepts of everything. Breathe in fresh ideas and thoughts. Inhale possibilities for you and the knowing that change can and does happen, and the Universe is far more supportive of change than it is of stagnation. Trust in death, so new life can emerge.

Death is the most transformative occurrence in the entire cosmos to cause evolution and forward movement. It's literally why evolution and growth occur. It's always for the highest good of all, and it never feels that way in the moment it happens. I am a medium, but more accurately, I am an observer of death, which is the ultimate and final phase of all transformation. So much energy and perfection are present in what we call the afterlife, and I want to focus on that so death is no longer scary, but celebrated and understood. Someday, I want it to be embraced and cherished for what it is, and not what it isn't.

Death opens us up into a new phase, and the process we call life happens all over again. This occurs throughout our cells, our bodies, throughout nature, and throughout the cosmos. It's a process that has been observed and duplicated in every single organism, from a quark (the smallest known observable particle) to the model of the Universe that shows us the Universe is expanding and therefore has no end. We are in a constant process of birth, death, and rebirth.

What does any of this have to do with your being able to connect to a loved one who has died? The more clarity we have about our true nature, the more we can begin to experience ourselves rather than get locked into believing the small truths of who we are. When we stay focused on the human self, we experience deep loss, inadequacy, and isolation, which are all ironically the exact opposite of what is really happening within us. And you will have a deeper understanding of not only death, what that other side really is, but you will also begin to live in a way that has you pushing through your own self-imposed limitations and creating a better life after your own death every day. You can become more familiar with death so you welcome it into your life and from that, you receive the Ultimate Knowledge, that there is no death. No linear beginning and ending in time. You become connected to the Infinite You and therefore can connect with the Infinite within everyone else.

Are you ready to have a whole new life filled with experiences rather than being a victim of circumstance? Are you open to seeing life in a way where you are willing to let go and die, every day? Are you interested in the afterlife of each moment?

Deborah Hanlon

12

You've Already Died a Trillion Times

How would you live differently if you fully embraced the real concept of death while you are still living? What if you truly comprehended the fact that you are on a continuum of living, and that you will never, ever experience a complete cessation of being?

You would see death as a constant transition. It wouldn't necessarily make it less painful, but that knowledge most certainly could relieve you of many fears, anger, guilt, and remorse. I don't believe the fear of death evolved with religions of the world, but it certainly didn't become less feared because of them either. The system is finite and wrought with hierarchy. The "advantaged" get more, the "disadvantaged" get less, and those who have enough money to sacrifice for forgiveness get ultimate paradise. Sayyy whaaat? Yeah. That's archaic in my opinion. It's a concept that comes from a materialistic mindset—in world of consumption and attaining "things" for pleasure. Maybe sharing a story from The Vedanta will help make this a little clearer.

The Vedanta is based on the Vedas, the sacred scriptures of India. Vedanta affirms the divinity of the soul, the oneness of existence, and the harmony of all religions. The foundation of the Vedanta is Hinduism, but The Vedanta is universal, and people from all countries, religions, and cultures find it equally relevant.

In the Vedanta is a fantastic story about death, our light, and the reason we don't seem to know who we really are. The story is brilliant and describes so clearly why as humans we just keep getting in our own way. I have taken the adapted story from Deepak Chopra's book, *Life After Death*[8], which is truly one of the ultimate sources on this topic written in Dr. Chopra's brilliant merging of the scientific and spiritual into one.

In the book, Savitri, a wife who has realized the Lord Death (Yama) is waiting to take her husband when he returns from work, seeks out the wisdom of a sage (Ramana). She is looking for help resisting Death's call for her husband. Ramana tells Savitri about a time when he found Yama's house and waited for him to return home. Savitri is horrified that anyone would sit and wait for Death to come instead of run from it. Ramana waits for three days before Yama returns and is distressed that he made Ramana wait for three days. After saying, "Not even Death can break the sacred vow of hospitality," he provides three wishes to Ramana, one for each day he waited.

Ramana's three wishes were 1) to know his way back home to the living; 2) to know whether or not Yama has ever felt love; and 3) to know whether or not the soul survives beyond death.

Yama told Ramana 1. the way back home is in the direction of the sun rising. 2. Yama reluctantly explained that the role of love is to create while his is to destroy, and so he had no need for love. And finally, 3. in response to Ramana's desire to know if souls live beyond death, he said with rage, "I will tell you the truth. There are two paths in life, the path of wisdom and the path of ignorance. The path of wisdom is to pursue the Self. The path of ignorance is to pursue pleasure. Pleasure, being born of the senses, is temporary, and whatever is temporary falls under the sway of death. Thus, the ignorant fall into my clutches. But the Self is the light of immortality. It shines forever. Few are wise enough to see this light, even though it is inside them and nowhere else. The Self is but the Light of your soul."

Savitri doesn't understand how one can miss finding the soul if the light of the soul shines inside each of us. Ramana explains by using a reflection in the puddle. He steps into the puddle, and the mud moves to the surface, making it impossible to see the sun's reflection on the surface anymore. Ramana says, "This is why people cannot find the soul. It is muddied by the mind's constant activity and confusion. When I destroyed the sun's reflection, I didn't kill the sun. It is eternal, and nothing I do can extinguish it. Now, you know the secret of the soul, which even Death cannot extinguish." The Soul, the Light, energy, can never be destroyed.

This story says it all to me. When we give way to holding onto so tightly to our worldly, physical selves, we can be opened up to see the timelessness of our Souls. The never-ending story of who we are and what this thing called life is all about. Much like the Christian traditions, parables and stories help us understand things that are quite inconceivable to the human limited mind. In this story, Yama was approached. Ramana didn't fear him; in fact, he waited for his chance to meet Death. He faced it, and he waited for it, for he knew, there really is no such thing as death. When greeted, Yama was forced to respond. In this story, he basically congratulates him for facing "that which is most feared," Death, the ending of our perceived self. He gifts him three wishes for spending three days awaiting Death's confrontation.

The first wish he asks, "How do I return home?" Now that he has faced Death, how can he return and leave its space? Lord Yama replies, "Face east, toward the rising sun." It can be taken literally, as all parables can, but "face the sun," meaning, seek the Source of Life, and you can return home. Seek the Light. Place your attention and focus toward the Source, and you will be home. The second question, "have you ever felt love?" is brilliant. Yama's response? "To love is to create, and I destroy, I have no need for love." In Ramana's compassion for Yama, he received a sense of what it feels like to be loved, directly from the loving source, of Ramana's pity. He flipped the script on Death itself, changed the feared purpose of finality, and turned it toward compassion. The final question is simply put and explained so eloquently that the greatest secret ever known was revealed by Death itself. We all know how magicians never reveal their tricks. Well here, in this story, the great magician of all time reveals the secret to his existence. He replies, "There are two paths in Life, one to pursue Wisdom, the other to pursue pleasure." He goes on to say that those seeking anything that satisfies the five senses, is temporary. But those who seek the Truth of thy Self will see the light of eternity.

Nothing ever ends when you are seeking the Truth of thy Self. Nothing can destroy or take it away. Death does not want us to know this because the fear of death causes us to stay small and scared. Death wants us to stay focused on the limitations of our hs. It is the motivation behind stagnation and non-growth. If we are the creators of our reality, and we come from fear and stagnation, we will return to our own Source of fear and stagnation, and Death will remain "real." When we face the true reality of the immortality of our soul, our spirit, the only thing that remains real is ourselves. We become more empowered, and we create more life, more evolution, more expansion. We create more Light. We recognize our HS!

Quantum Physics defines the basis of everything as light, energy, exactly what the religions and wise sages have said for millennia. Jesus Christ said, "I am the light of the world. Whoever follows Me will never walk in the darkness, but will have the light of life." (John 8:12) Could it be in fact that one of the most enlightened men in history understood our nature? I'm not a theologian, but so much of what Jesus, Buddha, and many other sages suggest makes sense to me—that there is a state, a consciousness, an awareness that is the source of all things. The "Light" is more accurate thousands of years later. Our technology is getting us closer every day to understanding what life is. Science is seeking to understand what *light* really is. Meanwhile, the ancient prophets, sages, wise people, knew it by experiencing it. Being it. No machinery, computer chips, and fancy scopes were needed to observe, just their own awareness of it.

So why is this state of being so difficult to find, now? How and why do we forget our True Nature? Because like Ramana said, stepping into the mud puddle, we are constantly muddying the waters with our conditioned minds, the minds of constant activity and confusion. The learned ways of being cause us to forget that "the sun, our light" is eternal. We can't be muddied when we remember our Source, but only when we compare ourselves to the finite objects—people, nature, and material "things" around us. The greatest tool humans have to be human, are our five senses, and the worst tool for Spirit are...our five senses. They help us navigate this world, and yet, they take us away from our Nature and Higher Selves. Can we learn to live with both realms? Absolutely.

We are conditioned creatures. Plain and simple. We do what we know until what we know is outdated and updated, or no longer viable. As two-year-olds, we might throw ourselves on the floor when we are upset, but hopefully, that behavior changes when we are say, twenty. We find a different way to get our needs met. We update our methods. Sometimes, the update is healthy and smooth. Other times, we have a rude awakening. To the two-year-old, the rude awakening might be, "Oh, no. Mommy isn't listening to me or giving me what I want when I do this stuff." Over time, that child changes his or her behavior for the better, developing new skills and emotional growth.

Take every behavior you ever learn and realize this is how you have developed (or not developed) over time. The child who hears prejudiced words at home learns to be and act prejudiced. When a child learns over two decades that a particular race or religion is wrong or bad, and then they learn what they were taught isn't true, it's not an overnight aha moment. Usually there is a process of understanding and figuring out what is true and what is not. There is an undoing of the former beliefs, a process which is very much like experiencing a physical death. Instead of grieving the loss of someone you know or love, you experience the loss of something you knew to be "true."

The hs, also known as the ego, wants to stay intact. It sees "change" itself as a death and the hs understands death as a finality, not a transition. This process is lonely and scary and takes a tremendous amount of trust in the unknown. It's like the trapeze acrobat who needs to let go of one bar, twist, turn, and tumble toward the unknown of a new truth. They pray the other bar, or truth, shows up, and they can land safely on the other side. Sometimes they fall into the net, and have to start all over. This is how leaving our old beliefs works. This is a facet of death. And we still don't like it when it's happening. We resist, until we can't any more.

Until the risk to remain tightly in the bud is more painful than the risk it takes to blossom. ~Anais Nin

Then, one day, we find ourselves on the other side of truth. And we are reborn. Renewed. Refreshed. Re-energized. We find new people, places, and things around us. We will often let go of a lot of the old self and everyone and everything formerly attached to it through this process. While we now understand that the death of anything is the doorway to something new, the process of walking through that door and leaving anything we used to know, as we used to know it, is painful. It isn't for the weak. The cool part about it is once you have some awareness as to what is happening, you can stay focused on the "other side," versus worrying about what you are leaving behind or what may change because of the process. This, is death, it's happened to you a trillion times—and look—you are still here. You have survived several deaths of a former self, have undertaken the process of change, and transformed into something new. There is no marking of a beginning or an end because there is none. The self is infinite. Life itself is infinite. Your progress, and evolution are infinite. We can seek to discover what the pivotal moments were that have caused us to think, act, and see things differently, but the moments leading up to that moment, were also all a part of that moment itself. It's been a flow, not a life of singular steps. One moment flows into the very next one.

Have you ever gotten into a habit of traveling a particular way to your home, only to have that interrupted by a change in traffic patterns? You most likely easily changed directions, went with the flow, and got yourself home. You probably didn't even think about it as anything more or less than an inconvenience. Maybe you hoped this change would be temporary. It's doubtful you thought about this change in your routine as an ending. Your mind just naturally changed along with it and continued as usual. There was a disruption, and then forward movement. It flowed naturally. You had no other choice but to flow along with it. Take this approach, this mindset toward all change.

Think about a time where you remember seeing a change or feeling a shift within yourself, when changes caused you to think and behave differently. I remember how challenging the process of my divorce was for me. I had to decide to end my old life and was terrified. I was nervous about how I would start a whole new life all over. I was concerned about leaving the old, and I couldn't fully imagine what the new life would look like.

My entire divorce process took more than six years from the time of making a decision to go forward with one, to today, where life is a very good, new normal. I am a completely different person on the outside than I was when I was married. I have changed many beliefs about myself, marriage, raising a family, and what a family is in general. Before, I felt I couldn't make a decision because I didn't feel right about not being happy. I felt something must be wrong with me. I fought that feeling for a long time, and in the end, I feel I made the right decision. The biggest thing that died for me during my divorce was my relationship with some of my family members. I didn't expect that to happen, and so, today, my concept of family has changed. Until I let go of my sadness and of my former belief of what a family is, I could not embrace (and then create) the family life I always wanted.

Growing and evolving creates massive changes. Every time. I had to let go of what was in order to gain what now is, and I will tell you, I hated every step of the process. Yet I was not going to go back to living out of my old (dead) self. And I finally moved forward. Life opened up for me in ways I never imagined when I let go and allowed the transformation to happen. Remember though, I hated it every step of the way. I never thought to myself, *Yay. This death process is fantastic, and at the end of this rainbow, there will be a pot of gold.* Nope. Not even close. Instead, I was really wishing my breathing would cease forever, and that I would die. Ha. Now, grasp this. I'm the one saying there is no death. I felt like a fraud, like something was wrong with me, and that I really didn't know anything about anything at all. All that self-talk was my trying to dissolve my former core beliefs about myself, and dissolve them, I did.

If life isn't changing for you, you aren't growing. Think about when you gave birth to your children. Everything in your world changed when you became a parent, right? Then think about the day when your children did or will leave you as an empty nester. You have to recalibrate your life and living as a parent, to living without a child in your home every day. This change was or will be a death to your own habits of living, and yet there is an afterlife. What about retirement? Again, there is or will be a death followed by a rebirth, a reconfiguring of how to live—the afterlife. We experience death like this on a regular basis.

On a physical level, death is occurring every single second

inside your own self via the cells of your body. We are constantly being renewed in our daily lives. The you that is you today is not the same make up of cells you were as an infant, a kindergarten graduate, a teenager, or who you even were when you started reading this paragraph. There is a constant flow of forward movement and change in the Universe. There is never stagnation anywhere in the entire Universe, ever.

Your body's cells are constantly dividing, dying, and regenerating. Red blood cells live for about four months, and then they die. New cells are created in their place. Skin cells live about two to three weeks before they die and are replaced. Your stomach is lined with cells, and since they are exposed to acid, they regenerate themselves quickly, about once every five days. The bones in your body take much longer to regenerate, completely replacing all their cells about every ten years. But nothing in the Universe stays stagnant.

In nature, things are constantly dying off or transitioning, too. In the fall, leaves change color before dying and falling to the ground, only to be replaced in the spring. Birds molt their winter plumage to grow breeding feathers. Snakes shed their dead skin and replace it with new. In the winter, particularly in the Northeast United States, everything goes into hibernation. The trees lose their leaves, plants die. Underneath all the cold snow, there is an awakening about to happen. New life. New seeds. New sprouts.

Regeneration and the death and rebirthing cycle happens everywhere in the universe, all the time. Mt. Saint Helens erupted, becoming the most devastating volcanic eruption in the history of America, leaving behind four cubic miles of rock turned to dust, ashes, gas, and soot in its wake. A picture in *National Geographic* a week after the eruption showed the area. It may as well have been a picture of the surface of the moon. Dead tree trunks stuck out all over the place, and little ponds in craters were scattered over the ground. The area looked as if it would be dead for all of eternity after such devastation. But just one year later, a photo of the exact same spot showed the dead trees and little ponds still in place, surrounded by newly growing, green life. The volcanic heat had burned away the brush that had previously prevented the sunlight from reaching the forest, and the warmth helped germinate seeds that had long since been buried in the ground. The Universe recreated new vegetation. The death of the old always opens a doorway for new. There exists an Afterlife in every moment to everything. Always.

13

The Human Experience of Death

So many times, people tell me, "I never feel my deceased relative(s) around me," but others seem to feel them all the time. What are those in the first group doing wrong? Nothing. It's perfectly normal not to feel them. We are used to living in the physical realm, meaning what we see, feel, hear, taste, smell, and touch are what makes things appear real to us. When a person dies, all of their physical components have died, but not the essence of who they are!

Their consciousness remains intact and lives on forever. We need to learn how to switch our connecting from physical to the spiritual. The fastest way to do this is through your thoughts. Just allow yourself to think about those who have passed on. Yes, you may feel sadness. That's OK. That's normal. Also, begin to notice the subtleties of signs from the other side. It's in the little teeny glimpses and moments. I call them winks. The more I tell people something is a sign a loved one is here, people get fixated on that particular sign. This means, they are ignoring, or not even noticing the other thousand ways loved ones can show up for you. So, when they are around, consider their small and subtle ways of communicating as a wink. They are simply saying, "Hey, you. I'm here. Hang in there."

We all want to know if the deceased are OK, especially if the death is sudden or unexpected. It's natural for those of us still here on earth to wonder if the deceased were scared when they died, if they experienced pain, or if there was anything we could have done to prevent it from happening or help them through it. Sometimes, yes, they have experienced the pain of their passing. Sometimes yes, they were absolutely terrified to die. Some were, yes, lonely in the moment of their passing. But as soon as they have crossed over (which happens immediately and often happens before the physical body has died) they are already past the pain. They are no longer questioning what happened or why no one was with them. All those sensations and experiences are of the human realm, and once your spirit leaves your body, there is an unprecedented peace and a superfast download of well, quite frankly everything. They have the good spot. They are OK. They are not upset, scared, in pain, or miserable.

When someone dies, we here are left not only with an indescribable un-name-able void, but, we are flooded with questions and panicked emotions. Disbelief. An overwhelming feeling of disconnect. We worry for the deceased, and we are worried for ourselves. We want to think of all the scenarios that could have played out and maybe, just maybe, we could have changed this destiny nightmare. People begin to call to express their sympathies. They come to visit. Families and friends share memories when this or that happened with the recently deceased. During these moments, we are temporarily lifted in a haze of this energy, brought to us by the prayers, thoughts, good intentions, and caring statements from nearly everyone we ever met and some from strangers.

Those of us left on earth after a loved one dies want to know where the deceased went. After someone dies, they are simply everywhere. They are no longer limited by the human form. We exist as a location/identity right now. It's easy to know where you and I are because wherever our body is, that's where we are. (Or so we think.) So, when people cross over, they are existing in a state of awareness of all things. They are everywhere. That is much better than their moving on to another particular location because, if they are in one space, then we would not be able to communicate with them at any moment.

Right now, notice where you are when you are reading this. Now, think of a family member or friend who lives in another country or state far from you. Sure, they exist. They are on the planet, but can you see them? Can you get to them instantly? Can you talk to them? Now sure, you can connect via electronics, but there are massive limitations on your interactions based on location alone. Think of having to communicate with a family member in the next room. Even then, yes, they are close to you, but they aren't able to share your experience of the now precisely with you because they aren't right there with you.

When we die, and we enter into the conscious space of everywhere, we are in fact sharing each and every collective experience around the globe. Try to envision that for yourself. Imagine your body being in every space in the Universe right now. Tune into any one location and be there. We can in fact do this as humans. It is often called remote viewing. But typically, we aren't able to exist in multiple places at once, and that creates the illusion disguised as reality of separation

When mediums connect with spirit, we need to have some sort of experience for them to show us so we can identify them. So, although they don't have a form, they will present it to us so we can see, hear, or sense them. But when we say, "Oh I see he has blond hair, or is tall, short," they don't really exist in that way anymore. They are just letting us know those things as they used to be for identification purposes. It is nearly impossible to feel them by using our minds. When a parent loses a child, it is rare for them to "feel" their children around them. My own parents have said they do not feel my deceased brother around them, and I also have a hard time recognizing his presence. Grief and logic tend to block pure connections because the heart hurts so much that we try to use our minds to sense them. Mind and spirit never mix, and so, we all come up short in trying to make those connections.

How can we sense our loved ones after they die, then? It's a practice. Your spirit and the spirit of your loved ones who have passed are always connecting with each other. So first, just know and believe it as much as you can. Grief will continuously remind you they aren't there, but our true matter, our spirits always know more than that. We are more than just our physical existence.

When you lose a loved one, just work through the grief at first. Acknowledge the sadness. It's OK to be devastated. How can you be anything but that right after you've lost someone? It isn't the time for you to be anything else.

That's the first step. Honor what is, right now, and that will allow the energy to move through you. It's a daily process that is beyond excruciating. I sit with people every day about this stuff, and yet, I have no personal clue what it is fully like for anyone who has lost a child, as I have not experienced the death of my child. There are no words I feel I can give another parent, as a human, as a mother, but I do know you will absolutely see each other again. I have no doubts about that!

Everything in the Universe is working together in perfect sync. When it is our time to go, everything arranges in the Universe to make it happen when it is time for someone to "die" or leave our physical bodies. On a day that has been a predetermined destiny for 250,000 people to die, the Universe will cause an event to make it happen, for instance, a tsunami. Life is cyclical - the cause is the effect. Everything is in a constant rhythm with everything else both biologically and spiritually.

Everyone has a time to go, and the Universe works in synchronicity to create that. When you accept that you can't change things, you feel peace. If we stand way back from our current moment and learn to observe what is happening without judgment, and recognize it is supposed to be exactly as it is, that initially creates a level of peace you haven't had before. You feel "all is well." We may not feel this right away.

When someone we love dies, we stand in front of the world with a cultural understanding of receiving love from all those who come to pay their so-called last respects. The line in front of the casket becomes the line of the same sentiments, over and over and over. It's filled with the "I'm so sorry for your loss." "May he Rest in Peace." "He/she was such an amazing person." We say out loud, almost robotically, "Yes. He is." Or how about, "I know he/she is flying above us right now with all the angels, my grandmother, and my old neighbor Ted who also passed away last Sunday." Or "He/she is in a better place now." Or we hear "Martha really wanted to be here with you, but she had tickets to a concert she bought a year ago and they were front row, so she couldn't make it, but she sends her love and unwavering support." Or the best yet: "Well, it was his time. The Big Guy must have needed him more than we did." It's a mind- and heart-bending, out of body experience that is awful.

As the line gets shorter and time dwindles down to the last few minutes of the wake or memorial service, your exhaustion begins to hit you. You don't even feel like you are there. There's numbness. Grief that can't be touched, and just a blur. People. Thoughts. Sentiments. And your loved one is there, in a casket. It's all a hazy horrible dream. You are grateful to have anyone around you until, they speak. And everyone's words cut with an innocent attempt to soothe you. Some words help. Most make you feel homicidal, but because you don't have enough energy to conjure up those emotions, you bury them, and into the haze they go, only to be revealed later.

You will begin to hear people talk about how this is all a part of your "journey" here on earth. And that there is a "lesson" to be learned in all of it. You will teeter between knowing for sure this was everyone's destiny, and that there are great moments to gain from it, to experiencing the heartache of how unfair it is and wishing it never happened. Or you will also beg for just ten more minutes with that person. You will torture yourself with mostly remembering the times you took that person for granted. You will convince yourself that you never let them know in any way, shape, or form, that you loved them, or that they mattered to you. No matter how often you may have expressed this, you will allow yourself to believe they didn't really know how important they were to you. This will prevent you from being close to others. This may paralyze you momentarily. These are the thoughts that come to you when you are alone, grieving privately. Your car will become a vehicle for expression and communication to the Other Side. You will pull over and spend a ton of time, sobbing, screaming, or just sitting praying that no one sees you. You also secretly pray, someone sees you and saves you from this. But that someone, is dead.

Everything becomes sentimental. Watching a Fruit of the Loom underwear commercial becomes heartbreaking because it causes you to remember that time in Target when you bought so and so the wrong-size undies. They were mad, you laughed. It was a simple daily task that now feels like the final bullet in your heart. *Why did I take that moment for granted? Why didn't I rush back out and get him the right size? Does he know I do care about him? Did he feel upset when I laughed it off?* Oh, the thoughts that get triggered from just about everything will bring you to your knees. Those moments aren't preplanned. They blindside you on a Tuesday afternoon.

You begin to question your faith and religion, if you were raised with one. You question God. You question why the good die and the bad live on forever. (They don't.) You will want to love again and be loved, and in the next breath, never want love again out of fear of this heartache happening again.

You hear about being able to communicate with the deceased. Depending on your background, how you were raised, and your religious beliefs, you buy every book about Death and The Other Side possible. You bought this book out of hopes of finding answers. How can we communicate with them? You vacillate between thinking and hoping all thing are signs, and then doubting any connections you have felt and calling them "coincidences." You get mad when anyone talks you out of something being a sign from them. You get mad when people say they have spoken and received signs from them, especially when you don't feel you have.

You either avoid places that have special memories with them, or you feel you can only go to that place. You either avoid the cemetery, or you deeply need to go there. These places don't help you. But it's an action and it's doing something. All of this is occurring internally within you, as well as with all the other people who are grieving the same person's death. Yet, on the outside, no one seems to be grieving the same. People will say, and do things that just seem flat out bizarre and will leave you wondering, what the hell? Usually, we keep quiet. We don't have the energy to question, or we are being empathetic and understanding that others have their own ways of coping, no matter how whackadoodle it seems to be.

There are few spaces of internal peace through this process. You either have deep love for those who are helping you through it or deeper hatred for those who just aren't getting it. This is Death's vantage point from the living, those of us who are left behind. There's no getting around it. When we are human, death is horrific.

Nothing can prepare you for this lonely journey that you embark on. The experience and subsequent process isn't pleasant. I wish I could tell you that everything will be OK and normal again, but you have established a new normal, and anytime anything is new, we experience pain.

What I can tell you is that there will also be miracles that occur to you and around you because of it. These small and large gifts will occur out of nowhere and sometimes leave you completely stunned, other times, fully validated. Ugh. I know. I hated these words too!

Ya just gotta' hang in there. Remember, the concept of an Afterlife exists in everything. They are with you whether you feel it or not.

Your loved one's physical body has died, and we humans automatically think their entire spirit and energy has died—that they no longer exist anywhere other than in our painful memories.

Grief is a battle between black and white. Reality and non-reality. There are times of extreme sadness that swing to moments of deep introspection and almost enlightenment, followed by bouts of depression. It is a process that leaves you feeling all over the map—a process I have understood from an early age.

14

I Ain't Afraid of No Ghosts

What do the deceased have that we do not? A better, clearer consciousness. A total lack of judgment. The ability to see life from all angles and viewpoints. When we die, we understand life from the truth of it all, and not from only the vantage point of our singular selves. We experience the Wave of Light and no longer just the small or particle self that experiences itself in comparison to the others around it. It has no ego, no more hs. Thing is, we only experience a small part of the whole in this form. We aren't capable of experiencing everything in life in one lifetime, so there is an automatic lack built into our hs experience. We see and do some things, but not all. We have opinions of our surroundings, based on what we understand and how we were raised.

The deceased have a consciousness that is both clear and evolved. They have shed a large piece of themselves that causes by laws of physics to vibrate on a lower or denser vibration. The process of our spirit leaving our bodies allows for us to instantly feel the release of all stress, tension, and negativity the body feels. The spirit is an expansive, never-ending field of energy. And what do we often do? We stuff it inside a small vessel, our bodies, and we make it small, dense, and limited. We do this by believing we are only our bodies, and by believing we are only capable of doing or experiencing so much. How does that happen? By our conditioning, our upbringing, our experiences from infancy.

The whole experience of being human is that we are animals who are conditioned for how to think, feel, and behave. Yes, we have our own views and understanding and perspective on things, but how often do we challenge our own perspective? How often do we snap out of who we think we are, and seek to expand ourselves?

People often confuse me and my work with that of a paranormal ghost hunter and believer. What are ghosts? Ghosts are another concept for humans to feel controlled and overpowered.

Ghosts are *not* your known loved ones. They are not creepy apparitions of a previously living person. They are aspects of *yourself* that are being reflected back to you in glimpses. Say whaaaat? I hear on a daily basis people who ask me to come to their homes or businesses to "clear" the negative energies (aka "Ghosts" that reside there.) I always immediately respond to them, "OK, done."

You do not need someone to clear negative energy that belongs to the disembodied from your home, ever! When you feel a foreign energy around you, it's an aspect of yourself that you are either currently very much in alignment with, or an aspect that you may be shunning away from yourself (or trying to). If you sense evil energy, that's an aspect of yourself that is resonating with fear or a sense of being scared about *something*. It's the part of yourself that continues to allow you to be unempowered, and you create a reason for it rather than addressing the old fear. We (unconsciously) project our fears onto something or someone else, and we are calling them ghosts.

We do this all the time. It's easy to think a fear is outside of ourselves because then we do not have to deal with it. Rather, we can stay outside of it—and remain a victim to it. Although that doesn't handle the issue, it does make us feel like we are still intact. We manifest these things in our environment to become aware of them and ultimately to grow from them. Problem is, no one knows about this. There is NO such thing as evil energy on the other side. When we are in spirit/energy form, we are restored to our true and pure essence. There is absolutely, positively no such thing as evil in the domain and space of the other side. There is no darkness in pure Light.

We exist in dimensions. As humans, we are in the dimension that is expressed and experienced on a physical, 3D plane. As already explained, when we die, we reunite with Source. And that source has been, is, and always will be the Pure potentiality of all creation. Potential is not the same as what is. It is the sum of everything, while expressing no visible or tangible evidence of form yet. So, in the field of potential, where nothing and yet the possibility of everything is formed, evil does not exist. When manifested, yes, it can and does exist, but again, that comes in form and not in energy terms. Once it's manifested, is when it's born into a particular lower dimension, and then it does it take on its identity or vibration of "good" or "evil." What am I saying? Evil exists within humans (hs,) not in our energetic (HS) selves.

So, what are people *seeing* when they see ghosts? Imprints. Imprints of yes, former people, but they are seeing them because their energy has become a mirror for themselves.

Let's look at this from another vantage point. The last thing I want to do is to continue to allow people to think of ghosts incorrectly! Remember, my goal is to help you understand Energy on a deeper level, so you can learn how to align yourself, mind, body, and spirit of being a creator and not a victim. That alone will help you live a better life! Releasing foolish fears frees up your energy fields to place importance on all you really do want to accomplish!

So, have you ever noticed that ultra fear-based people are the ones who constantly talk about being afraid of ghosts? They appear on paranormal TV shows and claim they were harassed and sometimes harmed by an apparition. Sometimes these events happen in their homes, and sometimes during a so-called ghost hunt. I find these shows... well, ridiculous. I haven't really heard many people proclaiming to be harassed by ghosts while sitting at their desks in the middle of a large office separated by cubicles. Or bus drivers, train conductors, taxi drivers, pilots, chauffeurs, being harmed and ridiculed while transporting people around. Why have restaurant service workers not *served* apparitions meals only to be denied their tips? Why have we not heard FOX news report, "Man/ woman killed by evil spirit?" Fear and the unknown sell.

I haven't really heard any verified stories of say, doctors, who are suddenly overcome by negative ghosts while performing an intricate surgery. Haven't heard it once at all where they are so distracted by an awful prankster apparition just trying to mess up their procedure. However, I have heard of people who have felt an *intervention* of energy during times of fear and need and helped a person overcome that fear and were able to perform at such a high level of focus. There is a difference between having one energy that lifts us up, and one that takes us down. If ghosts *were* real, at least in the sense that we as a society have been conditioned to believe in them, why don't they show up more often? Why don't they do more damage to all sorts of people? Why isn't *everyone* afraid of them?

Why haven't I been attacked by a ghost? Surely, you would think I, a person who connects every day with deceased energies would have met a bad one by now! What about countless other mediums like John Edward, James Van Praagh, Lisa Williams, Theresa Caputo, Suzanne Northrop, John Holland, and my personal favorite, George Anderson? Don't you think at least one of us should have by now come in contact with a former murderer? I actually have multiple times, so I am certain all of those mentioned above have as well. Then why didn't one of those negative energies just kill us while we were speaking? Or forget harming us physically. I would think at least one of them would have made us nervous, upset or, afraid, by now, right? Why hasn't it happened? It's because that is not how energy works. Therefore, it's nowhere in any one of our belief systems about the other side.

I could connect with a former mass murderer, and their energy wouldn't be any more or less negative than Mother Theresa. (I know, I know... That makes a lot of people very upset to hear!) They may come through as a mean, nasty energy, because that is how they allowed their energy to be known in *human* form. But he/she is truly no longer in this evil *state*. That all existed in the physical state of being and not in the spiritual. Ever. No matter what. What people like Mother Theresa already know is this very fact. That at the core of all of us, we are the same pure, pristine, creative energy. Our human selves by our conditioning, habitual living and awareness determine which side of the good-and-evil spectrum we live. Someday, I envision us being able to have compassion for all evildoers for choosing to live out a life in which their actions are harmful and cause pain. Life is hard enough to live when you are trying to be good and decent. I can't imagine how difficult it is to live in such a state of disconnect, and well, evil.

So, why are these ghosts showing up and bothering those who are already afraid? Because these people believe in the fear. They are actually drawing an experience of fear and powerlessness to them. "That which you are seeking is seeking you," wrote Rumi. If you believe in negativity, you will experience it. Often.

If you believe in negative experiences and ghosts, you will experience them. Some people were actually *taught* to feel powerless. In fact, many were. Some are actually taught to feel inferior to all things energetic or paranormal. The notion of there being an angry and discerning God in heaven who will judge us at the end of our lives creates panic and fear in our collective minds. It forces us to listen and be good. When people know, or at least think they are being watched, they "behave." If God is watching, I'll be good. Just like Santa and all other personifications of make believe and magic. Have you ever picked your nose while someone was watching? Probably not. Have you done it while you are alone? Yeah. Case closed. If we are being watched, we behave differently. How powerful is the notion of the Ultimate Watcher?

I adore retired Episcopalian Bishop John Shelby Spong, who very eloquently spoke to this very notion. He is quoted by *The Waking Times*[9], "I don't think Hell exists. I happen to believe in life after death, but I don't think it's got a thing to do with reward and punishment. **Religion is always in the control business, and that's something people don't really understand.** It's in a guilt-producing control business. And if you have Heaven as a place where you're rewarded for your goodness, and Hell is a place where you're punished for your evil, then you sort of have control of the population. And so, they create this fiery place which has quite literally scared the Hell out of a lot of people throughout Christian history. And it's part of a control tactic."

He goes on to say, "Every church I know claims that 'we are the true church' – that they have some ultimate authority, 'We have the infallible Pope,' 'We have the Bible.' The idea that the truth of God can be bound in any human system, by any human creed, by any human book, is almost beyond imagination for me. God is not a Christian. God is not a Jew or a Muslim or a Hindi or Buddhist. All of those are human systems human beings have created to try to help us walk into the mystery of God. I honor my tradition. I walk through my tradition. But I don't think my tradition defines God. It only points me **to** God."

I just love it. He is agreeing with the idea that religions are largely seeking to control people to get people to do what is declared as right. Perhaps the intention for that is good, and perhaps it isn't. That debate goes far beyond the scope of this chapter; however, we need to remember religions are created from the minds of man. We are the ones who created the rules, rituals, and beliefs surrounding them. Yes, as Bishop Spong suggests, they are all pointing us to God, but the reality of what God truly is, is inconceivable when we try to understand it through our human lenses.

He brilliantly says in a filmed sermon, "You and I are emerging people, not fallen people. Our problem is not that we are born in sin. Our problem is we do not yet know how to fully achieve being fully *human*. The function of the Christ is not to rescue the sinners, but to empower you and call you to be more deeply and fully human than you have ever realized that was the potential within you to be. Maybe salvation needs to be conveyed in terms of enhancing your humanity, rather than rescuing you from it."

How can we enhance our humanity with our limitations and all, rather than be victims of our humanity? How do we live and be our full and authentic selves rather than die every day never even knowing the depths of our humanity?

We are simply too limited to understand the magnitude of what "God, Universe, The Ultimate Being," etc, is. Religions are based on having a group of people scared enough to participate in rituals that keep them tied to a particular leader and stuck in a mindset that they aren't free or capable of being themselves without the guidance of a human who is higher than they are. Personally, I think that is downright scary. Dangerous. To me, that's a *soul murder.* To actually believe anyone has more power over yourself than you do is terrible. Sure, we always need others guidance around us. But wisdom comes from knowledge lived or known intuitively. No one person can ever be you and have all your experiences. We can bring in mentors, leaders, and people who can encourage us to dig deeper into ourselves, and then yes, that's healthy. But as soon as we think someone else is in charge of our self, we actually shut off our ability to be empowered and to connect to some Higher awareness and thoughts. We stop growing. We atrophy as humans.

People who are connected to their humanity are able to empower themselves beyond it. Empowered people are more honest with themselves and others. They are confident, even in their inadequate moments. Fear is a great manipulator for an angry, jealous, or insecure person to use over people they want to obey. Empowerment comes from people who see the benefit of all beings living and feeling their true potential - or at least letting people know they are capable of achieving more for themselves!

I for one, know I am way more useful when I feel good about myself and others than when I don't. When I am down on myself in any way, shape, or form, I allow those negative thoughts to leak into the other parts of my being. It takes me down, down, down. I don't want to do whatever I am good at. I don't even allow myself to believe I am good at anything! I don't want to participate in all of life when I am focused on the areas of my own personal belief of "I suck."

When we are unempowered, we take an apathetic stance in life. It breeds circumstances to do badly. Why not? The mindset of "No one cares about me and who I am" sets in, and that spreads to the external environment. Once a child loses their recess for bad behavior, do you think they are more motivated to do better in class? No way. They already lost what they wanted. The motivation to get it back is gone. Instead, negative self concepts creep in, negative thoughts about the punishing teacher set in, and no good can come of that. To incite fear and oppression is the exact polar opposite of love and expansion. And love is the energy field of it all. It's the soil of manifestation and potential. There's really no word to describe this space. Love is an energy that allows things to flourish and grow. It's nurturing and authentic. This is the energy field from which we are all created. It is at the core of all of us. How often do we operate out of that space?

So again, you will ask me, what IS a ghost? It's an apparition of a state of your own awareness. This could be a current awareness or an old belief. "Ghosts" are the energy field felt in a space that existed before. I often sit with people who have had traumatic lives.

They very often express to me they feel negative energies around them all the time. These energies are actually the remnants of their old feelings. Their old selves. If someone was abused, when they are no longer in the space of the abuser, they may feel discomfort or scared by a presence. It often sets them off into a panic attack. Or in the very least, keeps them from feeling comfortable in their own skin. This circumstance is a function their own cells having a memory of their past fearful situations. What happens to us in our lives becomes a part of us. It's stored in our memories. Stored in our cells. Stored in our consciousness. The fear is like a buried treasure getting dug up years later in an attempt to release it. But instead, our psychology and our society has us now transforming our past fears into something else—a fictional ghost, who now has power over us. We begin to try to now create a physical tangible reality of these fears! This is tragic. Ghosts, as you think of them, are no more real than your dreams. They seem real in the moment of experiencing them, but when you dissect the experience later, you can see connections between your former beliefs and fears, and quickly match how they line up and are projected onto a new beast, that ever illusive, scary, and uncontrollable unknown. One can reread Charles Dickens' *A Christmas Carol* more astutely and notice the hidden meaning behind each of the three ghosts who show up to poor Ebenezer Scrooge. Each ghost represents an unresolved aspect of Scrooge himself. Fortunately, in that book, Scrooge is able to finally see who he has become *because* of these ghosts and is able to make a major transformation shift by the end. He starts as a miserable, distrustful man who has no meaningful connection to anyone, and changes into a generous, fulfilled man who sees his purpose through *helping* others. I only wish our current visits from ghosts would provide us with such meaningful insights into ourselves and create such beautiful metamorphosis in our characters!

How can you heal yourself and move past trauma like Scrooge? How can you utilize the information from your ghosts (or your fear of them) to provide you with this insight?

Growth Opportunity

Personify your fears. Imagine your worst fears were a human being. What would this "person" look like? How would they act? What would they wear? What is their profession? How do they torment you? What is their motivation for their torment? How do you feel around their presence? Really engage your imagination and create a projection of all your fears in a human form. How or what do you need to do to empower yourself around this entity?

When you don't look at your fears and express and experience them, then they become suppressed and stored. They wait to come out when it's safe enough to do so. The ghosts you wish to believe in can help you resolve a lot of trauma within yourself, if you understand and know how to approach it. These ghosts are not outside you. They are you. They represent your fears, concerns, and stresses. They are embodying your fear. And you and only you can put them to rest or keep them alive. You are their creator!

Have you ever experienced something so traumatic (ranging from a difficult upbringing, to a car accident, to a burglary) and you kept your calm during it, but hours, or sometimes, days, weeks, even months later, that trauma rises to the surface? Post-traumatic stress is a real thing. Ask any soldier, victim of a crime, or anyone who has experienced anything jarring in their lives. In the moment, our body responds to stress with hormones to keep us calm, cool, and collected. Or it gives us the energy to run away.

This is what's known as the "flight or fight" response. When our brains recognize a stressful situation, the sympathetic nervous system responds by releasing adrenaline and norepinephrine. This makes our heart rate and breathing speed up, and it constricts our blood vessels while also tightening muscles. In a relaxed state, the neurons are fired minimally. But when we're afraid or stressed, that perception of stress is relayed from the sensory cortex of the brain through the thalamus to the brain stem, a route that increases noradrenergic activity and causes us to become more attentive and alert. The abundance of catecholamines at neuroreceptor sites means we are forced to rely more on intuitive behaviors that we generally use when fighting or escaping danger. When in the flight-or-fight mode, we have the strength needed to get out of harm's way.

Later on, the body recovers from this increased activity, calms down, and the reality of the stress sets in. When not dealt with, these emotions simply stay stored for a better time to surface. This is why in life, just when we feel life is good, and things are coming along so nicely for us, we are blindsided by anxiety or irrational fears. It's not that anything in our immediate reality has caused those emotions. Instead, the body has relaxed and actually feels safe enough to finally deal with these old emotions. This is the exact thing that happened to me when I was watching my brother's videos on the living room wall. The grief, sadness, and loss came up because 1. It was triggered by the videos and 2., it was a *safe* time for me to deal with them. Any earlier, and there were too many other things occurring around me that had to be handled. Just when I am feeling good about life, I get blindsided by very old grief. Good times. But knowing this happens is truly half the battle! You aren't crazy! You aren't constantly plugged into drama. You are processing what couldn't have been processed earlier.

The *ghosts* surface so we can confront and actually see and feel what ghosts are residing within. What fears and insecurities are you holding onto? What parts of you have not been allowed to die? What purpose do these ghosts serve you? Do you want to let them go? Do you want to listen to what insights they have for you? Or do you prefer to shrink in fear? Do you wish to cower in the corner and recite prayers, light sage, and feel scared? It's up to you. You can totally decide here. Which one feels better to you? Then that's the one you should do.

15
What Happens When We Die?

People are afraid of the process of dying and afraid of what happens to them after they're dead. In George Campbell's book, *Exit Strategy: A Textbook on Death and Dying*[10], he shares the answers from surveys about death taken in classrooms, where 50 percent of college students say they are scared of the dying process. The severity of our fear of death changes throughout the years, with the fear of dying being at a lowest point between the ages of fifteen and twenty-one, and that fear increasing as we get older and start to experience a decline in our abilities, and experiencing the deaths of friends and acquaintances in our age group.

People are also scared about what happens to them after they die. The unknown is always scary, and death is a big unknown for most of us. After you die, will you be stuck in a place you don't like forever? Rolling a rock up a steep hill, over and over for all of eternity? How will family members survive without you?

How can we really know what happens when we die if we do not have our own recollection of it from this lifetime? How can we know anything about it? Well, on one hand, we can't, not when we are thinking or worrying about death from our human perspective. We put too much emphasis of how we operate here on earth, and we think it's similar when we die.

Are you afraid of it? Are you worried about it? Are you worried that death means the final end? Are you worried about being alone or ceasing to exist? Or are you upset with it, only thinking about your loved ones and how they will survive without you? Have you thought about your own death and what that means to you? (And if so, I am sure this—I *hope* this has then caused you to question how you live.) Death makes us live when we allow it. I am constantly amazed at how many people are literally scared to death about death! And I crave to know and understand what is going on that is causing that. Besides, I'm more intrigued at how this intense fear of death paralyzes people so much that they literally fail to live because of it. Ironically, people who are intensely afraid of death end up being *deader* while they're still alive!

It is my hope that as you read what I'm sharing with you in this book and open your mind to new concepts of death and the Afterlife, you can begin to release your fear. Releasing the fear and having awareness of our interconnectedness can improve your quality of life now and help you experience more of a "heaven on earth" sort of lifestyle while you are still living in your human identity.

The number one question people ask me when someone dies is, "Can you tell me if my loved ones are OK?" As humans, we experience the physical separation when someone dies. Because we're tuned in at the physical level, when someone's physical body is no longer here, we say they've died. They're "gone." We grieve and feel the loss. Those people are no longer with us because of our beliefs about what death is. And we fail to realize they aren't thinking in these terms whatsoever! They are practically screaming their heads off with joy saying, "Oh My God! I'm OK! I'm here! I am not disconnected from you!" Only the physical body has died. Sadly, as humans, we rarely connect spiritually with each other while here, and we tend to only connect on the human, physical level. We rely on our five senses to experience everything. But can you just for a moment think of the energy of those you love and care about who are around you?

Let's try an exercise to help you do this.

Growth Opportunity

Stop reading for a moment, and think about the energy your circle or tribe (those with whom you spend your time) gives off. Feel it. Feel them. Know them through feeling how they are, which is different from feeling them as you want them to be. Rather than think about them, feel them. Imagine yourself connecting your core to theirs. Imagine a light energy that links them with you and you with them. Does that link feel good? What does It feel like? Get in touch with that feeling. Imagine being them. How do you feel to them? Take the time to really try this. Do this with family, friends, coworkers, and even strangers! The more you do it, the more you will feel the difference between your perceptions of people and who they really are.

But what really happens when someone dies, and what is experienced by the person who dies is the opposite of what we experience when someone else dies. It wasn't just about the physical all along. The people who have passed finally realize the spiritual connection that we've always had, the connection that always was and always will be—and they become more connected than ever before. That is why they are all OK. I promise you, every single person who has died is OK. They have learned the secret. They feel us, our true essence of who we are. They sense and know our intentions, our limitations, our belief systems, our thoughts, and feelings. They understand how it all has been in accordance to every other living organism in the Universe.

When someone dies, they realize the people they know are not just those people in their physical bodies. When someone dies, they realize that everyone is far more than their physical identities, and they connect to themselves and to everyone they've ever been around, all at the same time. It's euphoric. We are the light, and we all become one in this process. When we die, we truly understand The Collective Whole and our part in it.

There is no judgment. No anger. No animosity. No right and wrong. Those are all emotions that are caused when we have an ego and are experiencing life through our physical, human identities. Finally understanding this is what gives us the ultimate connection. We can experience this more and more every day as we practice non-attachment, the concept of no self, accepting what is in our paths, keeping a clear mind, and practicing full compassion for everyone. Or you can take the easier route and not transcend any of this and continue to do what you have been doing your entire life. If that is working well for you, then stick with it. But if you are unhappy, unsettled, more stressed than not, feeling inadequate, and feeling separated from not only others, but yourself, then this truly is the formula for you to take! It's definitely easier to be an ignorant human being, but not less painful. The coolest part is that it's your choice.

We often think about death as a moment in time. One minute we are alive, and the next, we are dead. Your lungs have stopped moving air, and your heart has stopped beating. It's at that moment that a person is clinically dead. But a number of scientific studies by neuroscientists are looking to prove that death is not cut and dry, like flipping the light switch on and off. That dying is actually a process, during which time we are conscious and having experiences.

Jimo Borjigin, a neuroscientist at the University of Michigan, discovered that when rats have been clinically dead for at least thirty seconds, during which time they have no heartbeats and do not breathe, their brains show stronger signals of conscious thought immediately after cardiac arrest[11]. The study suggests that our final journey into death may involve a brief state of heightened consciousness.

One in five people who are resuscitated after their hearts stop report near-death experiences (NDEs). These people are unresponsive, seemingly unconscious, and pronounced clinically dead. Yet when resuscitated, they return with stories of bright lights, memories, and meetings with people that they knew before they died. Many report they were able to hear conversations of people in the physical room with their bodies after their death. I've heard over and over through hundreds of readings, that many times, our loved ones have crossed over even before their body "died." Often, those on life support have exited their bodies while machines kept the body functions going. They report back many of the details that occurred in the room up until the moment where their bodies were clinically been declared dead. We are not in charge of someone's death, even when we have to make a decision to remove someone from life support. Our souls, have a predetermined time and day when they are leaving, and nothing intercepts that. I often find it such a horrible situation to put family members in to think they have all the control over when someone dies when the reality is, only our souls and our connection to the Collective Whole have that power, and they operate seamlessly.

Once I tell people that their loved ones are OK after they pass, and they are provided some proof of that message, people want to know what actually happens during the process of dying, or "crossing over." Now, as I've stated earlier, I have not had, at least not up to the point in time as I am writing this, ever had a Near Death Experience. So, no, I personally have not witnessed the feeling of my own direct crossing over. I have, however, understood the process of crossing over from the vantage point of the deceased who have come through with messages for their loved ones. I have read numerous books on NDE experiences. My first was by Dannion Brinkley when I was a young teen, and it left me wanting to know more, more, more about this phenomenon! Everyone's account of what happens shortly after we pass on is remarkably similar, nearly identical.

Dannion Brinkley writes of his experience in *Saved By The Light*[12], that left him with "special powers." He was electrocuted while talking on the phone during an intense thunderstorm in 1975 and was clinically dead for twenty-eight minutes. During that time, he experienced, a "crossing over." He saw the white light, had his life review, and was able to be connected to otherworldly realms. He was told it wasn't his time and was given visions of future events, and a mission here on earth.

In 2010, Todd Burpo published *Heaven is Real*[13]. an account of what his then four-year-old son, Colton, told him about what Heaven was like when he had a near-death experience. Colton, from very Christian family, described seeing Jesus, "riding on a rainbow-colored horse" and being seated next to Jesus' mother Mary as she kneeled at the throne of God. He began speaking to his parents about his experiences while undergoing surgery when he was three-years old. He said he saw an unborn sister his mom had miscarried years before his birth, and he knew details about a grandfather never discussed before. This book became a bestseller and was even turned into a box office hit movie. Clearly, the world is interested in this topic. I'm glad I'm not the only one!

Anita Moorjani, author of *Dying to be Me*[14] published her amazing account of her near-death experience in 2006. She was dying from lymphoma, was in a coma, and was reaching her final stages of life. Her account describes in detail what it felt like to be connected to everyone and everything. She states she could be in many places at once and realized she was so much more, that we are all so much more than what we perceive. She teaches of changing our focus in life to enhance our time here on earth. Her analogy of what she discovered when she crossed over is a great one. She says, imagine we are all housed in a huge warehouse. All of time and space is inside a large pitch-black space, and we are all like individual flashlights. Wherever we place our awareness is what we can see in the light of our flashlight. When she crossed over, she saw the entire warehouse and everything that was inside it both as separate flashlights and as a Collective Whole. The entire warehouse was illuminated, and everything became known to her in that instant. She remembers not wanting to leave this place at all, but was told by her deceased father and best friend that it was not her time, and she had to return to her body. She knew at that moment that when she did return to her body, she would be fully healed of her cancer. Her doctors have no explanation for how her lymphoma was nearly 70 percent gone just four days after this experience.

All these cases, as well as countless others that are well documented, have come under scrutiny from skeptics and scientists alike. It is to be expected. This topic borders of the unknown, religious beliefs and what science tells us is real. Many suggest all of this is an outworking of our human psyche and nothing more that happens at death. There has been the question of why do only Christians' report seeing Jesus and other Christian figures, while Muslims, and Hindus see their versions of saints and sages? Dr. Deepak Chopra, in *Life after Death*, discusses this question and puts it in perspective. He says, "Believers may go to heaven (or hell) that matches their religious backgrounds. In the afterlife, they will meet their most cherished version of God or gods. If they anticipate the afterlife to be euphoric, it will be, or will be sad if that is what they expect. Skeptics might find the experience to be exactly as they imagined. A space of nothingness. No life after death. No God. No Higher Power present." He suggests that since no one way of belief is present anywhere in society, why would the experience of the afterlife be any different? He says our choice and our conditioning will impact our experiences. All of this is created on the level of our consciousness. Where we focus our attention is what we will see. Again, we are the creators of our experiences, even after death.

Anita's story sounds exactly like what I have been told and experienced through sessions with people who have passed on. There is an awareness of the interconnectedness of us all that goes far beyond anything our human selves can conceive of. Has the other side ever expressed to me they have seen Jesus or any other religious icon? Absolutely! Many have relayed that their experience is exactly as they thought it would be. And many others say it's nothing like what they expected. This brings great comfort to their loved ones. Many former skeptics become believers in the afterlife once they have passed on as well! I've had quite a few stories where an energy expresses to their loved ones, "I can't believe this stuff is real!" Your experience of the afterlife may reflect the beliefs you held here on earth during your human form, but not always.

In Hinduism, there is a belief that the state of awareness a person is in when they pass is the state of awareness they remain in. I have mixed feelings on this. I do feel it's true in some respects although I do not sense from those on the other side they are spending eternity in a state of panic or disruption when a person is not prepared for their own passing. Rather, I notice the state of awareness we are in may be the state of awareness we are born into in our next lifetime. It becomes a part of the experiences here that we will seek to resolve. I firmly believe those who have deep fears of dying had a rough or disturbing passing in a previous lifetime. I do not have clear evidence of this, nor am I aware of any research done on the topic. This is a hunch I have had from sitting with thousands of people over the past fifteen years. There are themes and patterns in our lives, and they are all interwoven with previous lifetimes. Jeesh! That's a lot to consider! There will be more of this in the chapter on reincarnation.

When we pass on, we go through what I call a purifying process. This is the process when our soul recognizes that we are not actually our physical bodies. It is the moment when we recognize we are spiritual beings that were temporarily stored in particular physical bodies, so that we would be able to experience life. We are the stuff of God, energy, manifested in physical form, but that is not all we are! We realized we have been part of a very complicated and intricate web of interconnectivity (The Collective Whole) which far surpasses our comprehension. Every living being is in perfect synchronicity as everything else in the Universe. Everything is in the right place at the right time. We have our life review, and we experience life as the sum total of who we were and how our energy field impacted others who came in contact with us. This goes from the trivial moments of sitting on a train next to someone, to those moments when we cut someone off in traffic nearly causing an accident, to the moments with whom we spent most of our time on earth. We experience all of it from a vantage point of It All. We are the Cause and the Effect!

After that phase of our crossing is complete, and we finally pass on, the awareness of our true self, our soul, is a liberating and freeing event. We are released from our ego and the concept of "me and mine." We have clarity on our impact and purpose while here in the physical. We finally have the opportunity to really know and understand what all the events experienced during our lifetime were teaching us. We experience gratitude and compassion for everyone and everything that has occurred in our lives. We finally understand we were living out experiences that we asked for (this includes both good and bad experiences) in order to learn lessons and experience life.

Regardless of how the death is brought about, sudden illness, self-inflicted, accident, old age, there is a moment when you/your spirit experiences the separation from the physical body. This is when people talk about "going to the light." That light is actually our own energy. When people say they were going toward the light, we're actually reconnecting to our own light/spirit, rediscovering our own light. The light is that connection to everything and everywhere.

The light always feels good, calm, and peaceful, because that's your essence, and you're being completely reconnected to it. It's love itself, and it is truly the essence or the vibration that has made up everything else in the universe. We are finally reconnected to it as we go through it.

We say it is our own energy, but it's really a game of semantics. We perceive it to be our own because that is how we have experienced it up until that point, as ourselves, the *me* I think I am! The connecting from Self to the Collective Whole is what is largely described as the seeing of the light that is so commonly described by the NDEers. All along, we have been the light, cloaked in our personalities and persona. That begins to unravel via the life review, and we see the light, our true selves as a flowing stream of consciousness. The grasp of time itself becomes lengthened and expanded. We become aware that we are of no time and simultaneously of all time. There is nothing I am, and nothing I am not. Returning to this light or rather, becoming reacquainted with and remembering it, is euphoric, and it can't be described adequately in any human terms.

Science is trying to prove this: "I saw my life flash before my eyes." However, my first experience as a medium was experiencing someone else's life review. I didn't even know she was dying at the time, but later when I knew she was dying, I realized I was seeing her life flashing before her eyes. That life "flash" is an unwinding of your subconscious tapes. Everything you experience is recorded in your subconscious. Every sound, person we meet, taste, smell. It starts unwinding like a movie. It takes nanoseconds. When the tape is being rewound, we will experience anything and everything we've done for someone else during our lifetime through the eyes of the other person. If you help someone, save someone, make them smile, buy a gift for someone, help them have a good day, you will experience it all again in the way the person you did it for experienced it. This life "flash" of experiences will also reflect each of our negative deeds. Whether intentional or unintentional, you will feel it from the other person's perspective. This can only be described as intense, euphoric, and the truest reality check ever. It's what I call the Ultimate Download of information and experiences.

As a medium, my openness to communicate with those who have died allows me to also experience situations from the vantage point of the people who have died. If you were to hear the conversations I have with the deceased, this is what it would sound like from a person describing what they feel as they transition to the other side, that crossing over to "death."

"Oh wow. The light, the love, oh, Mom. Is it really you? And is that Grandma? Poppy? Buddy, my dog? Uncle Phil? Oh my god, the love is overwhelming! I never knew love and light like this existed! What…what's this? Whoa."

The download begins.

This is the part of our final human journey where we finally rewind the videotape and relive our entire lives—where we go through the purification process—experiencing our lives both from our own vantage point of living it and from the vantage points of everyone we have ever met, talked with, touched, and interacted with! We literally feel the ripples of every action we have ever made. We do not judge it. We just experience it in its full purity. This is our final "human" experience.

During this download, we understand the whys of life. We understand how nothing was ever what we thought. Sure, we feel the dramatic events of life, those we were the target of and those we caused. We feel the love and joys as well again. Remember making fun of Little Tommy on the bus? Guess what? We revisit that situation now, from Tommy's experience—that little boy who went home and cried. It will hurt. Badly. We will feel so sad we hurt him. We will feel sorry. We will understand deeply what we did. Then, we may also feel Tommy's joy that occurred twenty years later, as he became a spokesperson against anti-bullying for all he endured as a kid. Now, he goes to help others, and he is making a difference in the world. He is changing lives. One at a time. And you were a part of that. You created great pain to him, so one day, he would take it away from someone else. In his case, he taught hundreds, maybe thousands. And you can feel that accomplishment as well because you experienced Tommy as Tommy. And you finally got it. You saw this aspect of yourself that was hurtful, and you wished with everything you could have changed it. And therefore, you did, in spirit form.

Think about this for a moment Really. Stay with me here because this is intense. We re-experience every interaction from our conception to our death. Yep! Everyone your mom spoke with and had conversations with while you were in utero, you heard and felt through her. You picked up on her thoughts and feelings, and then absorbed them as your own. The person who delivered you, the nurses, the family members at your birth and your first days home. Your pediatrician, siblings, everything will be re-experienced from birth onward. Your every interaction—you feel it through your own eyes and from the other person's eyes as well. And it all makes sense.

Then you see and feel the experience and the ripples of every one of those situations. Every. Single. One. This is when the connection to everything starts to overwhelm us. This is when we finally understand what it is to be one. One consciousness. One Whole. The Collective Whole.

We finally understand that we're connected through each other, like a Grand Human/Spirit Puzzle. And all the pieces fit neatly into place. The puzzle is an energy field that no word can describe.

Imagine this scenario at your own funeral. *Oh look, wow, it's my funeral! Look at who came. Wow. I never thought the owner of my favorite deli, John, cared enough to come. Wow.* Then we relive our deli interactions. We hear what John says. *He loved that I always left a dollar in the tip jar every day? It was only a buck! I didn't know he turned around and gave that money to a homeless man for food. I made a small contribution and didn't even know it. My impact went on way further than I have ever truly realized. And wow.*

There's my dad. Poor guy. We never got to say goodbye. I am OK with him on that. I wish he knew that… I want him to know that. I will make sure I let him know that I loved him more than words could ever say. I flash back to memory of driving in his convertible playing the soundtrack of Dirty Dancing's Hungry Eyes while the air from the night sky cools me, but the heated seats are keeping me warm… Loved that night. It was Father Daughter Night one summer back when I was in sixth grade…

And that's when I plant that memory in my sibling's ear… and I watch her remind my dad of that memory. "Hey Dad. I just had this feeling like I should tell you… remember that night.. in your convertible. She talked about that all the time. She loved that ride… It meant the world to her." His tears turn to a smile. He remembers the good times.

The deceased have methods of getting messages to the humans. It never fails. There is great comfort in knowing we can send them reminders from time to time. We also understand they sometimes know these are winks from beyond, and that more often the winks go unnoticed. It's OK. We are still with them. More so than ever. We aren't disconnected in death. We are RE-connected. The feeling of peace, love, connection is… well.. there are no words for it. We watch our death. We understand why we had the life we did. We get it. We see it. Feel it. And understand it. And it's all OK. We survived the human adventure. We left our mark. We oversee our loved ones. We see how hard it is for them to carry on. We don't like it, but we also know it's necessary. We know what they will learn from it. We will see their soul evolve through this pain. We observe them with love. We push them forward with their transformations. We help to connect them with people who can relate. We watch their worlds completely change. We have the benefit of watching their lives and how it will turn up ahead. We prevent what is ours to prevent. We surrender to what is. We wait for them until they rejoin up completely in spirit. We greet them the moment they pass and we introduce them into The Energy Field. And it's all OK. The unborn children begin to interact with the living, and the cycle of life goes on and on and on. It is the Afterlife.

Your loved one's physical body has died. And to us humans, we automatically think their entire spirit and energy has died. That they no longer exist anywhere other than in our painful memories, but as you've been reading in this book, you know that is simply not the case.

During the process of "crossing over" the good deeds we did in our life will be felt, from the viewpoint of the person who was the recipient of our kindness. Ever give money to someone who truly needed it? Ever save someone's life? Ever hold the door for someone in the mall? Have you ever written a note to the teacher who changed your life? Have you ever complimented someone? Have you ever sat with a sick person just so they weren't alone? Have you ever walked past someone and smiled? Ever strike up a random conversation and connect with a complete stranger? Ever surprise a stranger and buy them a cup of coffee? Filled their gas tank? Or paid for their toll? Ever thank the A/C repair man for coming over right away to get your unit working? Ever over-tip a waitress because you can relate to working hard? Ever tell someone you love them? Help a little one tie their shoes? Ever run a fundraiser to help those in need? Or donate to a cause? Ever write to a lonely soldier? Have you ever done any good deed? Ever? Have you ever showed love, appreciation, and gratitude for someone? Ever connect with someone? When you cross over, you will experience the magnitude of those deeds from the vantage point of the person you helped. You will also be able to see the ripple effect of what that did for that person and any good deed, or loving action that came from them as a result. The ripple goes on and on and on. It's magnified. The love you gave to another, every simple and small act is recorded in the energy field, and it's returned to you, the Source of that love. You are the creator. And all energy returns to its source. Our actions resonate with our vibration. When we are kind, kindness comes back to us. When we love freely and deeply, that love is returned to us. When we are generous, that generosity is returned to us! Remember, you are the creator of your world!

Anything we do to another, or for another person, we are ultimately also doing for ourselves. When you pray for someone's good health or highest good to be placed into action, we are at the same time praying for our own highest good to be put into action.

Have you ever made fun of someone? Or hurt someone's feelings? Have you ever been rude, unkind? Have you deliberately ignored the needs of another? Have you turned your head away and chose to ignore a problem? Have you lived in denial of your actions? Have you inflicted harm on another? Have you stopped loving someone and didn't give them the reasons why? Have you cheated on a spouse or significant other? Or lied to a parent? Have you hit your children? Have you been deceitful? Have you ever acted in a way that hurt another? Let's take this scenario in an extreme case. A murderer will experience the pain they inflicted on other people whose lives they have injured. The pain of the person whose life they took, as well as those connected to the person whose life was taken. Imagine the magnitude of that pain. It too, ripples outward. We are all connected, so our pain is connected too. We are all creators of joy and creators of pain. How much we create of either one is our free will. There was a source that created that pain, and so to the Source that pain returns. That person, the murderer, will feel the collective pain he or she created. We will finally understand the other side of this dynamic. Because you are not just you on the other side, you are also everyone else's spirit. Once we feel the discomfort from what we have created, and we fully realize just how much pain we have caused, there is the opportunity to transform it. When we have grasped just how strongly our effect has had on others, we can lean into it and experience it, and that is when we experience truth. We are no longer coming from our egoic, individual self. We don't have agendas or mental illnesses. We aren't coming from a place of fear and dysfunction, which are all human aspects of the spirit. Instead, we are ascended to a space where we can understand our actions and thus create the opportunity for forgiveness. We transcend the human experience and enter into the Source space, the Collective Whole. We realize what we have done to others, was ultimately done to ourselves. The separation of you and me is clear: there is no separation. When you take someone's joy, in any capacity, you are only taking joy from yourself. We finally understand this concept as Spirit/Energy form. Imagine if we fully grasped this and lived this out in our physical form! How much better life could be! Although we are limited, we are capable of learning. We are capable of understanding that what we do to others, we are really doing to ourselves.

What will it take for us to apply this? Awareness. Meditation. Non-reaction to situations. The art of remembering who we really are at all moments. To not be offended by another's actions toward us. To remember we are the Source. We are creators. Reconditioning. Grace. Discipline. Faith. Love. Honesty. That is what it's going to take!

I repeat, which side do you want to be on? The creator of more joy? Or pain? What you do unto others you do to yourself. I often think how fortunate I feel I am that I have not chosen to be the Hitler in this current lifetime I am living. I can have compassion for those who are intentionally causing pain to anyone. For those people will receive a deluge of horror when they have crossed over. Yes, ultimately, they too will cross into "heaven" because the Source (God) knows the smaller hs has faults and limitations. Source knows that we are not fully conscious and understanding of the laws of spirit. But there is no way it can be an easy or good feeling of existence when you are constantly harming others. Energetically it goes against our Spirit nature, and somewhere within us, it simply doesn't feel good. I can be grateful I am choosing to be who I am in this lifetime. The Source does not discriminate against these energies, since they were born out of the Source itself. People hate when I say that the evil humans who do horrible things will also ultimately experience heaven. And I understand that. But when we can look at aspects of life from a much higher vantage point, we remember we are all the same learning curve in life. We aren't perfect here. We aren't meant to be. We are meant to live openly, freely, to propel energy forward. We are meant to learn. We are meant to love. We are meant to fight. We are meant to disagree. We are meant to make resolutions. It all works toward our evolution. It's all part of the birth, life, death cycle.

Many argue that this paradigm of what you to do others you are really doing to yourself is a self-centered pursuit to fulfill your own happiness and joy. But it's quite the opposite. When we seek only to make ourselves happy, then that is a self-centered intention, and therefore what will come back to you, is the purest form of what you have given out, a selfish pursuit of happiness. Remember, spirit knows what is True. Spirit knows the deepest core of all creation. We can't hide anything or fake anything in pure Spirit/Energy form. Ever give a false compliment to someone? You knew you weren't being truthful but said it anyway. If you said it to be condescending, the Universe knows that, and condescending remarks will be sent back to you. If you said it to encourage someone with the true intention of helping them, then that will also be mirrored back to you in life! Just be careful, when you give a false compliment, and it doesn't really help that other person, but instead keeps them stuck, believing something they shouldn't, then that also bounces back to you if what you said didn't feel good on the subatomic particle level in your soul. That is where creation exists. That is the space that our human existence is boiled down to, the core truth. And that is the source of creation. Honesty is a skill that must be fostered and encouraged. Creating a space to be *self* honest is key.

As you cross over and unwind the tape of your life, you start to experience the One-ness that we all are. Then you completely let go of all the physical, and you are suspended in that consciousness of

One-ness. There is no longer a physical body to confine us and create limitations. There is no more separation, and you realize all along you were actually everyone else too.

For those of us still here in the physical world, because we have such limited thoughts about what life and death are, our black-and-white thinking prevents us from considering that there is more to us than our physical being. It's hard for our human selves to wrap our minds around the concept that we are all spirit and energy that is simply housed within our physical bodies. The limited belief system most of us have automatically creates unhappiness and automatically creates the illusion of separation when someone dies. We believe we are just our bodies and the personalities. And when death happens, those things disappear from our sensory experience. The concept of gone is enacted, and complete death or absence of life is what seems true. The "you're either alive or dead" mentality is devastating. And it's completely false.

Do you know how computer programs work? Basically, you can create a computer program that does something specific. That computer program will do just that one thing, and it will not operate outside that one thing because it doesn't know how. It never has a "thought" to try something different or to expand its capabilities. Quantum computing is changing this. Finally, we are understanding the particle and wave theory! Our brains work exactly the same way, operating according to our current belief systems and things we've learned or thought we've learned over the years until we "reprogram" our thoughts. Unlike the computer program, our brain is capable of thoughts and expansion. We always have the option to upgrade our personal "operating programs" to rethink the concept of life and death and challenge any belief system by introducing new information and experiences. You are doing that right now, whether you realize it or not, simply by reading this book.

When you begin to think of death differently and to realize that it's a transition instead of "the end," you begin to understand that the stresses of your day-to-day life don't matter as much. You don't stay fixated on them, as you will easily recognize the trivial to the profound.

Once you get to this stage of awareness, you can decide which human moments do matter. Where do you want to focus your energy? Is it the great car? The house? Or is it the people in your life? Creating a family and a network of supportive loving people around you? You get to choose what matters to you, what is real, and what feels good. This is how you start creating your own heaven on earth. You can start to find honest pleasure in the things that matter to you and let go of the things that don't matter as much in the big scheme of your current life. When you redirect your thoughts to the things that matter and bring you pleasure, you'll experience more of it and less of the things that are negative.

The Beyond, Other Side and Afterlife are all within. It's been there the entire time, fully accessible by merely shifting your focus on it. Again. "It's been here all along!" is the mantra of Dorothy that we must adopt!

Deborah Hanlon

16

Reincarnation

If we talk about life after death, why don't we talk about
life before life?
~Goswami

Let's now throw a monkey wrench into everything. Let's talk about how we have all done this living thing already and in fact, multiple times. Have you ever had a feeling you have been here before? Have you ever even considered the idea of a "recycled soul?" I remember when the concept of recycling was really becoming popular. (Crazy to say, I remember when we didn't have modern-day recycling.) As the idea of taking a previously used item and using its essence to make something new out of it emerged in popular society, it clicked inside me. I know it sounds overly simplified, and perhaps it is. But I remember feeling inside me, maybe I was recycled.

Maybe I have been here before in a different incarnation, and when a new need for me arose, I was born into a new body, and a new use for me was made. I personally love that idea. You may not. It may make you feel insignificant. It makes me feel connected to all of time, all people. Everywhere. It makes me feel I belong, but not to any one particular race or religion, but to the world and all of time.

I love the concept of reincarnation. It reinforces that there is no end for me. I am useful and have value. I'll keep coming back, and I'll continue to have purpose and create more meaning for myself and others. I'll continue to be a small, yet significant part of the whole. I'll always belong. I'll always come back, do my part. It will come to a conclusion and then happen all over again. I think it's kind of amazing. And we are all a part of this cycle.

Or again, is this even the case? Are we recycled, or are we having memories of the brief moments and for whatever reasons, are we holding onto someone else's stuff and confusing them as our own? When we come from Source or the Collective Whole, is it possible that we are somehow taking an individual memory or experience that we witnessed while we were there?

If the Collective Whole contains all the information about what has come before, what is currently happening, and what will come, is it then possible that reincarnation isn't really in fact, being born again, but rather a snafu in the cosmos where we remember and confuse someone else's life as our own? Are we tapping into a small portion of history? And if so, for what? Why does that happen? Is it here to help us and teach us? Or is this a glitch in the Greatest Computer of all time, the Universe? Or, as humans, are we tapping into a prior individual through the Collective Whole?

Reincarnation has been a concept known to sages for thousands of years. It's not a new concept, and it's a natural mindset in many parts of the world. It's only a fairly new concept in the United States. The song *Galileo*[15] by the Indigo Girls is about reincarnation! What a brilliant song to bring to the masses via music.

Can we understand that we are so much more than the memories in this lifetime? Can we understand fully the continuum we are all working in? Life doesn't end with our death. Our cells, our energy fields carry information from physical lifetime to physical lifetime. If we understood that perhaps some of our fears and irrational concerns and phobias were born in another lifetime, we would have so much more insight and thus control over ourselves. I believe we would have an incredible amount of peace and opportunity for healing across generations.

Imagine having an unexplained fear in your current lifetime of being afraid of flying. (Thank you Indigo Girls!) Once it's discovered the fear came from a previous life, where you have died in an aviation crash, you can not only heal your fear in this lifetime, but on some level, I believe we also have the chance to heal the prior lifetimes' fear felt right before that impending death. Wrap your head around this one. So, say the above scenario occurred. In a prior life, you died in a plane crash, but in this lifetime, you were able to revisit it and bring healing to it. Say, through past life regression, and/or other techniques, you were able to communicate a sense of peace to your former self to assure yourself that all will be well. Perhaps, once your current self does this, it changes the entire experience. Perhaps the angels and presences that are often described, seen, and felt at the time of death are the future versions of yourself. Go ahead, read that again. Yes, your current self, in trying to heal an earlier wound, can actually communicate to your former self to set things straight. How? Because, we are a continuum, there is no such thing as time. The you that you are right now is still the *you* you were.

All of it is happening simultaneously, and the illusion of life having a cause-and-effect stream isn't true at all. The cause is the effect, and the effect is there for the cause. It's intermingled, happening at the same time. Just as we learned we can place ourselves in other energy fields by thinking of them, we can also place ourselves in other aspects of our past lives.

In fact, new research from the Emory University School of Medicine reported in *The Telegraph*[16] shows that our memories can be handed down through our ancestry. Generation to generation, we can pass down fears, phobias, and experiences via our DNA.

"Researchers at the Emory University School of Medicine, in Atlanta, found that mice can pass on learned information about traumatic or stressful experiences–in this case, a fear of the smell of cherry blossom–to subsequent generations. Scientists trained mice to fear the scent of a cherry blossom by using an electric shock. The offspring were also found to fear the scent as well even though they were never around it before. They had no logical reason to fear this scent, other than the fear was passed down through their DNA. This suggests that experiences are somehow transferred from the brain into the genome, allowing them to be passed on to later generations," according to Marcus Pembrey, Professor of Paediatric Genetics at University College London, who said the work provided "compelling evidence for the biological transmission of memory."

This brings up an entirely other discussion of how and where memories are stored in humans, if in fact they are even stored. How and will we ever be able to measure and "locate" consciousness. Thoughts, memories, and beliefs? What in fact are they anyway? There is nothing tangible (as far as we know at this time) to prove these thoughts, beliefs and memories exist, but clearly, they do and are manifested in the physical world as such.

There is nothing more powerful than being regressed by a true professional. It's is one thing to have a psychic or medium tell you what or who you were in another lifetime, and it's an entirely different thing to have yourself actually experience it. When you feel the emotions and problems you experienced before, you activate the memory or consciousness sharing in this lifetime. You bring it to the top of your awareness, where you are able to then process and either accept or erase a prior participation in life.

Carol Bowman, renowned past-life regressionist and colleague explains that we are not born a blank slate but rather "a soul rich with wisdom from many lifetimes." On her website, she further details how our past-life memories carry an "energetic charge" and can continue to affect us.

A regression is a full sensory experience. It is through the actual participation of going back to these lifetimes that creates the ability to heal the possible negative charges attached to those memories. If things were left undone, we have the advantage to allow it to be so, or to fix things in this lifetime. When we make any memory conscious from this lifetime or another, we can heal it. She states PLR (Past Life Regression) is a spiritual healing as it is completely separate from any religious teachings. It is perhaps mistakenly linked as a religious belief simply because we are dealing with the soul's journey and getting in touch with it. You do not have to be a religious person, a follower of any human-created way or method of describing or explaining your soul self and human self. When you are regressed by a professional (as recommended by Carol and me—Do not go to just anyone for this), you are not just entering a juxtaposition of your current soul and your former self. You are touching the in-between lives as well. It's powerful. People cry, have rage, relive trauma, all for the purpose of opening it up and releasing it. I also see how compassion for all is created when we fully understand PLR. It sets up the forum for no longer allowing ourselves to judge one another for our human actions. Who is to say I wasn't once someone who inflicted great harm on thousands? I can often get to a place of pure compassion for those who "choose" to do evil in this lifetime. I actually embrace the concept of gratitude that I did not choose that past this lifetime. But am infinitely aware that it could have been me who chose the lesser paths in times gone by. I have been both the murderer and the healer many times! Who am I to judge? We are only here to learn. We waste time on judgments.

I've been regressed numerous times by Carol Bowman and by Dr. Brian Weiss, another pioneer in the field of PLR. I've experienced a dozen or so lifetimes, all which revealed very pertinent information for me in my current life situations. Those regressions provided me, if nothing else, deep insight on certain dynamics of current relationships and why certain relationships are either as strong or as weak and why. There were roots to so many of my interactions with people and knowing what those were provided that last link of information for healing for myself in this lifetime. I constantly wonder what else I've been and what I've done in other lifetimes that have all led up to my writing this book. What has helped me do what I do and be who I am. I often think about my energy field. Did I do this in another lifetime? Or were the tables flipped? Was I a perpetrator? Was I a murderer? And today do I sit with my previous victims, only in this life, my job is to help heal them rather than harm them? Are all my clients people I've harmed in some other way while in another body? Or was I shaman in another life working with the same masses? Have I sat with and had mutual healings before? Am I to continue my work from another lifetime? Or does what I do and who I am today have nothing to do with any of my previous lifetimes? How will my work and identity in this lifetime manifest in the next one? Again, I don't have empirical evidence other than what I feel I know. I think there is a thread. All lifetimes end up being the same one. Eventually we are all linked by experiences. We are the giver and receiver. We are the perpetrator and the victim. We are the healer and the disease. We are the child and the parent.

Through regression, I have extracted key components to situations in previous lifetimes to current relationships and jobs I've had here. I've understood current relationships on a much deeper level from experiencing myself in previous incarnations. I experienced another lifetime with my ex-husband. We were married before in another lifetime. In that life, he doted on me, was very wealthy, and I apparently betrayed him. I believe, to a degree, that we were placed in this lifetime in an attempt to heal that wound to him. Unfortunately, I may have simply reopened it this go around! Not because I betrayed him though, but because our marriage dissolved, and we went our separate ways. Or, maybe it is in fact healed, which is why we went our separate ways. You would have to ask him his thoughts on that. I feel healed. But perhaps it isn't, and we must go again in another lifetime. Yikes!

I've experienced a deep understanding of my relationship with my niece and why I felt such a strong degree of responsibility for her, even though I was only twelve years old when she was born. I remember feeling that she was mine. And, in another lifetime, she was. She was my granddaughter, and I her grandfather. I was her main caregiver and I didn't prepare her to be able to live without me. On my deathbed, I watched her grieve for me terribly, and it was in that instant of my passing, that I knew I had to come back and fix this separation anxiety. I had to show her that I would be here even when I wasn't with her in this lifetime. Having that session helped heal me of a decade or more of deep guilt for all the times she was taken from me, meaning she had to move and live with her parents rather than me, her aunt. Every time, I felt I was failing her and letting her down. After this regression, I was able to understand the dynamic more deeply and put things in their natural order, and I believe we have healed the relationship in this lifetime.

Do you suffer from unexplained phobias? Have you ever met a person you just instantly clicked with? Or do you know someone who drives you crazy and upsets you for apparently no reason, someone you just do not like and really have no logical reason to? Have you ever met someone you didn't really want to get to know, but you ultimately felt you had to? I had this feeling about my ex-husband. Something inside me told me I had to go out with him, even though I initially wasn't interested in him. Well, that led to getting married, having children, and voila! The rest is history. Now in hindsight, I can see how perfect the Universe created for me, for us, what it needed to.

Have you ever traveled to a new place only to feel like you have been there before? Do you have frequent historical time period-related dreams? Do you or your children have a propensity for learning about a particular era or have extensive knowledge about a particular topic without formal education regarding it? Have you ever felt you weren't supposed to be in the body you are currently born in? Did you ever hear a child speak about "when I used to be big"? Or say to their mom, "when I was your mommy"?

How does reincarnation play into all this? What does it have anything to do with our current lives and subsequent death? Notice interactions and themes that occur in this lifetime. They may tell a story of another time.

How do you know if you have been here before? Notice the clues!

Growth Opportunity

Can you think of all your relationships in your current life and notice any themes? Do you tend to attract a certain type of person to be around you? How do you react to certain personalities? Do men make you anxious? Or women make you feel inferior? Do you have a fear of getting pregnant?

Many women with that fear when regressed find out they died in childbirth before. I find that astounding. Sometimes, all that is blocking a woman from conceiving is a deep fear of death stemming from a whole other lifetime. Some have reported being able to get pregnant after they had a successful regression to rid them of the initial cause of their fear.

Sometimes we keep attracting the same people, scenarios, and experiences into our lives to resolve them. We are constantly given a new life and new opportunity to create something different. How do we do that? With awareness. If you continue to see yourself as the one finite being you are in this very moment, the opportunity for deeper connection to everything else is dramatically lessened. Once you remember that you have, are, and will continue to lead several lives, you will begin to see life as just that, the Continuum. And life isn't as perplexing. You learn to go with the flow, have less resistance to what is, gain a healthy and natural curiosity for life and learning. You won't be as easily offended. We take much less personally, doubt ourselves less, and understand things at an almost indescribable level of consciousness. Sounds good, right?

Some may argue that our interactions with one another come only from our current lifetime and experiences. We can absolutely ask, is this all coming from this lifetime of conditioning? Perhaps. But what if it's deeper than that? What if our conditioning itself is a role played by our parents and caregivers given to us in order to work out past lives? What if, everyone you meet, everywhere, at all times, is a role being played to help you overcome the past? What if life is really like the movie *The Truman Show*? In this film, Jim Carrey plays the role of Truman Burbank, a made-up identity of a child who was raised to believe his world was real and true, when really in fact his entire life is a script. Every inch of it was recorded and filmed. All of the players in this life were actors, playing the roles alongside Truman. The only one in the entire fictitious town of Seahaven who didn't know this was a TV show was Truman. The object of people's voyeurism, Truman lived a harmless, predictable life. But eventually, he began to question his humanity. He began to dream of traveling to faraway places like Fiji. Unfortunately, his going to Fiji would end the program, so instead, the producers tried to manipulate Truman's fears by setting up a fake storm at sea when he was a young boy. The seas swelled, and his "father" fell into the ocean. This was choreographed for Truman to develop a fear of the ocean, which would hopefully stop him from ever wanting to leave the island town. It didn't. In fact, this discomfort in life, caused pain, which caused him to question the outside world even more.

It was through this pain and questioning and challenging what was formerly assumed, that Truman was able to discover his true reality. He was merely a player, and his world was a stage, just as

Shakespeare suggests. He found his truth, that his identity was only based on what others put on him, and yet, intrinsically, there was a drive to know himself and his world on a deeper level.

Like *The Truman Show*, we are all holding roles. We get to decide our own roles, but so often we get lured into these roles as givens and truths. Rarely do we challenge or transcend them. But when we do, we undergo a metamorphosis. In *The Truman Show*, everyone was playing their part to get Truman to believe a particular truth. What if that is exactly what life is like here for us? The only difference is, everyone here is playing their roles unconsciously. We don't even know we are doing it! At least in *The Truman Show*, everyone understood their roles *as* roles. They clocked in, played their part, and left. It was clear- for everyone except Truman. Under this paradigm, our roles, would be even more dramatic. We are all playing into each other's beliefs, without even knowing it.

Yikes! Does your head hurt? Because mine sure does. What I am suggesting, is what if you had certain themes, fears, issues, whatever you want to call it, to heal from another lifetime. This lifetime, your caregivers are "chosen" to get you steered in the right direction of healing. What is the right direction? Well, at first, it's to experience the pain, so that in the pain, you seek to find a different route—a different alternative or truth to what was previously understood. Pain ultimately leads to healing. Pain can be the mind/body/spirits' watchdog, when we listen. It tells us something isn't right and hopefully causes us to remedy that before more pain is brought on. Everyone is helping each other with this process. How amazing is that?

All of this is stuff we learn and co-conspire as humans. The human selves (hs) are running around playing these roles with little to no awareness. It isn't until we consult the Higher Self (HS,) the Soul, that we can make connections and put things together. There is no drama in the upper realms. All things exist to balance out everything else everywhere. Nothing is seen as wrong or bad. But instead, each experience owns its own timing and placement. Again, do you want to live as a human—basically blind and filled with so much uncertainty? Or would you rather open yourself up and come from a much larger, connected picture and realize you are everyone, and everyone is you? There is intense power in that space. That is where we reside when we die. This is the space of perfection, of being in the collective whole, while being in human form. That is again, the space, the mindset, the consciousness sharing, whatever you want to call it, that we must become acclimated in order to stay above the lower-density vibrations of being in the third dimension, also known as the material world. This is the space where all is well for the goodness of all.

Your personal healing will occur when you align yourself with the goodness of the whole and stop worrying about all the itty-bitty details of the here and now.

Deborah Hanlon

17
What is Healing & How Do You Do It?

What is healing? It's a restoration of Self to wholeness. What is wholeness? It's the existence of being in alignment with everything. It's a reconnection to all of it, the Collective Whole. Life is training us to RE-member that we are more than our small selves. We continue to sign up, if you will, for these experiences in the attempt to grow and learn from them. Each experience reminds us we are alive. And when we are connected to being alive, we are in alignment with the continuum of life, rather than a finite process of life and birth. But again, guess what? We are already healed. We are already in perfect alignment with all that is, both inside ourselves and outside in the outer realms. Why are we so desperately seeking to be perfect when really what we need to realize is that we are already an expression of perfection? We must learn to come closer to acceptance, and realize the agenda of our hs really is short-sighted. We must remember, there is always a higher, bigger, better picture working through and around us. We would drastically reduce our misery meters if we could do this even just one percent more of the time.

If we are choosing to manifest ourselves into a body, we start taking on the identity and forming the thoughts and beliefs of being human. We live our lives, and when we die, we reconnect to our source again. All along, we've been this energy field, and we realize that when we die. When we reincarnate, or when we're reborn, we realize we're always being reborn.

Imagine that people/spirits are all the ocean. When we're born, it's like taking a cup of water from that ocean. When we die, we're returned into the ocean. Every time someone is born or dies, they are returned into the ocean or taken out of the ocean. Because we're all one. Our spirits are like the ocean; it's all the same. Ultimately, all particles of the ocean will mix with all other parts. We remain separated and yet whole as well.

Metaphysical healing is based on the belief that our thoughts create our reality, and that there is a connection between the mind and body, and if you want to have a healthy body, you must also have a healthy mind.

According to metaphysics, if we have negative thought patterns, then we are more likely to become ill than someone who is in the habit of positive thought patterns. When someone becomes ill, metaphysical healers will encourage them to reverse their negative thought patterns and become more positive. It is believed that metaphysical healing occurs both on a spiritual and physical level. You'll see evidence of successful metaphysical healing even in western cultures where doctors treat illnesses with medication and surgeries. Doctors encourage their patients to remain positive throughout their treatments, proving that to improve the health of the body, a person needs to understand and connect with energy.

Metaphysical healing (sometimes called spiritual healing) encourages the individual's own spirit (or energy) to heal the physical body it is housed in. It puts the power of healing in your own hands, under one of the main laws of metaphysics: The Law of Freedom, which says that each person is responsible for his or her own thoughts, actions, and energy. This makes us accountable for our own illness, and pain, but also puts us in the driver's seat as the person able to cure our ailments.

Some negative thought patterns and habits contribute to the type of illness or pain you experience. If you have chronic lower back pain, for example, you're probably spending a lot of time worrying about money and the lack of money. Under the Law of Freedom and metaphysical healing, you could change your negative patterns of thought surrounding money, make a budget, and meditate to relieve yourself of the back pain.

Emotions of anger, guilt, and resentment will lead to illness or pain. Emotions of self-love and self-worth lead to healing.

When people say they have been healed by God or Jesus, it is considered miraculous healing. There is generally no medical explanation for people who have experienced miraculous or faith healing. Many people believe that a ritualistic practice of prayer can cause divine intervention in the form of spiritual and physical healing of disease or disability.

Sometimes a process of spontaneous healing, or spontaneous remission occurs. A person might be in the hospital with cancer or some other terrible disease. Doctors may say they only have a few weeks or even a few hours to live, and then, suddenly, the disease is gone, and there is no explanation. Proof of this is Anita Moorjani's previously mentioned book.

People come to me hoping for answers, messages, validation, hope, forgiveness, peace of mind, a last chance, or just to know they are OK. To hear anything. When someone dies, no matter what the circumstances are, we all always feel there was more we could have said or done for them. We feel, for whatever reasons, real or imagined, that that person didn't really know how much they meant to us. It kills us.

Healing comes from being free. Free of toxins, or toxic

thoughts and feelings. Free of worry. Healing comes from being in the present. Being OK with what is. Being able to know that all is well. Healing is a state of mind, and it affects our bodies, minds, and spirits. When you know your loved ones are more than fine, then you can begin your own healing process. The focus can be on ourselves and each other here, rather than worrying about all the woulda, coulda, shoulda. Your grieving is the vehicle for healing. I promise you this.

As I've already said, there's no right or wrong way to grieve. People ask me all the time when they can first come to see a medium. Is there a timeframe where someone won't come through? Every medium is different. I have a harder (but definitely not impossible) time feeling someone who has passed within two to eight weeks. Some mediums say not to come to them until it's been a year since the person has passed. I don't have a full explanation for this, and it's not consistent for everyone. And yet, I have connected with many people who have passed within this timeframe.

People have mixed emotions coming to a medium, especially for the first time. For one, when we think about it, no one wants to *have* to see a medium. No one wants to experience the pain and disconnection from any loved one. Upon entering our doors, people sometimes become emotional. The reality of what is about to transpire, or the expectations of such come to a head. I've been told in sad tones and angry ones, "You know, Deborah, I do NOT want to be here with you. You know, that right? This sucks that I am coming here with you." And I get it. It does suck. Big time.

My advice for everyone about to embark on this journey is to become aware of all your expectations prior to your appointment. Everyone (including me, as a medium) wants to hear very specific information, details, code words, nicknames, specific messages, memories, distinguishing characteristics, etc. Make note of all of these expectations. And try to let go and detach from them. Very hard, I know, but so often we are all so hooked on hearing what we want to hear that we initially miss out on all the messages they are trying to convey. People send me emails weeks, months, and sometimes years after a session to tell me they didn't hear the messages the very day of their session but were able to make sense of it all later, when they were able to process it all differently. Just remember that!

I am not a fan of mediums who allow clients to come back over and over and over too soon. I have a six-month rule, and oftentimes, even that is too soon to keep coming back. I feel once a year is more than sufficient. After that, I notice sessions become more about the here and now, and how to move forward with all your new personal tools of strength and growth that have occurred for you while grieving. Connecting with your loved ones on the other side most certainly can take the edge off your fears and sadness, but it cannot, in my opinion, be used as the *only* way to cope. We must learn to transition from having a physical/human relationship to a spiritual one. That process takes time and lots of introspection, expression, and sorrow. There is no quick fix to your grief. The process is not fun, but it lends us the ultimate way to take massive strides in our growth.

Deborah Hanlon

18
How to Create Heaven on Earth

Whether you think you can, or think you can't, you're right.
~Henry Ford

So, how can we create a sense of Heaven on Earth? What is it about the consciousness of the deceased that makes it heavenly? As we just discussed, when we die, we are returned to our essence, our spirit, our normal, natural, good, and pure energy, which puts us all at peace. We are restored to our full whole selves. We are returned to our Higher Selves. We are aware, finally, of how connected and truly the same we all are. We release the need to be "right." We acknowledge the fact that everyone has a world view, and no one's is incorrect, it's simply theirs.

Nonjudgment. As I see it, the key to creating heaven on your earth lies in the art of nonjudgment. You can begin to create your own heaven on earth by doing just that. Release your need to be right. Realize your opinion. While it matters, it's only just that, one opinion among millions. Recognize that no matter what, your actions matter, and everything you do has an effect on everyone else in the world. Your reactions matter just as much.

Most of our issues and tensions come from interpersonal reactions to each other. We get sad, frustrated, angry with others when they don't see our point of view, or when someone is blatantly rude or mean. And that's going to happen. We get closer to heaven when we don't take personal offense and when we don't create a story around why so and so did such and such to us. We don't need to create reasons, whether justified or not.

We are quick to judge others. The deceased recognize there is a learning curve, that we all do things we may not understand, but at the end of the day, or at the end of our lives, we see that, for the most part, we are all trying our best, and we do the best with what we know at any given time. We can give ourselves and each other compassion. Understand that sometimes humans act without compassion or awareness of others. It's going to happen. Embrace your inner asshole so you can see that in others. There is no need to generalize that all people are selfish. We are all selfish at different times. Hopefully, not too many people are around catching us!

Yes, we get uptight about the actions of others, but we must release that. Do your part. Be your best self and recognize that not even you are perfect. There have been moments where you too were perceived as an a-hole or uncaring. There have been times you didn't act perfectly, and while we want to have fewer of those moments, once we can see the non-perfection in ourselves, we will release our need for everyone else around us to be perfect.

Have you ever yelled out at someone while in your car driving because they cut you off? Or have you ever been standing on a line and someone just blatantly cut in front of you? In these moments, our egos get quite upset. We feel someone personally and deliberately decided to take our place. Whether that is true or not isn't the issue. What is the issue, is have you ever unknowingly cut someone off while driving or in a line? No? How do you know? I'm pretty sure, there have been times where you too have been so stuck in your own head that you missed moments when you were unconscious. If you say, "No, I've never done that," that tells me how completely unconscious you really are. Of course, you have. We all have. So, perhaps in those moments where someone cut you off, they were simply acting unconsciously. Yes, that's frustrating, but it's not about you. And again, when we recognize the moments we have been less than stellar, whether deliberately or not, we will have less anger toward the actions of others. Instead, we can say, "They are simply unaware in this moment." That's a lot better than saying, "What a #(*$&^ JERK!", and then holding onto the energy of that for who knows how long.

Tolerance, acceptance, and compassion are the keys to how we must treat others and first, ourselves.

Time. The deceased aren't caught up in a concept of time. They are in a space of conscious awareness that is literally eternal and timeless.

We, while in physical form, do absolutely experience the concept of time. Seasons may come and go, our bodies age, things "die." We are sometimes petrified by the concept of having no time to accomplish things, and yet, we get paralyzed by the concept and never do anything about it. If you feel you don't have time, then that is all the more reason to create time for things you want to do. The deceased realize that everything is temporary. Each moment is just that, a moment. And nothing ever stays the same. Being able to become present in each moment allows us to see things more clearly. When we experience the current moment, everything is OK, even when it isn't. We may not like what the current moment is, but when we are in it, feeling it, and not running up into our heads to try to either escape it or explain *why* it's happening, the moment is much more bearable. Actions become clear. Everything simply is what it is, rather than our hoping, wishing, waiting, filling ourselves with desire to experience something that isn't right now. So much of our grief, and pain come from our avoidance of what is, rather than facing it.

Sh*t thinking. The deceased are clear on what is happening. They aren't entertaining what isn't happening. They exist only in each moment. Humans are so hung up on what isn't happening way more than what actually is. This causes us tremendous amounts of unnecessary stress and unrest. We are literally creating our own uncertainty by entertaining negative scary thoughts of doom and gloom every day. I'm certain if you had a recorder of your thousands of mindless thoughts a day, you would hear yourself thinking about the what-ifs way more than the what-is. What if so and so passes away? What if I never get married? What if I don't have a job? What if I get sick? What if I never recover from my grief? What if people think such and such of me? What if I fail? What if? What if? What if? Why do we not think in terms of what-if in the positive? Have you spent time observing your thoughts saying, What if everything works out? What if I get a raise? What if I get into the college of my dreams? What if I meet the perfect partner for myself? What if I have a wonderful peaceful and abundant life? This is how we are meant to think, and you are the creator of it all.

There is nothing either good or bad, but thinking makes it so.
~William Shakespeare

Apologize and have forgiveness. The deceased have also had the opportunity to truly understand the ramifications of their actions on earth. Does this mean everyone gets to experience bliss, even those who did bad things here on earth? And while I promised to not get all religious in this book, I am intrigued by words stated by Jesus.

In the hours before he died, Jesus assured his apostle he would be with him in his heavenly Kingdom. He later promised a condemned criminal: "You will be with me in Paradise" (Luke 23:43)

People normally do not like to hear this when I say it, but yes, even those who did bad deeds here on earth get the benefit of being restored into their purest selves. Finally, in death, we see who we were not in life. Jesus seems to have been one of the Ultimate humans who understood the difference between Human and Higher Self. My favorite line in the Bible from when I was a young Catholic schoolgirl, and I didn't have a clue what all these religious traditions were really about, was from Jesus when he was on the cross nearing his death.

Then Jesus said, "Father, forgive them, for they do not know what they are doing." (Luke 23:24) I loved this from the beginning, and today have a deeper connection to these words than ever before. In my interpretation, he is saying, "Universe, forgive these humans, for they are too small to understand what they are doing. They are limited and only know what they believe and nothing more. Once in the Kingdom of Heaven, they will understand."

Trust in the unseen. There is a level of trust, a suspension of the logical mind that is required for us to experience Heaven on Earth. In order to receive and actually witness the miracles that can and do occur for ourselves we must trust in the process. We must remember that the "Universe" is smarter than we are. It has the Collective Whole in its highest good. We must believe and trust that we are always going to be placed in a situation that is the best possible for us at any given moment. Then, we need to let go. Let go of our desire. Let go of things having to be a certain way. Remember, our way is limited. The Universe's way is pure potentiality!

Growth Opportunity

What are your concepts of heaven?
If you're going to create heaven on earth, you need to figure

out what "heaven" is for you. If you didn't have any religious upbringing, you're either going to really struggle with this, or you're a blank slate, and you have the advantage to understand. Identify what holds you back here in the physical. Pinpoint characteristics about yourself you would like to upgrade or let go. Ask yourself, "What is holding me back?" Imagine your life, and describe it in detail of what life would look and feel like for you if you can let go of what limits you. What are you telling yourself are the reasons success, happiness, peace, or whatever else you are seeking are out of reach for you? What is your excuse? The parts of your life you are living from your head, your egoic self, are undoubtedly are what is causing you grief stress and tension. You can let these aspects go. You can live in a more heavenly state of mind.

Some people will visit a psychic in order to find out if and when they're going to find true love or get a new job. When the psychic tells them, yes, you will meet someone next month, or you will get the new job you're applying for, that thought gets so planted into the conscious and subconscious minds that it literally happens because the person began believing in it so strongly (which is half the battle). We create our realities with our thoughts, feelings, and beliefs. We are what we believe, and we manifest what we believe. This is why it is so important to recognize some of the old thoughts and belief systems you're carrying around, so you can choose whether it is a belief you want to keep or change.

You don't need a psychic to tell you something is going to happen in order to shift your thinking and believing. You can do that for yourself and learn how to create the reality you want for yourself and to recognize and listen to your own intuition. It's time to create your own "Heaven on Earth."

Think what-if, and think big in terms of happiness. Press yourself on what it is you feel you want and need in this moment to help you feel better. Heaven is just that. What you have done all along with all of your negative what-if thoughts is imagine into living what hell is like. It's no wonder our lives are complicated, stressful, and draining. We often create them to be so. We have created a hell on earth and can equally create our heaven. It just all depends on where you choose to place your focus.

Growth Opportunity

What is holding you back? Free write a list, or paragraph of the things that are preventing you from living the life you really want. Write down everything. Do not hold anything back! If you feel raising your children is holding you back from having a career, but feel guilty for feeling that, write it down anyway. Get real and honest with your responses. What is holding you back? What has to be obliterated from your life in order for you to expand?

Next write what you fear may (or may not) happen if you lived your own Kingdom of Heaven? Sometimes, we hold ourselves back not because we feel incapable, but because we are afraid of what will or might change if we decide to live a more authentic life. I remember knowing deep inside that as I upgraded my self-esteem and personal goals, I would no longer want to be married. I allowed this fear to prevent me from taking any steps forward on myself for years. In my situation, I did end up getting divorced, but that is most certainly not everyone's path. I allowed this fear to slow me down and literally almost prevented me from my current Heaven on Earth. It became my opportunity to either create heaven or hell. Today, my ex-husband and I have a good relationship, and we manage our kids' full lives well. For me, this is heaven.

Transcending thoughts and beliefs that hold us back. In order to overcome the thoughts and belief systems that hold us back and prevent us from reaching our goals or living our personal dream lifestyle, we need to understand that we are always spirit, even while we are human.

We believe what is "true" because of our human identities, our childhoods, and the thoughts and belief systems we've established throughout our lifetimes. Again, go back and think about your childhood. Much of your identity and what you believe has come from your first nine years or so of life. Did your parents/caregivers frequently express concern about not having enough money? You might have the belief system that you will never have enough money to do the things you want to do as a result. Having this belief doesn't mean you can never change your mindset about money. Once you recognize what this belief system is, you can start taking steps to create a new mindset.

It does take work! Magical thinking will not land you in a new life. Your new life requires commitment to a new way of thinking and stepping out of your comfort zone as often as possible. It requires work and effort. Usually the hardest part, is identifying your old patterns and creating a new world-view template to follow. Once that framework is set, you need mindful attention to what you want and the belief that it's possible put things into motion. That's the effort! My Energy Transformation Awareness classes go more into depth on how to make all these changes and expedite the process.

So, let's get this straight. If we are naturally Perfect and Whole, and we have the potential for this level of peace and perfection as humans, why do we need to go through all the negative stuff? Why even bother coming here if we have to work at creating Heaven on Earth? Why don't we just stay in the Energetic/Spiritual form in bliss?

We are here to awaken from the illusion of our separateness.
~Thich Nhat Hanh

We all come to this planet to experience ourselves! When we are contained in the Collective Whole, we don't experience ourselves as individuals. Sometimes, we like to experience ourselves on the smaller scale because once we are small and limited (or we perceive ourselves to be), then we crave the return to our intrinsic form of whole and infinite. And once we are infinite, we desire the experience of separateness again. This ebb and flow of our reality is what causes forward movement. Evolution. We continue to gain back an aspect of ourselves that feels missing when we are born into our lesser selves. We continue to raise the stakes and push our limits, which expands the Collective Whole, which is the literal force that creates infinity. The CW expands forever, because it's fueled by our desire while we are in the limited mindset. We are the expansion that brings us back to ourselves, being whole. Did I lose you? Think water cycle. The water from the oceans, evaporates, rises up to the atmosphere, become either cooled or warmed by the air, travels, rains, or snows back down onto mountains, flows into the rivers and streams, only to find its way back to the ocean. The Water Cycle is our survival. We can say we are all a part of an Energetic/Spiritual Cycle that sustains life.

Once here, we must learn predetermined lessons to enrich our experience. These lessons often show up around the aspects of our life we feel we left out on our return to earth. It is up to us to be conscious enough to recognize what our lessons are, and with that, comes the power to choose how we learn that lesson. Although our overall lessons are pre-programmed, the way we learn them is not.

This is why the awareness of who we are and why we do what we do, along with the power of positive thinking, are so important. Example: If one of our lessons in this lifetime has to do with lack—a belief that we do not have enough—experiences of lack will keep showing up until we recognize it and change our thinking about it. If we believe we don't have enough, then that will always be our experience. If we stop focusing on lack and start to affirm in our thinking, statements that affirm, "There is enough to go around," "I am taken care of effortlessly," "I always have what I need and more," and "There is no limit to what I can have in my life," we can change.

The lesson of lack can present itself in many forms—lack of wealth and ability to support oneself, lack of love, nurture, and guidance, lack of self-worth, lack of ability. Once you change your perception of what is possible, you will change your experience and bring the heavenly experience to earth. And you will have mastered one of your lessons on this planet. And then, we do it *allll* over again.

19
Grief: The Final Frontier

What to expect when you are grieving.

First. Expect nothing. Nothing of yourself. And Nothing of others.

One day you are OK, and the next day (or moment) you are falling apart.

Nothing makes sense.

Everyone is handling your grief and their own very differently. Some people are extremely uncomfortable around grieving people, and others swoon in and get too close. Recognize your needs and expectations as just that. When they aren't upheld, it doesn't mean anything. Try your very best to realize everyone is in different spaces at different times. Never undermine your own grief, or another's. No one can fully understand and manage another's grief before their own. This will be quite a challenging feat to realize. Frustration, anger, sadness all come with this.

Grief is also such a personal adventure. It's the final frontier of any particular stage of personal transformation. We experience the lack of the physical presences of our loved ones, and we miss them. And since we are social creatures who experience death on this side, we see death as an ending. And it is. It's the end of what we wanted as a relationship that keeps going and growing. It stops the awareness of the continuum of life that was once purely taken for granted. Whether the death was anticipated, or sudden, the end of a life creates a black hole in the fabric of your own personal cosmos. And our thoughts and emotions get sucked down that hole, suffocate us, and squeeze us into new beings. Eventually, you will feel the momentum and movement of life again. Eventually, you will be moving at the speed of light and emerge on the other side of that hole. You will be quantum-ly transformed into a newer version of yourself. That version will still experience sadness and life again, but it will become deeper and wiser. The parts broken within become the places where it is strongest.

While you are in the black hole, there are few spaces of internal peace. It's not designed to be fun or euphoric. We typically don't go into a black hole of life thinking, *Oh wow, I'm so looking forward to the insight and the outcome of personal depth all of this pain is going to give me. This is going to be a great ride, and I'm going to buckle my seat belt.* No. We don't think of that. We may have glimpses of hope for that, but rarely do we hang onto those thoughts. Or at the very least, they aren't consistent enough at the beginning of the excursion. Believe it or not. You probably won't recognize it as such at the time, but when you reflect on the years after death, there was a magical potential for tremendous growth happening to you. But until that point, you either have deep love for those who are helping you through it, or deeper hatred for those who just aren't getting it. You most likely will feel bad for feeling that way and question what is wrong with you. Then you spiral. And again, you enter into the haze.

You think this stage will never end. You're very being rises and collapses like waves hitting rocks at high tide. There are moments when it all seems like you have nothing left in you, and then, you gain a surge of energy that tricks you into feeling everything will be perfect and fine again. Then the grief hits you all over, and you are knocked down on your spiritual behind again.

There is nothing that can predict or can give you consistent pleasure. Happiness itself feels wrong, and yet is deeply craved. It feels as if this craving is so far beneath your soul that is either shouldn't or will never again exist. But it will, and it does. Your joy and ability to be around people in casual settings will come back. I promise. But there are no timeframes for that. Everyone is different. Which is really just another super annoying sentence you will hear a thousand trillion times from everyone you meet and will want to eventually crush someone for it. Yeah. Good times.

You will encounter all sorts of people and their God-given expert advice on how to fix your grief. The "Do what I did to help my grief, it worked" advice will make you either really want to try what they did with desperation and hope for some relief, or you will revolt at what sounds like a ridiculous attempt at covering your own pain. Or you may just simply go numb. There will be a very stubborn part of you that does not even want to ever again be OK. If you can't have so and so back, you don't want to ever again experience anything, not joy, not happiness, pleasure, pain, nothing ever again.

There's also a sense that if you let people think you are OK for one second, they will forget everything you are going through and just glaze over your state and never worry or think about your needs again. So, the pain and grief can keep you feeling stuck. Your Soul wants you to heal, but it also knows everything. It knows when it will. And it goes with the flow. It's brilliant, connected, and it has your back 24/7. However, your mind will keep you stuck. It's afraid. Afraid of living again. Afraid of experiencing pain again. Afraid of healing. Afraid of never being able to be the same. Afraid of expressing what is really true for yourself at any moment. You don't want people to get sick of you, and yet, you don't people to just think you are fine. Your state of being changes in every instant sometimes. And you don't want anyone to think anything about you at all. You just want to be, and most likely, life doesn't allow for that. We have work and a life to return to. Sometimes, that's the best part. Sometimes, it's the worst. Which will again, make you lose yourself in it, fall away from it or go in "go mode," a numb pseudo state of being that seems neither good, nor bad. None of it will feel right.

You will hear people who have super good intentions tell you they remember when their pet rabbit passed, how heartbroken they were. And how much they understand how difficult the passing of your child/spouse/parent/sibling is because when Mr. Hippity passed, they couldn't even look at rabbit food. Politely, you will stare back at them, most certainly disconnected in every way, and nod, maybe even force a smile. Inside, you will want to smash these people.

You will hear people tell you it isn't fair to your loved one who passed if you are sad for them. That this sadness and grief holds them back on the other side. Well yeah. That's just a rotten thing to say and couldn't be further from the truth. Your grieving is perfectly normal and critical for your mental, emotional, physical, and spiritual health! We are humans, and while in human form, we grieve. All animals grieve their loved ones! It's been that way since the beginning of time. Every culture, every species, human and otherwise, have their own methods of expressing grief. Basically, since we are here in physical form, we want our loved ones to be here in physical form. End of story.

Even the choice of words people use around you will make you crazy. Semantics and vocabulary will make you homicidal. You will hear "It was their time," or "All this is a part of their journey," or "I'm sure they are at peace now," or "They are looking down at you right now not wanting you to be sad." Or—and here's a frustrating one, "If you were them, what would you want you loved ones to grieve?" "It wasn't your fault," "It couldn't have been prevented." "The universe is perfect in every way, and this was a part of that perfect plan." "Everything happens for a reason." (I'm guilty of that one, because I know it's true, but ugh! When I hear myself say it, I want to wrap my mouth with duct tape. I do believe this is true. My mother had to die so I could go on to help others understand death.) It goes on and on and on, and these ridiculously limiting thoughts, statements, and questions leave you semantically mugged. They beat you up and leave you on side of the grief highway. Or they trigger your inner serial killer and make you want to unleash a rage on people. And nope. I'm not kidding on that.

Or, you don't feel any of these things and just feel completely connected with everyone around you, and you feel so grateful for what everyone around you is doing and saying. The point is, the process (another word you will hear and use a trillion times ad nauseum.) is absolutely different for every single person going through it. Sure, there are similarities, and moments of connection, but no two scenarios are ever exactly the same, and somehow you will always find those differences and harp on them.

Death is isolating on two fronts, our own inner thoughts, and feelings, and then again with our outer worlds. I hear so many people expressing frustrations with how their world responds to them after a death. Upon returning to work, school, clubs, etc., people in general and our own families just don't know how to respond. There are the typical quick hugs of "Oh I'm happy to see you are back. How are you?"—silent, flat questions that aren't truly meant or felt, and then they run away from you. One friend described returning to work and social life felt as if she had a disease. No one wanted to come near her because they didn't know what to say or do. There were awkward interactions. I also remember my mom saying how after my brother Chris died, she would see people purposely avoid her in grocery stores so they didn't have to deal with her. People don't like death and do not know what to do with people who are sad. It's crazy. Here is what to do. Say hi. Do what feels natural for you. If you are uncomfortable with talking about it, then don't. But go ahead and say you are uncomfortable with it, and that you don't want to say the wrong thing. Be honest. Say it out loud. Address it. Don't assume you have to have all the answers for that person, because you don't. And they aren't expecting you to. Just be real. If you are a person who needs to take action to show someone you care about and are thinking of them, then do that. If you are a cook, make them meals. If you are someone who likes to write, send them a card. If you don't have a clue, make a donation to a charity in their name, or if money has become tight, then pay a bill for them. Bring them coffee. Send a text. Or do nothing. That's OK too. Just do whatever you are doing with compassion and awareness of your own awkwardness, rather than running away. Honesty and truth are always helpful when dealing with those in grief. Grief has this magic ability that leaves you so raw that you can spot a fake sentiment and a phony intention from a thousand miles away. People know who is true and who truly cares, and who just can't.

Death's vantage point from the living is one of separation and ending. We consider ourselves those of us who are left behind. There's no getting around it, death, when we are human, is horrific. No one likes it. It's the marking of an ending of a relationship that we probably, at one time, took for granted. We all do it. We all forget to remember how precious life is. We often forget to say the I love yous and the I'm sorrys. Or at least, after a death, we can't even remember if we said these things enough, even when we said them all the time. We take for granted when our lives are running like *Groundhog Day* and everything is same old same old. We only realize how wonderful boredom can be when we are no longer bored. When tragedy pops up in our lives, everything makes us regret the days we took for granted. This is normal. I'm not saying it's good or right, but it is what we all do.

After death, we have a different view, but over time, we most likely slip back into our daily grinds and forget again. I've spoken to many parents who have had multiple children die on different occasions, and every parent has expressed to me how angry at themselves they are for taking their lives for granted, again. They thought for sure after their first child passed, they would never yell again at any of their other children and never get flustered at the little things in life. They would be supportive, loving, and present all the time. And yet, none of them did that. Not perfectly. Not every day. They once again got upset and angry at choices and behaviors. They yelled or expressed their opinions about something, made them do something the kids didn't want to do again (take out garbage, get a job, call your grandmother), and they feel terribly guilty for returning to life with the thought that it's all back to being predictable. They stopped thinking, for a moment, about how precious life is, because life had to go on. The garbage man was coming, and stuff needed to get done. That's called returning to normal. And we often end up feeling so guilty for doing that. It's a function of our human selves. We do this, and it stinks. But grief holds no one back except you—because you are human, and you are sad. Devastated. In shock. Alone. Angry. And scared. If you weren't all of the above, you would be dead. Yup, that's right. The deceased have the good spot. They truly are fine. They are no longer trapped by the limitations of their minds, which creates pure and true heaven, bliss, nirvana, peace, whatever you want to call it.

Grief is a powerful emotion. It's awful, actually. The one thing I want to be sure you know that I am in agreement with is that even though there is life after death, and even though we are made of spirit and therefore we never die, even though our loved ones are OK and at peace on the Other Side, and even though they are with us and are still experiencing life with us, we miss them.

I am not writing this book in hopes of getting people OK when someone around them dies. No. Rather, I am writing this book to help you know more about life, death and your Afterlife, so you can feel more comfortable and connected than you currently are. No matter what, when someone we love, admire or know dies, we are sad. And no matter what, we are human, and we are used to and conditioned to understand our world in the physical, and when something is taken away from us, we grieve it. We miss it. We love people. We love our interactions, and at the very least, we love our predictability of our connections. You may not love a co-worker. You may not even like that person, but if he or she passes away, you miss them. You feel the absence of their presence. And that is sad. The physical loss of a person changes dynamics we take for granted. What always was is what we expect to always be. When our predictable lives change, it causes discomfort. Sometimes a little, sometimes a lot. We take a lot for granted until it's gone.

Death causes a family to go haywire. Death changes a dynamic of personalities, no matter where it is felt. Paolo was a very integral part of my Sunday-night meditation class. After his passing, his physical presence was no longer there, and we felt it. This was a man many of us knew only in the walls of the center, and his absence is felt deeply. We all know his seat and we often keep it empty just for him. Imagine how it feels for a family when someone dies. When daily contact is a given and it's taken away, everything gets toppled.

Nothing can prepare you for death and grieving, and there are no one-size-fits-all instructions on how to handle it. It's a lonely journey that you embark on, one which will reveal you. And it changes day by day. And minute by minute. The experience and subsequent process isn't pleasant. I wish I could tell you that everything will be OK and normal again and for you to believe me. But you have established a new normal, and anytime anything is new, we experience pains. We often do not like change, particularly when it's thrown upon us. And especially when we don't like the changes that have happened. What I can tell you with full confidence, is that there will also be miracles that occur to you and around you because of it. These small and large gifts will pop out of nowhere and sometimes leave you completely stunned, other times, fully validated. This, I can promise you.

Ya just gotta' hang in there. And you need to shut off your brain. You probably won't, but it's important to know how much the mind inappropriately interferes with grieving. The mind is typically where we rely on our logical practical linear minds for emotional feedback and connection. Not a good idea. But communicating with anyone and anything is not as hard and is certainly not impossible. Once you learn how, it's effortless actually. It is only our minds and what they tell us that gets in our way. And that's the good news! I have created a meditation CD to help you get in touch with your grieving loved ones via guided mediation. Grieving is probably the number one interference of them all with feeling energy and feeling connected, but it's all part of the plan, and it's actually a perfect design. We grieve, because we have to.

Remember, "Every new beginning is another beginning's end." Grieving marks that end and opens the door for a new frontier. Just trust me on that. Please.

So yes, you can absolutely be sad and devastated when someone dies. I'll say this a thousand times… I am a medium. I connect people with their deceased loved ones all the time and guess what? I do not like when people die! I know without a shadow of a doubt they are still with us. I know they are OK. I know I can talk with them. But that doesn't matter to me when I am only coming from my human self. We want to touch them. We want to continue to go to the movies every week with them. Or play tennis. Have a drink, or just sleep next to them. We want to listen to music, laugh, eat, cry, and see and talk to them. That's normal. That's how we are made. So, when someone dies, there is grief. Deep grief. And it affects everyone differently. There really are no right and wrong ways to grieve. There's no timetable and no predicting how you are going to grieve. And as soon as you do understand a level of your grief, and accept it, it changes. There is nothing you have to do to find your way to acceptance other than grieving as you are in each moment. Acceptance is like Oz. Grieving is the yellow brick road. Just keep following it, and you will come to the Emerald City.

It's triggered by the craziest sights, sounds, smells, music, street signs, and lost moments. It doesn't end either. It morphs you. It makes you feel crazy. Then it makes you feel numb. It makes you angry. It makes you feel silly for being sad. It makes you hate people who don't seem to get it. It makes you cling to those who do. It causes you to either shrink and shrivel, or go out and find something, anything to help take away the pain. Sometimes we do both. Shrink, and beg for something new. Sometimes we become reluctant to go anywhere. Sometimes we feel guilty for not wanting to be around anyone. Sometimes all we can do is be out and stay busy. We think we are being selfish for being sad and not wanting anyone to try to make us happier. We think others are selfish for wanting us to be happy. We want to be happy, but sometimes, we just can't or just don't want to. Sometimes we fill the void with habits, shopping, eating, drinking, gambling, over texting, over socialization, or withdrawal. People try grief therapy groups and hate them. Other people prefer them and feel they have saved their lives. Some want no part of seeing a counselor. Some seek out religion. Others damn all religions and hate God. Many feel incredibly guilty for not trusting God and feel they ashamed to say that to some people in their place of worship. Some act out. Some implode. Some gain weight, and some lose it. Some resent the end of life for the person who passed because they no longer have control. Perhaps the deceased didn't listen to you when you harped on them to please get checked out, and they didn't do that in time. Others feel they didn't do enough and they should have visited more. Others are sickened when their family members couldn't die comfortably at home, while others really needed some help from a hospital staff and didn't get it. Some families grow closer, and many split farther apart. No one can predict how it's all going to go down for you. You just move through it, and that's how you find out.

My mentor, Anne Quinn, describes family dynamics brilliantly. She taught me to imagine that family is like a mobile. Each person adds weight to the mobile, but if you remove one person from it, the mobile goes lopsided until it recalibrates. We are so unaware of family dynamics. But if you take some time to understand your own family dynamics (who is the dominant energy, who is the rebellious one, who listens and follows all rules, who is aggressive, passive, the fun one, etc.) you will see the pattern of behavior has been disrupted. When this happens for any reason, (dad goes to rehab, child moves away for college, parents get divorced, etc.) the roles change and everyone falls into a new pattern. When someone dies, and the change is permanent, the entire family is thrown into turmoil simply from the dynamics shifting, let alone the grief and multitude of emotions that follow. Add financial stresses on top and whoa! Come on! I'd be angry at all Higher Powers too!

I often sit with grieving families who are having a hard time showing their emotions in fear of setting off another family member who might be seemingly OK that day. So, everyone becomes locked into a pattern of private grief. And no matter how many people you have around you, you still often feel alone in your grief. So many people think someone is just doing OK when they are actually not openly sharing their emotions out of fear of setting off another one. Grief is personal and unpredictable. And there tends to be a lot of miscommunication. Usually, I feel that's because emotions are tough to get in touch with. Sometimes we would rather ignore them, or bury them. There tends to be so many hidden emotions, things people are so scared to admit to.

It's imperative to get with a good grief counselor to help you navigate you through it. I also recommend staying in some sort of counseling for at least one year! Seeing family patterns, understanding them, and then changing them in a healthy way takes time. One session, or one month will not be enough to sort things through. Being able to communicate, and to learn your feelings matter no matter what they are, and to understand those feelings will vary throughout any given day during this process is critical for a healthy recovery process. Trust me on this! Please!

Yes, seeking the help of a medium is helpful as well. I always say it can definitely take the edge off, but any reputable medium should not and will not allow a person to use mediumship as therapy. Yes, it's helpful, and there is a lot to be gained from it, but there is so much more to learn and understand about yourself after experiencing a death that I feel only therapy and deep introspection and a commitment to yourself can help with. I do believe in and encourage people to take classes on meditation and personal development workshops to help you learn how to handle daily life. You need an army of people and support around you. We are often isolated and alone, even with family around us. In modern society, we tend to be very bad about supporting each other after death. We are sent back to work immediately and expected to function at normal levels nearly right away. That alone is devastating to our physical, mental, and emotional bodies. There is very little self-healing and nurturing. In tribal communities, this isn't the case. A person is allowed to grieve in and with the community. Literally the entire village will cry and emote with those suffering the loss.

People make sense of what is happening in their world through social interactions. Think about it, when something devastating or exciting or important happens in your life, you don't usually just sit back and quietly think about it, do you? No, you probably reach out to your friends or family to talk about it with them, to gain support and help! In today's world, we post it on social media and get the word out there. Facebook/Twitter/Instagram/ Snap Chat and whatever else is out there is flooded with our experiences, some mundane to some extremely tragic or profound. Grief experienced when someone dies is not something that just happens inside of you. It happens through the interactions between people. In cultures all over the world, rituals take place to help the surviving family and friends find meaning in the deceased's life, and death. Unfortunately for modern Western cultures, these rituals from earlier times have all but disappeared, and that feeling of togetherness we used to experience has faded. We now hurry ourselves up. Funeral are done quickly, and life returns "back to normal" way too quickly.

Now, think about your current support system. Are the majority of your closest family members nearby? Who is going to be there for you should something happen? And who are you available to should they need you? Reflect on this for a moment. See yourself as a part of the fabric of society that is important at any given moment. You have the power to help another at all times, and be ready at a moment's notice. You know how we constantly put off doing something fun because we are all too bogged down with responsibilities? I find it amazing when all those responsibilities and rules get thrown out the window when a tragedy occurs. Recently, my son had to be brought to the hospital for pain in his abdomen. I have a bizarre fear of appendicitis. I've never known anyone who has had it, let alone died or had complications from it, so I have no clue where this fear came from, perhaps another lifetime? But naturally, I thought my son was having an appendicitis attack. I rushed him to the hospital and cancelled my appointments quickly that day. Funny how I had no problem (or little problem) cancelling sessions with people who have waited for their session and have taken a day off from work or arranged for a sitter to meet with me. It's a huge inconvenience, and yet, in times of emergency, we drop everything and take care of what is right. Stop and recall when you have done this for another and when someone has done this for you.

There seems to be a slight pattern of experiences in grieving that I have observed over the past fifteen years. I am describing a pattern I have seen, and this is in no way, shape, or form an absolute way of grieving. This is what I have noticed as a generalized pattern of grieving as observed by me through my work. That's all. You may resonate with it, or not at all, and if you don't, it's simply because you don't, and does not mean you are doing anything wrong, or that I am wrong.

The first year after a death is a blur. It's the time when you are in fact aware the person has died, but there is still a level of disbelief that it happened. It makes moving on disorienting. Your patterns of living and being with this person in your life, has been disrupted. Basic daily tasks are done differently. Life changes in the blink of an eye. But it's not only for the deceased. The living has had a part of them, their daily routine, and expectations, die as well. And yet, they have to keep going in a foggy haze of grief and returning to life as usual. I've seen it all too often where people are afraid to open up to people about their real feelings. They feel selfish for staying in grief. They feel they have to either hide their feelings, or simply not talk about it all the time. People are afraid of turning others away, and they also observe who remains in their lives. Grief has a way of weeding people out of our lives. It changes dynamics and relationships everywhere. Things once tolerated by others becomes unbearable. Again, grief is a major vehicle for transformation for everyone.

The disbelief is disorienting as one minute you can be feeling OK, and in the very next second, something can trigger you and bring you to your knees. This lasts for a while. Again, it's different for everyone. It's also different depending on what type of death occurs. When my grandmother died at one hundred years old, we were happy for her. Of course, we didn't want her to have to die, but she had lived a rich life, and was done here. She suffered by hanging on and losing all of her freedom in the last six years of her life. It was more than past her time. So, when she died, while we were sad, we were also relieved. For her and for us. It was time. For me, and my children, there weren't so many series of triggers to make us sad when we thought of her. It was different for my mother. She did have those moments of deep sadness. For the rest of us, it was easier to say goodbye to her. A sudden unexpected death or the death of a relative or close loved one obviously hits with an even greater impact on our lives than say a family member who was hardly known.

It's also difficult to grieve within a family unit. So often, everyone is on a different page. When one person is having a basically having a good day, they don't want to be around or get triggered by someone who is not having a good moment. It leaves people feeling splintered and alone. Again, relationships change.

Within that first year, there is a constant need to remember "last year at this time we were...doing such and such..." It's painful to remember last year or a time when... Everyone seems to think or hope that once the official one-year anniversary passes, things will feel better. They don't, and sometimes the anniversary makes everything worse. Now there is one more (perceived) thing in between you and your loved one. Time.

The second year, things become real. The disbelief begins to wane, and the reality of having to live without this person is on your mind often. You are thrown into having to pick up your pieces, while many of those who were keeping you company have mainly gone back to their lives. Your new and future life is foggy. Desire to make all the changes needed can be overwhelming. Being paralyzed by non-clarity about the future is the norm. The second year is when you are all too aware of the new reality, but you are most certainly not at peace with it. You think it's time to start stepping forward and coming up with a new life plan, but more often than not, you will be halted by something that just stops you from moving forward. Or at least in a way that you can measure. You are moving forward, just by being alive and with your grief. You just won't feel like you are. You will feel stuck, with little or no true motivation to make any changes. The second year is tough, but I typically see the hardest time happening in the third year.

I see the most clients for the first time in either the first few months after death or in the third year. This is when time is getting longer, and everyone seems to feel like they should be over it by now, or that others think they should be. (This isn't true. People who understand grief, get it, and those who don't, are lucky.) The old life isn't completely over, and the new life isn't in its full fruition. You are working hard to create a new rhythm. I promise you, this will pass. Surround yourself with people and take time for you as much as you possibly can to help you through this point. Do what works for you (granted as long as it is healthy).

The fourth year is where you can finally truly see your growth and evolution. You begin to take your new life in a semi stride. Nothing is ever the same, and it doesn't mean you don't miss that person. It just means you have emerged from your cocoon of grief and are beginning to fly again. When you take the time for yourself and grieve as you need to (which most of the time, you won't really know what that is, or what that looks like), but eventually, you will have pulled your pieces back together and a new you will have emerged. You are still sad; that part really doesn't go away, but it does get less intense. When? That's different for everyone.

Of course, there is an aspect of grief where all the opposite of the above happens. People find who are truly there for them, and relationships that may have been distant before, become even closer. There is a clarity that is eventually gained when the initial stages of deep grief are traversed. Eventually, although there will always be a space in your hearts, minds, and memories that misses a person, there will be a day when you have come to see what a journey grief has taken you on and how much you have changed. You will be opened to learn and see life in a completely different way. You will, I promise, be able to see a strength in you, and all those who supported you. There will be a day when your focus of loss will get redirected to your personal growth. This is where there is the greatest Life After Death Experience takes place. Your life. After death. The Afterlife. Because the deceased haven't died, just their patterns, conditioning, beliefs, and egos have disintegrated. They have been freed from all of that and unleashed. Their purest state of their selves exist and are now an additional source for you to connect with. Their true selves will go on forever! A new you has emerged. Your loved ones couldn't be happier for you! In his book, *Promise Me, Dad: A Year of Hope, Hardship & Purpose*[17], Joe Biden says about grief, "One day, you will turn a corner."

Deborah Hanlon

20
The Afterlife is the Presence of Proof

Why do we constantly say, "I have had a lot of loss," as if no one else has? That is what happens here. We must change our mindset around that. We can't continue to lament over that fact. We know it's a given here. Life will change. It will constantly change. My father abhors when people say, "I lost my dad, or I lost my son/daughter etc." He says, sometimes a bit too emphatically for my tastes, "No you didn't. You didn't lose them because I'll bet if you lost them, you would still be out looking for them. They died." Some people shake their heads in agreement, others think about it, and still others let it go over their heads entirely. It's true. You didn't lose the person. They aren't lost, but you probably feel you lost something. You lost a connection to them. That's a loss for sure.

Loss is another word for change, and while I think it's an appropriate word to describe your feelings, it may not be a great word to continue to focus on. My dad is actually partially correct. If you lost them, you would probably go out to find them again. Yes, oftentimes, that's precisely where people are stuck, looking for them in all the wrong places and forms that you were familiar with from the past. If you tried to look for your five-year-old self, you wouldn't find her/him. That child existed, but that child has changed. You need to learn a new way to access your former self rather than looking for that black-haired (insert your color hair) little girl/boy playing in the dirt who was formerly known as me. You can access her/him through her thoughts and feelings. She/he may only remember little details about herself/himself from long ago.

Yes, we all want the details of our lives to verify identity. However, try not to forget to receive the rest of the information they are giving, like how they are doing now. Does only my nickname matter when I am looking for my literal former self? I'm guessing it does not matter. But if I am truly looking to access my five-year-old self, I would really want to know what she is thinking and feeling, and I really wouldn't worry about what she is wearing. Same goes for the deceased. Learn to access them as they are now rather than "Does she still like it when I make her coffee in the morning because we always did that, and I don't want to let her down and make her think I'm not thinking of her now." Or "Does he think it's all right if I date now? Are they mad at me for living again?" Let me tell you, they want to express how they are now.

They want you to know how all right they are and how they think and feel, which is better known as how they are consciousness itself! They want you to know they are connected to everything, to infinity itself! They want you to know how they finally see that nothing matters, unless you make it so—how they understand the rhythms and insanity of life, and how happy they are to have risen above it all! How they can and do still experience you, only now, they experience it all from a much clearer perspective. They know you love them. They know you miss them. They know when you couldn't deal with the loss anymore. They get it all.

If you want to keep accessing the past with them, (which is

fine too and necessary at first), I'm going to promise you, if you keep your interactions with them and only want to know about and talk about the past, you are only ultimately keeping yourself in the past with them. However, it's time to get to know them as they are now, so you can get to knowing yourself as you are now. We are told to never look back and stare, but only to glance to see how far you have come. That is my wish for you.

Life is a series of fun times mixed in with some negative stuff right before you depart and transform into a higher state of consciousness. A lot is going to happen to you here—a lot of good, a lot of pain. Experience each moment just as it is, rather than what it isn't or what you wish it to be. Remember, each moment is temporary, fleeting, and it's catapulting you to grow. When you can incorporate that into your psyche on a daily basis, then you find Heaven. It will be easier to do this at some moments than at others. And you have to remember that too. Sometimes, you can be quite Zen. Other times, not so much, and that's all right as well.

You will lose people you love, physically and emotionally. And it will hurt badly. You will grieve. You will question your faith, question what this is all about and will either sink into a depression or learn from it. You may do both. You will support another. And sometimes you will betray and hurt someone. Sometimes this happens consciously, sometimes you have no clue about it, until it's too late. You will celebrate births or grieve infertility. You will bury your parents, or you may bury your child. You will have jobs, perform tasks, and basically meld into the rest of society. You will follow fads, become fans of celebrities, or get politically active. Or not. You will do laundry. Lots of it. You will eat, most likely too much at times. You may discover a relationship with alcohol or drugs and then may learn not to have a relationship with either. You will experience a plethora of emotions ranging from loving euphoria to deep depression. You will have times when we feel we don't belong, and times when You feel adored.

Life is a range of experiences. It's supposed to be. The more the range, the deeper the experience. Climb high mountains, whether it's in your mind or in reality. Go to a desert. You will do both, metaphorically while you are here, so you might as well go to these places physically. You will be on the high from falling in love, or hitting a desert as middle age creeps in with no partner. You experience it all. The more, the better.

Set higher expectations for your life and living. That's why you are here. If things are crap, they shouldn't stay that way. That's the key. If you have juggled the same problems over and over, then you must take a deep look at yourself and get ready to get brave. Recognize there is a problem, and that problem may have a lot to do with the fact that you need to upgrade your thinking. Upgrade what you think is real and true and possible. Oh, so much more is possible for you. So much.

Think of it this way. Something that has been basically told to us that is impossible, is to survive death, the afterlife. No matter how much of a believer you are, most likely, there are still moments of doubt of an afterlife. You have been taught, dead is dead, and, well, science and mediums are proving that completely wrong every day. If that is no longer on the impossible list, what else is now deemed possible? What else is possible for you?

Your loved ones who have crossed, are doing well. They have surpassed all the toughest part of existing—being human. They have been resurrected into a Higher State of awareness, one that you too, can attain. You can at least be aware of the proverbial carrot to which we are all working toward. You know there is something greater, and then you can "pay your dues," stay present, and seek to make this life as great and fulfilling as possible. You are already where they are. You just haven't focused your intentions that way. You are particle and wave, human self and Higher Self simultaneously! If you don't know how to change your entire mindset, then you reach out to people who already are, and they will show you, by example, how to expand your greatest desires. Your loved ones will send you winks to let you know they are around. You will miss most of them, until one day, something will change your faith like nothing ever before. Get ready for that.

Expect the unexpected. Believe in the impossible. There is life after death. After every death. Life is an infinite wave of possibilities coming to a peak, and then falling away. We change. We grow. We evolve. We create. We destroy, in order to create. It is all a continuum. Everything is cause and effect. And it is all working out for your highest good. Every moment contains potential for growth and change. For that is all time is, a measurement of potential for change. Make yours matter. Make yourself matter to you.

You are not wrong, or broken or flawed. You are human. But you are also so much more than that. You are energy. You are infinite. It doesn't all end here. In fact, this is only the beginning.

How do I end a book that is ultimately about never having endings? How do I sum it all up? How can you put an ending on a book that is ultimately about infinity, a time of no endings? At the time of this writing, more than forty-two years of my life has passed—years of growing, learning and evolving. I have a passion to understand, to learn, to reconnect to those missing parts of myself. And I have a passion to teach you about yourself. All that has come before has led us to this moment. We are experiencing infinity through each other at this very precise second. Everything I experienced caused me to write this book, and everything that has come before you had cause you to be reading these words at precisely this moment. We are infinity expressing through each other!

This project has been a process in and of itself, and it alone taught me more about life, death and the Afterlife than almost any other aspect of my life combined. At times, I thought it would never get done. At times, I was confused. And honestly, at times, I was just so bored that I wanted to give up. There were times when I felt stupid for admitting I was writing a book out of fear of what others would think or say. There were times I was mortified to think, what if I am wrong? What if they laugh at me? Ironic, isn't it? Here I was falling into the old traps. Once realized, it became clear to me. We are all always overcoming the dark shadows of our thoughts. It's a natural component of being human. And it's one we must stay vigilant about. No one has it all right all the time! Being in the moment and staying aware of our true nature helps us to ignore those lying messages in our brains. They open us to think better thoughts for ourselves and our future. We don't need to be stuck as the people of our past. We cannot be.

When we can connect to ourselves on a deeper, kinder, and meaningful way, we gain clarity. When we can finally be open and honest about who we are, what we want and need, to whomever we need to, we begin to live in health. We gain connection. Connection to ourselves, and ultimately to each other. When we understand who we are, we can relax. Life has meaning simply because we are in it. That's our purpose. Just to be here. We are the unique expression of the Collective Whole. And we are all a part of it, not separate from it.

Be patient with yourself when you react poorly, and be kind to yourself. Just keep observing, growing. Get yourself out of the Cave, over and over and over. Turn toward the ever-growing light as often as you can. That's what it's about here. What has always been does not have to be what will always be.

And in those moments when you are low, and feeling stuck, those are the moments when you must take your awareness and remember you are connected to a system so much larger than your small human self. You must remember that you are always looked after, and the Universe seeks to keep your best interest at stake. It may not seem this way in the moment, but this is when we challenge our human minds and go into a our deeper knowing of how the Universe and our Higher Selves work. Those moments are the moments of a new birth, a process of dying begins. There are grief, struggle, anguish, anger. Every birth follows this process. Then comes the miracles, the spontaneous interactions with true angels on earth—people who have been there and get it, people who lift us up in ways we never knew we needed. People begin to help us reshape our visions of the world. And a newness is born. We save each other. Every moment of every day. We serve our purposes, millions of them, through each other.

Have you even given this much thought? Do you see how miraculous and precious we all are to each other? Have you noticed? Have you expressed this to another soul? We are literally here for one another. Just being who we are in each moment. Infinity in each other. Are you able to create your own personal heaven on earth? Are you willing to be, know, and do it?

Ironically, I learned that I was my very own monster at the end of this book. Endings always conjure worries. Have we said enough? Have we said it all? My thinking about the end, has been the scariest monster of them all. The end of this book. The end of our lives. And it has been yours, too.

Change your thinking. Embrace all the monsters. They are there. At the very end of all this physical worldly stuff, you are the monster, and you will absolutely love and embrace him/her with all your heart and soul, as will the rest of the Universe. Why not just get to know that monster today? Why not change that monster into your own personal superhero? Why wait until your physical death to finally feel at peace? Don't be afraid to turn the pages of your life in spite of the fear of what is coming. Instead, decide in advance to embrace all of it, even the possibility of the worst. Know you will survive all of it—because nothing ever dies. You are the Afterlife.

I'm in the Presence of *that* Proof every day. And so are you.

NOTES

1. Jon Stone (1971). *The Monster at the End of This Book*: Western Publishing Company.

2. Bruce Lipton, PhD. (2005). *The Biology of Belief:* Author's Pub Corp.

3. Tomie dePaola (1978). *The Clown of God:* Sandpiper

4. Malcolm Gladwell (2008). *Outliers:* Little, Brown and Company.

5. Napolean Hill (1987). *Think and Grow Rich:* Fawcett Books

6. Alain Aspect, Philippe Grangier, and Gerard Roger "Experimental Realization of Einstein-Podolsky-Rosen-Bohm *Gedankenexperiment.* A New Violation of Bell's Inequalities." American Physical Society, July 12, 1982.

7. Dr. Amit Goswami (2013). *Physics of the Soul:* Hampton Roads Publishing.

8. Deepak Chopra (2006). *Life After Death:* Harmony.

9. Vic Bishop "Retired Bishop Explains Why the Church Invented Hell." www.wakingtimes.com, May 12, 2016

10. George D. Campbell. III (1996-2016). *Exit Strategy: A Textbook on Death and Dying.*

11. Jimo Borjigin "Surge of neurophysiological coherence and connectivity in the drying brain." National Academy of Sciences of the United States of America, August 2013

12. Dannion Brinkley (2008). *Saved By The Light:* Harper One.

13. Todd Burpo (2010). *Heaven is Real:* Thomas Nelson Publishers.

14. Anita Moorjani (2012). *Dying to be Me*, Hay House.

15. Emily Sailers, performed by Indigo Girls. (1992) *Galileo*, Rites of Passage, Epic/Legacy. Vinyl EP.

16. Richard Gray "Phobias may be memories passed down in genes from ancestors." *The Telegraph*, December 2013

17. Joe Biden (2017). *Promise Me, Dad: A Year of Hope, Hardship & Purpose:* Flatiron Books.

ABOUT THE AUTHOR

After the death of her four-year-old brother, then three-year-old Deborah Hanlon embarked on a life-long journey of discovery of science and self to find proof of what she knew deep inside—that life after death exists. She knew her brother was "still around" as she was able to communicate with him. Possessing an insatiable interest in science and spirituality and a commitment to deepen her awareness, Deborah has become a trusted expert for matters of our hearts and souls. Her focus as a medium is to help the living transition to their own "afterlife" following the loss of a loved one.

Deborah's confidence to pursue mediumship on a professional level was ignited after winning a spot on the Sci-fi Network TV show, "The Gift" in 2006. She has since spoken to thousands of people across the United Sates in private appointments and large gallery-style forums. She has appeared on numerous morning radio shows taking live callers and answering questions regarding their deceased loved ones and life's challenges and goals. Deborah takes what is often seen as a heavy topic and eases hearts and minds with her authenticity, genuine care and sense of humor.

Her passion for teaching the living how to recalibrate themselves after loss inspired her to open her Spiritual space known as The Center for Being, Knowing, Doing in Newburgh, NY. There, Deborah teaches workshops on meditation/visualization, intuitive development, mediumship, personal development and energy awareness.

Deborah receives the most joy, insights and purpose from being a mother to her three sons. She lovingly calls them "The Caveteens," for their Neanderthal-like behavior and often expresses how they humble her into reality on a daily basis, keeping her real and authentic.

Learn more about Deborah at www.deborahhanlon.com, where she offers insights on her blog "Daily Dose of Deborah." Follow her on Facebook as Deborah Hanlon and Instagram as @imdeborahhanlon

Your Proof

Your Proof

Your Proof

Your Proof

Your Proof

Your Proof

Made in United States
Orlando, FL
17 July 2022